"This fascinating memoir

ence (NDE) researchers in the world, who herself benefited from three separate NDEs in 1977, is a wild ride, indeed! With a loose and free writing style, her life unfolds as that of a true ambassador to the world of spirit and unconditional love."

—Eben Alexander, M.D., former Harvard Neurosurgeon and author of *Proof of Heaven, The Map of Heaven*, and *Living in a Mindful Universe*

"*Edge Walker* is a shining reminder that sometimes our very being is the best gift we have for others. Spiritual researcher and global lecturer PMH Atwater brings the honesty of herself to this fascinating memoir of her experience-filled life, from her Rocky Mountain childhood through business, science, metaphysics, marriage, motherhood, to near-death experiences and more. For readers who have not already encountered Atwater's unique perspective, the book will be a wonderfully readable introduction. To her many devoted followers, *Edge Walker* will be like holding hands for a walk along the rim itself."

—Nancy Evans Bush, MA, president emerita of the International Association for Near-Death Studies, author of *Dancing Past the Dark: Distressing Near-Death Experiences*, and other books

"In this fascinating and outspoken book, PMH Atwater shares her 'memoir-autobiography' with us, writing about the many mysteries and miracles of her life, and about her misfortunes and setbacks as well. Being a near-death experiencer plus a near-death researcher has been both complex and wondrous for her. Looking back, she really had an incredible life indeed. Highly recommended."

—Pim van Lommel, cardiologist, NDE researcher, author of *Consciousness Beyond Life*

"PMH's near-death experiences themselves are undoubtedly remarkable. The devotion to her life mission of helping others to alleviate the fear of death certainly warrants our respect. What equally deserves our admiration is her penetrating insight into the nature of the phenomenal world. She never fails to grasp the totality of Creation wherein she saw Love continuing to spring from deeper realities through symbols and signs. This book is one sheer voice of Divine Love spoken to humanity through an often painful and yet ultimately victorious life of God's beloved daughter."

—Dr. Young-hae Chi, lecturer, University of Oxford

"*Edge Walker* reveals for the first time the real PMH Atwater in the raw: not just the near-death experiencer and prolific author, but the spiritual human struggling to fit into a culture that rewards conformity. *Edge Walker* provides an honest, no-holds-barred account of PMH's life-long transcendent journey and her fight to be heard as the voice of a different reality, how she became an 'Edge Walker,' someone who walks between worlds and tries to build bridges between them. PMH Atwater recounts how the incredible gift and curse of experiencing unconditional love both uplifted and crushed her. This book is guaranteed to open your eyes—if you let it—your mind, illustrating how integrating spiritual truth and logical thinking is both impossible and essential for us all. *Edge Walker* is, in my opinion, the most astonishing of Atwater's many books."

—Bruce Greyson, M.D., Professor Emeritus of Psychiatry & Neurobehavioral Sciences, University of Virginia, and author of *After: A Doctor Explores What Near-Death Experiences Reveal about Life and Beyond*

"PMH Atwater's work has had an impact on a lot of lives. I know that I'm not the only one who's been deeply touched by it."

—Marie-Noëlle Baechler, active in France with NDE experiencers

"PMH Atwater is a genius, brilliant writer, and one of the world's leading experts on the phenomena known as Near-Death Experiences. In her book *Edge Walker*, Dr. Atwater shares with the reader several deeply personal tragedies which led to many harrowing encounters with death. These universally relatable experiences emotionally bond the reader with the author. We join her in understanding what awaits every human beyond physical life."

—Mark Anthony, JD, Psychic Explorer, and author of *The Afterlife Frequency, Evidence of Eternity*, and *Never Letting Go*

"PMH Atwater's *Edge Walker* is the book that her many friends, fans, and followers have been waiting for. In it, PMH finally tells the story of her amazing life, and it is really a mind blower. Now one can finally see the vastness of her truly multi-dimensional being. You will find her story absolutely riveting. Don't miss it!"

—Kenneth Ring, Ph.D., author many books, including *Lessons From The Light*

"The wisdom found in Chapter 31, titled 'In-Betweens,' makes reading *Edge Walker* worthwhile. This autobiography helped me understand my own NDE journey."

—Peter Panagore, Minister, First Radio Parish Church of America, and author of *NDEr*

"As Elbert Hubbard once quipped: 'The problem with theologians is that we have to die to find out whether they're right.' Well, PMH Atwater did die—three times! And, as a skilled investigator and communicator, she went on to interview thousands of other near-death experiencers and write about their accounts. While theologians parse the meaning of ancient texts and offer only speculations, PMH delivers experience-backed insight into life's greatest mysteries. In her many books examining NDEs and other extraordinary phenomena, PMH has told pieces of her own story. Now, in *Edge Walker*, she reveals all. A courageous trailblazer, her bold personality shines through on every page."

—Sam Torode, author of *Living from the Soul: The 7 Spiritual Principles of Ralph Waldo Emerson*

"*Edge Walker* led me on a fantastical journey that was agonizingly poignant and surprisingly joyful and uplifting. It's a pragmatic take on how a mystic and psychic can also be a skeptical detective and hard nosed researcher. Her elegant navigation between physical and nonphysical realms made me fall in love with her all over again."

—Scott Taylor, Ed.D., President, Expanded Awareness Institute, retired President Monroe Institute, author, guide, researcher on Near-Death and Shared-Death Experiences

EDGE WALKER

The Many Lives and Deaths of PMH Atwater

P.M.H. ATWATER

RAINBOW RIDGE BOOKS

Cover and interior design by Frame25 Productions
Cover photo © David De Lang c/o Shutterstock.com

Published by:
Rainbow Ridge Books, LLC
Virginia Beach, VA
www.rainbowridgebooks.com

Library of Congress Control Number: 2023936966

ISBN 978-1-937907-75-4

10 9 8 7 6 5 4 3 2 1
Printed in the United States of America

Contents

Facts

- Born Twin Falls, Idaho—1937
- Two mothers, five fathers—differing worldviews
- Did first double-blind study with a control group, age five
- Guided by Spirit Keepers of Idaho's deserts and canyons
- Married local farmer/pilot—1956, divorced 1976
- Birthed three children, later in life miscarried three
- Employment history: secretary, administrative assistant, writer, newspaper columnist, editor, creator tour-guide programs for State of Idaho/Scouting badges, bank analyst
- Died Boise, Idaho—three times in three months, had a different near-death experience with each—1977
- Met Elisabeth Kübler Ross, M.D. at O'Hare Airport—1978
- Left Idaho, zig-zagged across the nation to Falls Church, Virginia—1978
- Began research of all aspects of near-death phenomenon—1978

- Married media/communications specialist, spiritual teacher—1980
- NDE research discovered by Kenneth Ring, Ph.D.—1981
- Met peer group in Storrs, Connecticut, and studied their research—1981
- Joined International Association of Near-Death Studies (IANDS)—1981
- Wrote *"Coming Back"* Column for IANDS newsletter for five years and that became background for *Coming Back to Life*, my first major book—1988
- Earned Doctorate in Humanities, Montreal, Quebec—1992

Edges

I love them. For me, the most perfect place in the world to stand is at the very edge of a yawn between rock sheets that define a canyon. One move out of sync with the moment is all it takes to be swallowed by the thunder-spray of a gorge hundreds of feet below. It's comfortable here. Nice. Canyon tops baked naked by a large sun remind me of my youth. I played on them as a child and well into womanhood—on edges hardly wide enough for the tuck of my shoe.

One day, as I stood on a canyon edge remembering the passage of decades, I saw something hovering in the air above a nearby waterfall: a crowd. It was perfectly balanced. Every soul I'd ever known since childhood, everyone who had ever come into my life (even for a short time), loved ones, those that frightened or hurt me, every single soul—they were all there smiling at me. No words, good or bad—just all the people who had been a part of my life suddenly in my life once more.

Never had I seen, read, imagined, or heard of such a thing. But it was no mirage. Even in the heat. All of these people helped me live a meaningful life—and they wanted me to know how happy they were to have been a part of it. They made certain I suffered, laughed, screamed, and skipped through each squeeze of air my mind sculpted. Like players on a stage, they ensured I never missed a cue. This now, right now, was when I absolutely knew the game of life was love.

Chapter 1

Rainstorm

"Hope is the bird who feels the light and sings while dawn is still dark."
—Rabindranath Tagore

Way past midnight. Hardly anyone knew of my birth. Hush. Hush. Childbirth out of wedlock was considered a crime in 1937, so my mother fled Kansas to be near her two sisters living in the reclaimed deserts of southern Idaho. No support. Damned by her sisters' husbands. Dark omens.

I was born in a private clinic near the city of Twin Falls and the Snake River Canyon gorge. As a child, Shoshone Falls (higher than Niagara), was my favorite playground whenever water was diverted away from it for farming. I climbed it and many other waterfalls when I was young—reaching for burning skies, hugging cliffs and pressing against jagged rock faces as if born of them. A life defined by edges. Nothing full frontal.

My birth intertwined with the lives of the Sogns—Norwegian folk—who were once extremely wealthy before the stock market crash. They found themselves stranded in Twin Falls because of a business deal gone sour. One day a gypsy fortune teller offered to read Momma Sogn's tea leaves. She saw two things: Daddy Sogn—while outside doing yardwork—would be offered a job and he would do that job until he could work no more. And the daughter they'd both prayed for would come to them in the middle of a rainstorm.

Bull's eye exact. A few days later, while outside trimming a hedge, a veterinarian walked up to Daddy Sogn and offered him a job at an animal hospital. He took it and worked there until old age and poor health forced him to retire.

Soon after Daddy started working at the animal hospital, the fortune teller's second prediction came true. Daddy was downtown in the middle of a rainstorm and saw a young woman clinging to a lamppost and crying. Curious, he approached and asked what was wrong. Her tearful answer: she'd just had a baby, her landlady had kicked her out, and she had no place to go. Moved by the tragedy before him, he invited her home, saying his wife could care for the infant. As you might guess, I became the Sogn's prayed-for-daughter. The Sogns even kept my crib in their bedroom, not my birth mother's.

I was four years old when I learned that the pretty woman going in and out of the house, hardly paying any attention to me, was actually my real mother. I couldn't handle it. Nor did I learn my legal status until years later. From the very start, I'd cry whenever she touched or held me. Photos taken at the time, even as a babe, show me trying to get away from her, screaming to get away. She blamed the Sogns for spoiling me, never thinking the cause of my behavior might be something else.

Although the Sogns read the Bible every night of their lives, they (like me), still openly accepted "things mysterious" as true. I would often play with fairies and giggle as they spun in whirlygigs of wind across my open palms, through leaves and bushes, near the roots of big trees. I would gaze at the "rivers" that flowed across open skies, predicting weather to come. Stuff like that. Always accurate. Always very much okay.

When I was about five years old, a minister came to call. He heard me talking to God at a tea party in what had become my bedroom. He asked if he could take a peek and see for himself. Sure enough, he saw me at my little table passing pretend cookies and tiny glasses of milk to God as we busily conversed. Momma Sogn said the minister glowed when he left, convinced that all he saw and heard truly revealed the presence of God. No need for questions.

I was always the odd kid. Other worlds were very visible and deeply real to me. I'd dwell in those places, sometimes as much as this one. Often, I'd sit on the edge of windows and sing to worms. Whenever it rained, I'd sing to them. No one had window screens then. Open a window and you could sit on the ledge, unprotected—daring, yet comfy.

I had a noticeable mole on the right side of my forehead. One day I climbed up to the mirror and spoke to the mole, angry that it was so far to the right. "You're supposed to be in the very middle, straight up from my nose. Move." As if one order would fix it, I forgot about the whole thing until about three months later. Another look in the mirror revealed that the mole had moved, right to where I'd told it to go. That pleased me.

I was about to begin grade school when innocence suddenly turned black. Death was everywhere around me. People were talking about it, some were crying. The news spread far and wide on radios, newspaper headlines, and movie reels. Men felt like failures if they were turned down at recruitment centers. They wanted to fight. Save our country. No matter where you were, who you talked to, everyone was involved. Some ran right outside their doors onto the open streets so their screams could be heard.

World War II. President Roosevelt asked everyone to help—even children. In households across the nation, empty food cans were washed, flattened, and set aside until the metal could be collected by the Army to be used in the war effort. People planted Victory Gardens. If you didn't grow your own food you didn't eat much. Going to a grocery store in some parts of town meant taking your own food with you and canning it while at the store. There was little else there. Check-out meant paying for the tin you used to can your food, along with what few items you bought.

Mama Sogn made sandwiches for the beggars who would pound at the back door. They lived in caves that spanned Rock Creek Canyon, outside Twin Falls. Daddy Sogn would scold her. "What if you get raped? You don't know these men." She never stopped sharing what food she could spare though. "You need to take care of people," she'd say. I'd help her when I could. Nothing bad happened to either of us.

Neighborhoods devised a way to handle food shortages and help those in need. If you had extra food, you'd put it in a paper bag, set it on someone's porch, ring the doorbell, then run. People were proud. You didn't want to embarrass anyone.

When I was about four, maybe a little older, Momma Sogn and I were in the downtown area when, suddenly, I couldn't walk anymore. I fell down, and, when I was finally able to stand again, my legs wobbled. Momma Sogn insisted that my mother take me to see Dr. Valdi Fundling for tests. Verdict: polio. Luckily it was a mild case, because after a few months I was almost back to normal. During that time, however (and when no one was looking), I'd slide off the bed and practice using my legs. No doctor could tell me I'd never walk again. No way. This determination steadied my resolve. I practiced more each time. Pain didn't matter. Walking normally again did. According to my birth mother, my quick recovery proved that I made the whole thing up. I had done it for attention.

A simple fact soon became very apparent to me: like it or not, I had two mothers, not one. Each expected different behaviors and responses (and there would sometimes be unpleasant consequences if I forgot who expected what, when). Momma Sogn's version of living life meant love and forgiveness. My birth mother's was about strict obedience, always.

Still, I envisioned myself part of the Sogn family—a good Norwegian—and vowed that someday I would visit the Sognefjord and walk the paths of Viking lore. After all, I ate raw fish for breakfast like the rest of them. I also ate sweet soup (figs, prunes, tapioca pearls, plus a jigger of whiskey, slow-cooked for hours), and that special desert they made from the milk of a cow just freshened (baked in a dish sitting in water until the milk turned into custard and cake all by itself). Pastries for breakfast. Never dinner. Always choices of cheese. Yes, Norwegian. Me.

No matter my heart, the truth is . . . I was my mother's mistake. Just admitting this, writing it down, catches me. I never really thought of my situation that way. Born into a world chock full of curiosities—well, that seemed enough. Contradiction crowded every inch, every minute of my youth. Curiosity reigned. I did my first double-blind study with a control group when I was about five. Mud pies. I wanted to know why some were one color, others another. Texture too. What controlled that? So I set up lids and cups of different kinds of dirt from everywhere I could find. Some in shade. Some in the sun. All contained some degree of water. I tried the experiment several ways. My discovery? The sun caused the variations in colors and textures: it didn't matter what kind of dirt it was, where it came from, how much water was added, or the size of containers I used.

Endless questions. Clever experiments. My big reveal? Trust only what you can verify yourself. Nothing else is true.

Chapter 2

Pearl Harbor and Gold Stars

"Life is not intended to be safe. A safe life has too small a name for a creature of eternity. Life, at its noblest and highest, has a hazard about it."
—Ethel Waters

Scary air raid drills happened fairly often. Wailing sirens meant lights out. Wardens would pound at your door until you let them in. They had the authority to check your house, room by room, and make certain there were no lights on. Smoking wasn't allowed either. No exceptions. So much was rationed: butter, gasoline, nylons, sugar, sheets. I loved the music, and grew up with the Andrew Sisters, Bing Crosby, and Fred Astaire's dancing. There were a lot of large, free-standing billboards on downtown streets . . . *Buy War Bonds. Help Save your Country. Rosie the Riveter. Woman Power.* And women did indeed leave their homes, some to make war supplies. Even in our little town, this happened. This bothered Momma Sogn. She couldn't imagine women doing anything but taking care of their families, cooking, cleaning, and looking beautiful for their husbands. When Daddy Sogn came home each night from work, Momma would splay herself across the sofa—best dress, best jewelry, looking every inch a movie star. Maybe it was their age. They were way past old. Both exemplified Victorian values and excesses.

I wore mostly taffeta and velvet as a child, like a princess. My birth mother often complained to Momma Sogn. She said there was no need to buy all those fancy clothes and would sometimes ask why Momma Sogn charged her for looking after me. After all, Momma Sogn loved me, right? My birth mother was a waitress, and that was her only source of income. Tips. I flatly refused to believe the arguments I heard. Kids know. You can't feign love.

My birth mother eventually re-married (a mailman) and took me to live with her. Home was now right across the street from the Sogns. Each day after school I could be with the Sogns for a while before I had to walk over to my birth mother's house and be something I wasn't—afraid.

Washington Elementary seemed forever away. That long walk to school terrified me more than the man I now had to call "dad." It haunted me for decades . . . because the street was a walk of death. Pearl Harbor. Gold stars on people's windows. If anyone died in the war effort, the government gave their family a large gold star decal to put on their window in honor of the sacrifice that was made. On my walk to school, there were stars everywhere. Kids know what's going on. Those gold stars were death stars. One morning five or six new gold stars appeared on the window of a home I regularly walked past, and I just stood there, staring, sobbing. I don't recall a single morning in all of first grade when I didn't have to stop my tears and quiet my shudders just to walk in the door of my classroom.

Throughout my elementary years, I did everything I could to avoid getting a 100% score on school papers. This insured no gold stars from any teacher . . . no death stars. The horror that gold conveyed stayed with me throughout my school years and even into adulthood. I never made peace with the stuff until well into my fifties. I couldn't wear gold or anything the color of gold until I was sixty-plus.

But that's not all. When I entered my first grade classroom, punishment greeted me. I turned out to be the only kid in class who could smell color, see music, and hear numbers. "Liar, liar, pants on fire," kids yelled. Everything was literal to me, so when a girl wished she could play in the large puddle forming near the school entryway, I simply pushed her in so she could have the fun she wanted. In my mind, I did her a favor. She felt the opposite. So did the school principal. I never understood why I received punishment for doing a good deed. Many times I'd have to sit on a tall stool in front of the class, halfway between the teacher's desk and the classroom door, as an example of a bad child who told lies. Sometimes, while sitting on that stool, the teacher made me wear a tall conical hat that said "Dunce" on it. Everyone laughed—except me.

The principal did whatever he could to kick me out, including berating my mother. The two had special meetings. She prevailed, which meant I stayed in school. At year's end I had become so angry, livid actually, that I stated with full strength, right then and there, that adults were stupid and I never wanted to be one when I grew up. I dove back into testing things, not trusting anyone except the Sogns. I cross-compared and studied every little thing to find out why my world differed from everyone else's. I carefully observed how people walked, what they wore, how they spoke, and who they were with (and when), to find out if I could learn anything from their traits that might help me with mine.

As fate would have it, that first grade teacher turned out to be my Homeroom Counselor in the seventh grade. It took real courage for me to approach her, to ask if she remembered me. She did, and laughed about the whole affair, tossing it off as though it were nothing. I just stood there. Silent. Decades later I learned that I was born with synesthesia, an elaboration of the limbic system in the brain which enabled kids like me to sense in multiples. Everything that happened in first grade finally made sense. Not to my birth mother though. That first grade debacle, along with her earlier denial of the polio verdict, convinced her she was stuck with a worthless child—her punishment for the affair she'd had as a teenager.

Back and forth I'd go after that. Mom (my birth mother) with her latest man. Me back at the Sogns. Grade school tucked in-between. All the men in Mom's life made threats against me. One even helped her "kidnap" me from the Sogns late one night: Suitcase full of clothes. A long drive to Colorado. Not sure where. I remember screaming daily because of constant constipation and a strange man threatening to beat me up. Mom ended up selling her fur coat for bus money so she could send me back to Twin Falls. I was back with the Sogns again.

Mom eventually returned to Twin Falls and began dating a police officer. He treated her fairly, loved to talk to her, and he liked kids. She married him, and he adopted me. Later came two newbees—a girl and a boy. I was jealous at first because it seemed like they got all the attention and there was none for me. I finally made sense of this and came to love them both. It took me three years to accept my "nuther father" as the saint he turned out to be.

Our small home near the edge of Rock Creek Canyon had only one dirt lane connecting it with the highway. Girls weren't allowed to wear pants, so my legs often froze on the long hike to catch the bus for school. I'll never forget the winter when snow piled higher than the school bus roof. I spent weekends building snow tunnels, along with ice castles and snow diamonds.

Mom worked a part-time job selling tickets at the Radio Rondevu—the perfect stage for big bands and lots of dancing. Sending me to the movie house 'til it closed cost twelve cents—much cheaper than the many dollars a babysitter would charge. You guessed it—I saw a lot of movies, as well as Saturday morning adventure series, cartoons, cowboy films, and the latest newsreels (usually of Hitler banging on a podium as his "goose steppers" paraded by). Seeing all of those films got me thinking about morality and I soon began to ponder one of life's Big Questions: what is good and what is evil? Big Answer: I decided the difference between good and evil had to be love . . . 'cause Hitler ran around destroying things, while cowboys sacrificed themselves to help others.

Reading for me turned out to be horribly difficult. Words danced around and letters sometimes changed places. Kids would laugh every time I tried to read out loud. I dreaded such exercises. It took me several years to teach myself how to read. No one helped. I invented all the "how-tos" I needed by sensing what felt right to do. I stood on orange crates for a stage, then drilled myself out loud, hour after hour, with comic books and Sunday funnies, matching what I saw on the page with what I said. I'd have to sneak in the time to do this, so no one would guess what activities went on in the "milk house". . . that small cinderblock building once used to house a separator (a large contraption that separated cream from milk), now only storage. Today this reading anomaly shows up only if I'm too tired or don't feel well. My three years of "whenever I could practice" paid off. But my sensing differences—the synesthesia—quietly slipped into everyday normalness.

I did a lot of house cleaning during my preteen years. When done, Mom would don white gloves and run them across the window sills, doors, and floors. Any dirt meant I'd have to do the job over again. Cleaning up the hen house proved to be pure horror. Why? Pick up a carcass and maggots would swoosh out. I'd scream and run back up to the house. Nope. Had to clean up everything myself. Nothing I did pleased her. Often she'd yell: "You're worthless, you're a liar."

For solace I'd walk up to the high pasture where the Spirit Keepers were, sit on a log, talk to them, and learn from them. They would emerge from the land as a mountain builds: large bases sloping upward to peaks on top. Huge. I'd imagine faces, bodies, hair, but none of that applied. They were energy beings—transparent, yet I could both see and hear them. Their words filled my mind at the same pitch as if they'd actually spoken out loud; their energy packed my soul. They showed me how they held each speck and particle of the planet together. Air-glued. They taught me how to walk through cliffs and packed earth; be a rock. I didn't really like doing any of that though—too stuffy, too cramped. The full range of vastness was better. More choices. More mystery.

Mom knew how to cook and bake her own bread. Watch and learn, she'd say. So I did. Got to be a good cook myself—except I loved spices and garlic. She didn't, and neither did Dad. For them: bay leaves. The whole family ate well on the poorest of budgets. Asparagus was plentiful on roadsides. There were berries, fish, and elk in the mountains. Milk cows. Chickens in the barnyard. With a hatchet, Mom would kill good bakers and boil water for removing the feathers. I'd gut them. If there was a hen, I'd find a lifetime of eggs, all she'd ever lay, tucked inside her breast (from the one that would have been tomorrow's egg, to those that were progressively smaller, coiled, and waiting). This fascinated me. I wondered if all females (people, animals, birds) had all the eggs they'd ever have at birth—sort of a gift supply without extras.

Dad's great Uncle (the one who provided the place where we lived), sometimes visited. He once ran large flocks of sheep. A master of sourdough cooking, he often wore a starter (a live culture of natural yeast and bacteria that makes baked goods rise) around his neck.

I was almost nine when I finally met my biological father. He was tall, handsome, had a great voice, and drank Scotch by the case. His mother and I bonded. She lost her husband from diabetes the same week insulin came on the market and helped her dad raise her brothers and sisters while mothering a son and daughter of her own. She also ran for County Clerk and won, and even had her own radio show where she and her kids sang. Her voice, by the way, even the dead could hear. A gutsy woman, she succeeded against all odds . . . consistently, daily. Her letters to me always urged me on—do more, learn more.

School became my mecca, a place where I could experience new things and truly be myself. Sometimes that worked out well and sometimes it didn't. I only passed second grade because my teacher was afraid she'd get me again the next year—so she fudged my scores.

My police officer father was different. He seemed to really care and tried to get along with me. I stone-walled and did everything I could to make life miserable for him and everyone else. No one could handle me. He gave up one day and told me off, saying I was my own worst enemy. That touched a chord deep within me. As he walked away, part of me went with him. I don't know when he took up drinking. Maybe he always had. I only know Mom yelled at him one day: stop drinking or leave. He stopped.

When I was ten I began stealing. Merchandise at the Five & Ten was difficult to reach—all of it covered by glass—long tables of it. High shelves toward the back were better for kids like me, where

I could disappear into what seemed like worlds of "stuff." Thinking no one could see me, I pushed all the small dolls I could grab into my pockets, then calmly walked away like another happy customer. Word got out.: "Police officer's daughter seen stealing from local stores." I had no idea anyone ever saw me, or that what I did would reflect in any way on Dad. He could lose his job. I could be labeled a thief and put in jail.

Desperation called for desperate measures. On a Saturday, my parents took me to see Momma Sogn. They didn't give me a reason, but I knew something was up. By then the Sogns had moved to a different part of town. I entered their large living room and noticed that the open door hid a desk behind it. When the door was closed, Momma went over to the desk and started reading her huge copy of the Bible. I walked to the far side of the room, sat on the sofa, and waited. No sound. Nothing said. Then Momma pointed to something in the Bible and started crying. Still nothing said. She just cried. When I couldn't take any more, I carefully tiptoed toward her, frightened at what I might find. She never moved. I peered over her shoulder. There, in words like poison darts, it said, "Thou shalt not steal."

Those words arced from the page and stabbed my heart. Whoa, I couldn't do this. Never, never again. I told her so. Promised. We huddled like silly kids and hatched a plan where the two of us would return everything I had stolen. We could sneak it back and no one would be the wiser. Silly I know, but when the day came, I stuffed everything into a brown paper bag and hid it between my legs. No one noticed. Like stooges in a movie, we went to the store and carefully "restocked the shelves" with the dolls I'd taken (all the while dodging clerks and customers). No one caught us. Deed done. It seemed as if my heart missed a few beats in the process. Yes, I kept my word. I never stole again.

Chapter 3

Nixes Mixes

"The world will persist in exhibiting before you what you persist in affirming the world is."
—Emma Curtis Hopkins

My birth mother began school on the mean streets of Chicago, and was ridiculed constantly because of how she looked. A child of Belgian immigrants, poverty defined the family, even when they moved to a farm in southwest Kansas. There were ten of them. All worked. No holidays. No extras in life. My mom's mother (my grandmother) once had to deliver one of her own children because the midwife fainted while her baby was being born. There was no denying the toughness of the times.

Mom's feet always had frostbite because she had to trudge to the bus stop without proper shoes or socks every winter during the school year. Her first and only gift ever was a guitar, given to her by her oldest brother after she finished school. He had returned to Chicago to make a life there. Mother's stories of growing up were absolutely awful to hear. She worked so hard. Yet several of her sisters poo-pooed her complaints, saying she, as their dad's favorite, always got the easiest jobs. I wondered about this during the only trip we took to Kansas to see the folks and the farm, including my birth father's kin. Kindness was everywhere. Maybe because hard times had passed.

Tales are that whenever my mother's father (my grandfather) rode a bus anywhere, for any reason, he'd know everyone on that bus (*and* know about their families, jobs, and dreams) by the time he reached his destination. No matter where or when—even after the folks sold the Kansas farm and bought one near Kimberly in Idaho—it was the same deal. He never quit reaching out, meeting people, learning. His inventions and creative ideas were ahead of his time. Too bad he never took out a copyright. He'd be wealthy if he had. Geniuses packed the family tree—highly creative, innovative people, including an aunt with a photographic memory.

My grandfather frightened me as a child though. I'd cower in corners trying not to be seen and just watch him and listen to his debates. My mother's claims of his harshness as a father (and how he never allowed any holiday to be celebrated), was, to me, over-the-top cruel. Yet he uttered only my name when he died. My mother never forgave me for this, as though I was somehow responsible. Not until I was an adult, when I worked for certified public accountants who'd had him for a client, did I learn of his brilliance. Grandma hardly ever said a word, yet her strength, her power, her steadfastness "owned" each moment and the very air we all breathed. She was an awesome woman, the daughter of a music professor in Brussels.

Like it or not, I had a family tree wider than most: this included my dad's side, my mother's side, and the Sogn's side—going all the way back to the Sognefjord. Daddy Sogn never spoke a word of English until age twelve. Although born in this country, he lived more like an immigrant; his people settling in the midlands of this country, prospering mightily.

Having three families—two mothers and five fathers—turned out to be more than a bit confusing. I always had to behave and present my questions of what, how, and why differently, depending on who I was around. But I never knew for certain who to be. Even the beautiful portrait done of me at about age three (hand-painted, fancy frame) hung in the milk house. My mother refused to have it anywhere it could be seen. Just storage. My life was like that portrait.

I envied the love given to my sister and brother. How lucky for them. My trips to town for visits with the Sogns were now strictly limited because I had once tried to run away. The cab driver I'd called to help me leave knew my dad and called him.

Trips to the mountains made everything bearable. What else does one do on a police officer's salary? We'd stock the cheap camper on the pickup with food, sleeping bags, and bug spray—and away we'd go. The Sawtooth Mountains, past Sun Valley and Red Fish Lake . . . heaven. Folks would take off and go fishing along mountain streams, but not before giving me strict orders about my behavior: don't stray too far. Well, you can guess how long those orders lasted. Since dad taught me direction finding, I had no hesitation about exploring riverbanks, abandoned mines, and mountain slopes. Sometimes bright energy spinners would appear in the air, right there or nearby. Portals to other worlds. I'd watch them. Never tried to enter one though. Didn't trust where they might lead.

I was always back at camp in time for the catch of the day. Eating fresh fish that was fried in a cast iron skillet over a pile of pinewood charcoal: super good.

One day I was reading the latest issue of *Life* magazine (a gift from the Sogns) and found myself staring. I must have been eleven or twelve at the time. The article, called "The Best Dressed and

Undressed Men in the World," included a full-length photo of a nude man, penis and all. Mother caught me staring and immediately grabbed the magazine while screaming insults at me. Then, for no reason I knew of, she started accusing me of trying to break up her marriage. She screamed louder than loud, using words I'd never heard of before. I froze. Once she left, I went straight for the dictionary. Shock. Never could I ever be such a person, do such things, be that. She lied. To be fair, the Sogns had indeed spoiled me. This made a huge difference in my behavior, pros and cons, but to call me a sexual pervert just for staring at a photo?

Mother's constant accusations against me had the opposite effect. One day I decided to lie on purpose; tell a real whopper so folks could see the difference. Since my grandparents came from Belgium and my Granddad claimed he had once proposed marriage to then-Princess Wilhelmina of the Netherlands (she turned him down of course), I considered myself no less than a Princess of Belgium; and I said so—in my elementary school classroom—in front of everyone. My plan boomeranged. Instead of teaching my mother a lesson, I became the laughing stock of the whole school. Once again, my mother had to meet with the principal. After this, I rolled up into a dark ball, lost in a world I could neither describe nor fathom.

One quiet Saturday while everyone was gone, I stared at myself in the bathroom mirror. I had recently finished grade school and so much pain was locked up inside me, it had literally twisted my face. Humanness was gone. I pointed at that face in the mirror and yelled: *I don't know how to change you, but I am going to change you.*

I swear the air has ears. Everything shifted.

Seventh grade. Junior High School. Wow!

I engineered all kinds of plans and pranks, all creative (none destructive), including talking my entire biology class into walking out on our teacher after she had taken a brief hiatus. This backfired when she told us in the hallway that everyone who participated in the walk-out would be flunked. Kids practically ran back. Utterly incensed that she would punish the whole class for my idea, I went straight up to that woman, told her I was the cause of everything, and said that if she was going to punish anyone it had to be only me. She sighed and said she'd been warned by my previous teachers to look out for me. I said they were right. She told me to sit down and shut up.

My English teacher turned out to be a French woman who didn't care what we did for assignments, as long as projects where creative and unusual. I flourished. Straight A's.

My math teacher, a football coach who hated teaching math, had a unique system for giving good grades. He'd give us a problem to be solved and the first one up to his desk with the right answer got an A+, second an A, third an A-, fourth a B+, and so on. The catch to his system? At any moment he could call on you and you'd have to stand up and show the entire class what you did to get your answer. Yup, I got straight A pluses—every time. Yup again, my turn came to stand up and teach the class my system. And I did—by describing how the numbers and I got acquainted, agreeing to jump over fences or crawl under them, even skipping when it mattered. The answers always revealed themselves as we played. I wish I had a photograph of my teacher's face when I finished my story—his mouth wide open, words stuck between his teeth. Finally, he muttered: *I never taught you anything like that. But as long as you get the right answers, keep doing it.*

Sweet success.

One day our school offered students a special project: anyone wanting to know how the various parts of our government functioned could work in one of their administrative buildings for a day. I jumped at the chance. For real. I got to wash windows for the mayor after cleaning up his office. Not sure I learned much, but I certainly had an opportunity to view the world around me through another lens.

Oops, almost forgot . . . in the latter part of grade school I concocted a story and told my parents that, as a school assignment, I had to visit every church in town and write a report about what I learned. There was no such assignment, but did I ever learn a lot. Different people. Different beliefs. Reading about topics like this was never enough. I had to do it—experience it fully—see things for myself.

Once I started high school, my plans and pranks became even more ambitious. During Social Studies class, on my teacher's birthday, I gave her a beautiful card and boxed gift (the class was in on it). She thanked us for our thoughtfulness, opened the gift . . . a loaded mouse trap. "April Fools!" we all yelled. My junior year I participated in a school walkout. School was unfair. It was like *Gulag 13* (the TV show). The walkout almost worked, until the principal threatened all of us with expulsion.

Next project: it bothered me that our school had Miss Twin Hi contests but no Mister Twin Hi. Not fair. So, all by myself, I put together just such a contest. I went around town to get prizes—good ones. Contestants had to complete three challenges: make a batch of chocolate chip cookies, take a quiz on proper house cleaning, and show how to set a table. Suddenly I had all the help in the world working with me. People everywhere were excited about the contest and it made the papers and news flashes. There was a big show in the auditorium and awards were presented. Never once did I seek out or receive credit for what I did. Personal satisfaction was enough. We now had a Mister Twin Hi contest that lasted several years. I don't know if the school still hosts such contests.

One afternoon I was doing some homework in the school library and I glanced up at one of the bookshelves. Not many books were there, but (to my surprise), one in particular stood out . . . mine. Somehow mine. Immediately I just knew that someday there would actually be a book I wrote on a shelf in a library. I never gave that vision a second thought until, as an adult, a Sheriff's Deputy read a sample of my writing and said I was in the wrong job. I should be a writer. Crazy.

Red Fish Lake was a go-to spot for campers and high school students. One particular day became mysteriously special as I sat on a large rock watching a guy in a speed boat making circles in the water. He circled again and again, as if he wanted me to see him. We met the next night—he a doctor's son getting ready for college and me a dummy who knew precious little about sex or dating. Since he and his family lived in Twin Falls too, we began to date—more and more often—until he proposed marriage and I said yes. Instead of plastering the air with shouldn'ts, both my parents began to query: do you know where you're going to live, what you're going to do while he's in college, or how you're going to graduate and pay for things? No on all counts, but we'd figure it out. He gave me a beautiful engagement ring and we began planning. In little more than a flash, he joined Special Forces and became a spy. I returned his ring. What had begun in sheer joy and wonderment, crashed. Utterly stunned, I focused again on school but couldn't concentrate. I felt lost, lied to.

Because of this, I missed the upper 10% of my graduating class by one point. I told everyone I graduated in the upper 11%. My goal: college. Make something of myself. Dad pounded on the table, saying girls only go to college to snag a guy. Don't worry about what happened with the doctor's son. The next guy would be better.

I found a job at a local real estate and insurance sales company thanks to friends who put in a good word for me. I had to accept less money at first because I wasn't eighteen yet. I moved baggage into a room at the Sogn's that I had to pay for as a renter. Time to be fully adult. This meant a whole new wardrobe, bank account, hair style, and learning curve. I had to walk everywhere I wanted to go. No such thing as a teenager like myself owning a car. Long walks were good exercise, and I walked a lot—sometimes late at night to work things out in my mind and sometimes just to see my city from another vantage point. Alleys included.

One night I walked by a bar and stopped. Inside were all kinds of people having fun and laughing. It was a colorful place with great music. I wanted so much to walk through that open door and join the others. Be like everyone else. But my legs turned to concrete. Really, they did. I couldn't move until I quit fighting whatever held me back, and then I walked on by, complaining all the way.

It wasn't until years later that dad admitted he watched what I did every night from his cop car as he cruised around. I didn't know whether to be pleased or shocked when he told me. It was nice that I had an "angel" keeping watch, but, double-groan, I never had the privacy I thought I did.

Another revelation happened at a Methodist Church I'd begun to attend as a way to meet more people. I even joined the choir. One Sunday the minister announced that anyone seeking to make God central to their life should come forward, be baptized, and accept membership in The Most High.

I was sitting in the choir loft during this announcement, minding my own business, when I was suddenly lifted by two invisible hands. I found myself walking the length of the loft, down the stairs, and to a place in front of the minister. At that moment, a beam of light broke through the skylight near where the congregation sat, arced over to where I stood, and shone only on me. Impossible—storm clouds filled the sky. Impossible—no beam of light could arc like this one did. Impossible 'cause the moment that the beam hit me, I lifted up and traveled through the beam itself into a light not of this Earth. In that light-filled world, twelve children danced with partners, each delighted by their assignment: once adults, what they did would help untold numbers throughout the world. I danced with a boy about my age. The two of us were thrilled to have the job we would someday do—both apart and together.

I blinked several times, surprised to see the minister in front of me, shaking my hand, congratulating me for making the commitment I just had. The church was full. People were reaching over to touch me and pat me on the back. In my mind there was only one thought: that arc of light meant the storm clouds were gone, the sun was out, and my friends and I could go hiking. It took a while to reach the front doors and run outside.

No. This can't be true!

I stomped up and down the sidewalk feeling betrayed. The sky had darkened. The clouds were heavier than before. No way some heavenly beam could have broken through the church skylight and shined only on me. Yes, my life had been crazy and mixed up since birth, but it was still my life—good or bad—and I had the right to live it. At that moment I rejected everything mystical or different or odd that had ever happened to me since birth. I had a mind and I would think things through . . . like everyone else.

Chapter 4

Smack Into Love

"We are people who need to love, because love is the soul's life."
—Hafiz

I decided to take up skiing.

I'd recently graduated from high school, had my first real job, and was earning enough money to support myself. I went on a few dates. Did a lot of dancing. Loved to jitterbug. Two-timed it (that means you dance twice as fast as the music). I managed to survive a three-timer, but really, slow music meant you could cuddle up, be a little sexy. Others bragged about ski trips and the challenge of high speeds on two slats of wood going straight down a slope. Driving north took you to Sun Valley. Driving south meant Magic Mountain and a range of mountains closer to town with a lot to offer. I rented what I needed in equipment and left with a group of friends, ready for fun.

Grabbing a tow rope took you as high as amateurs could go. Dumped off, I managed to maneuver over to what looked like a run. Managed? Ha! The lessons I had taken proved woefully inadequate. Fear ran through every inch of my frame. What now? I said a prayer and let loose. Halfway down, some fool bent over to adjust his boots . . . right in my path.

Smack!

I can honestly say that when I met the man who would be my husband, we fell for each other.

He spent the rest of the day teaching me how to curve around, slow down, and stop. We hit it off and dated often. Real often. I heard "bells" ringing in my head when he proposed marriage. Yes, he's the man I'd live my life with. I just knew. I said yes. Five months later we had a big church wedding which we paid for ourselves (who else could help on my side?). We had it all planned. After cutting the cake, we would quickly change clothes, make a run for the airport, climb aboard a Cessna, then head for Reno, where we would leave the plane, transfer to his (now our) car and head for southern California.

What we didn't expect was for a line of police cars to chase us all the way to the tarmac. Dad. He had planned, as a joke, to arrest us and put us in jail for who knows how long. We suspected he might pull some kind of prank, which is why we planned to hightail it out of church and head right for the airport after the wedding. But a car chase, like something out of the movies? Even I didn't think he'd go that far. Luckily, we took off before they could catch us. And the plane? My new husband belonged to an airplane club. Back-country airfields were common in Idaho. He flew most of them, knew mountain air, updrafts, downdrafts, and sky trails. Sometimes he taught. He sharecropped on a farm near Filer, and baptized each of our three children to flight when they were three months old. With babies aboard, I learned to carry screw drivers, picks, and a can opener in my purse should we ever be forced down. We were. Several times.

Our first child, a boy, arrived the year after we married. I spent two days in labor with pains five-minutes apart. The actual birth took two-and-a-half hours. Our baby weighed almost ten pounds when he was born. But, horror of horrors, he had a long narrow head shaped like a banana with red hair the shade of blood, eyes puffed shut, and scars all over his face from useless forceps. A freak. The doctor joked, "Looks like a boxer who lost his first round." The next day, pure magic. Not only did he suddenly have a normal head and the scars were gone—nurses joked about his unusual strength. He could lift his head and chest up from his bassinet and look around, eyeing the nurses and following everything they did. He studied things. A wunderkind.

Next year, back again. Only this child zipped through, arriving so fast I almost had her in the hospital elevator. A nervous kicker, always in a hurry, she grew to be Miss Fixit. At the age of nine, she repaired our television set when it went out. She just studied the thing, then figured out what needed fixing and did so. It worked perfectly after that. Fixed my steam iron too. She took it apart, laid everything out in a single line on the kitchen floor, studied each part, then put the iron back together. It worked like a charm afterward. There was one left-over screw, though (we never figured out the what or why of that piece).

I never figured out why my husband constantly teased our son either. Vicious. Everyone tried to stop him from doing it. Even doctors. That teasing became a lifetime threat to the boy's speech, as if he somehow didn't want his son to succeed in life. Despite this, our son was strong in every way and he "knew" music. He was always strumming something.

Years later, a second daughter came. She was sort of a combination of the first two, but she lacked the ambition and push they had. Small and delicate, she slept in a doll cradle. An uncle on my husband's side was unusually attentive to her whenever we visited.

He took her into his bedroom once. A pedophile? Even his own daughters grew to despise him. We could never prove our suspicions though. Family secret. Like what happened to me when I was hardly five (by an uncle who was married to one of my mother's sisters). Equally cruel.

That childhood abuse never kept me from enjoying sex with my husband or exploring what is possible with orgasms. As it turned out (and much to my husband's delight), I could reach climax from having my nipples rubbed in a certain way, clitoris, sides of my vagina, and, wonder of wonders, my cervix. I was able once to maintain an orgasm for nearly six minutes which pleased him immensely. I felt godlike, every cell in my body exploding into universes of universes. True, I had to go to the doctor afterward and have my cervix cauterized. Rubbed all its "skin" off. I did that several times before I realized that maybe I should tone down sexual pleasure somewhat and give my cervix a break.

We never had enough money, so I eventually had to consider seeking employment. I fought that assessment time and time again, as I did not want any of our children to go through what I did as a child. I wanted them to always have an involved mother who really valued their presence and who would kiss and hug them often. I took sewing classes and made many of their clothes, learned how to weave, and made pillows. I grabbed hammers, nails, and wood blocks to concoct a way to build toys from scratch. I had real trouble finding a way to make doll house chair legs stay on seats though. The girls loved them anyway.

I tackled gardening—had a large one, lined with flowers, the kind that protect veggies. It's called companion planting, and I never had to use bug sprays. I always left ten percent of my crops for bugs. They need to eat too. This kind of mutual respect netted abundant crops. I canned everything I could. I even took our son to the canning kitchen when he was barely a toddler, put him in an open box with lots of toys, then went about my business. Other women at the canning kitchen would wonder why I visited that large box so often, and they laughed when they saw a happy baby inside having a great time. Fallen apples in orchards became applesauce. I used peaches for breakfast and pies and made syrup from berry bushes (the wilder the better). Asparagus grew along fence lines. Sometimes my husband won on the elk draw, which meant meat for the winter if he made his shot. I tried churning my own butter. Once. Too much work. I usually canned around two hundred quarts and pints of food per year, sometimes closer to three hundred. The most I ever paid for a month of groceries for a family of five was $14 and fifty-some cents. And that was December when I bought decorations for cookies as an extra.

We all had an understanding that if we worked with nature, nature would work with us. I got a taste of this while still with my parents. Whenever the time came to kill an animal for its meat, we'd all sit on the ground near the barn door and watch as the butcher shot the steer right between the eyes. If we did this, the animal died instantly and its meat was tender and sweet. If we didn't, the animal would fight, be difficult to kill, and it's meat would be tough. On one particular elk draw, my husband, our son, and a friend went high into mountain country. They saw several bucks with large horn racks. After the first shot, the animals scattered—except for one. My husband shot and missed. The elk moved closer to him. He waited. Shot again. Missed. Before his third shot, my husband swears he heard that elk say to him: "Take all the time you need. I will be your family's meat this winter." The animal fell. Honestly, the tenderness of that meat was unbelievable, almost sweet.

On our farm, located in the Sucker Flats area near Filer, we struggled to meet yearly assessments. It was named "Sucker Flats" because rich bankers in Illinois bought up large tracks of land knowing nothing about farming or how long it would take hard-pack to become rich loam. My husband had been working the land for several years and felt only two more years were necessary before our farm really produced. To hurry things up, we took in herds of cattle to fatten up for markets, in addition to working crops. As fate would have it, that year it rained so hard and for so long, animals got foot-rot. Medical expenses exceeded profits. We lost big time. One day, around twelve noon, the sky blackened. Bright red licks against a no-find horizon meant one thing: range fire. I ran out of the house, grabbed a large wash from four clotheslines, rounded up the kids, and barely made it inside. Eerie. You could see flames from the living room window. Land Management crews barely snuffed out the danger in time. An omen. I remembered then our marriage date: May 13th. We were warned repeatedly to change that date. Maybe folks were right after all. I wondered . . .

In our part of the county, heart-breaking deaths occasionally happened. One man suffocated when a haystack fell on him. No one heard his screams. I woke up early several mornings in a row to bake muffins and fry eggs for the surviving family. Farm people take care of each other.

Fall meant the Twin Falls County Fair, and that meant baking competitions, circus rides, and bull riding. I usually won a few ribbons—mostly for bread making—and my specialty: burnt-sugar cake (tastes like butterscotch). One year my little brother took first place in the bread competition and I took third. I screamed. He grinned.

I regularly taught a large Sunday School class at the Filer Methodist Church. Our family was active and involved in many church activities. We said grace as a family before each meal. We also baked English Tea Rings at Christmas: put a candle in each loop, then lit each one as a reminder that all the joys of Christmas led to Easter, the crown of thorns, the death of Jesus, and his resurrection.

We needed extra income, so I eventually had to stop being a full-time mom and start working again. I got a job working for a bean broker who sold large quantities to Cuba after Castro took over. It both fascinated and horrified me to see how quickly a Communist government could fool its own people over and over again.

We were forced out of farming, even custom farming, by changing times. We lost the lease on our farm. Big sale. Standing as a family, kids in hand, we watched our life leave. My husband turned to his life-long love of flying and became a construction pilot near the Seven Devils mountains, where they were building a dam. He later began crop dusting—becoming the best in the state. At that time, bees were protected by law. That meant all crop dusting took place at night (when the bees go to bed) and ended come morning (when the bees woke up). The challenge: fields lined by tall popular trees planted by pioneers. Ground crews would stake out rows with powerful flashlights. The pilot had to suddenly lift high, miss trees, then go straight down, follow row lights, abruptly pull back up, aim high, avoid impact, turn, and then do the same thing again for each spread of rows 'til finished. He did this for years. I sat an extra plate at the dining room table for "death" during this time. We wanted our children to grow up with a rightness about this sort of thing —that death is not an enemy, but simply an arbiter of another way life can be lived. This worked fine with the oldest and youngest, but backfired with the middle child. It took her decades to make peace with death.

One evening my husband begged off a particular run because he had a gut feeling that he shouldn't fly that night. He decided to stay at the hangar and listen in "just for kicks" though. The man who took his place crashed into a rival company's plane mid-air, creating a fireball that fell straight down into a farmhouse where a woman was sleeping. There were no survivors. This nightmare so deeply impacted my husband that he quit flying.

Not long after that, we moved to Boise. There were more opportunities there, and staying in Twin Falls was becoming too painful for my husband. What had once been his home was now a constant and traumatic reminder of that plane crash.

During the many years that my husband flew assignments in all kinds of terrain, friends died. We'd visit families afterward and pay our respects, only to discover the deceased displayed the same behavior pattern—each time, each person, no matter the conditions before dying. Basically, here's what we found: people knew they were about to die and displayed that knowing in a pattern of behavior cues. And those cues matched exactly what I had previously observed in dad's police work, in the insurance job I'd once had, and throughout our various trips and engagements.

Here's the pattern: usually about three months to three weeks before their death, individuals start to change behaviors that are normal for them . . . subtle at first, this behavioral change begins as a need to reassess affairs and life goals, a shift from material concerns towards philosophical ones. This is followed by a need to see everyone who is special to them. If visits aren't possible, they begin writing letters or calling people on the phone, maybe e-mailing . . . as time draws near the people become more serious about straightening out their affairs and/or training or instructing a loved one or friend to take over in their stead . . . there comes a need, almost a compulsion, to revel secret feelings and deeper thoughts, to say what has not been said, especially to loved ones, accompanied by a desire for one last fling (to do what is most enjoyed). This need to settle affairs can become spooky, on occasion morbid or unusually serious . . . usually about 24 to 36 hours before actual death, individuals relax and are at peace, often exuding a peculiar strength as if they were now ready for something important to occur . . . and they often have a "glow" about them.

I've found a few exceptions, but, overall, folks seem to know the unknowable when the time comes to leave Earth life.

Once, as a young wife and mother, I had a chance to accompany my husband on a special tour with the Air Force Association to see the hanger of the Atomic Plane (a nuclear powered aircraft that was still in its planning stages). Near Arco, the mammoth hanger, and how it was built, was almost beyond comprehension . . . including curving windows of the thickest glass I had ever seen. The plane never flew though—it was cancelled by Congress. Whatever became of that hanger and how its huge expenditure simply "disappeared" from our nation's budget, I never learned. Yes, I asked.

The following year the Atomic Energy Testing Station opened its doors to the public for its first-ever tour. I was right there.

Once inside, I had to walk through a special door frame that picked up anything suspicious, then I was given a badge that I was supposed to wear at all times. Other than that, I was by myself . . . like a kid in a toy store. I usually aimed for the off-line nuclear reactors, where irradiated pools glowed an eerie blue and mechanical arms were used for picking up and moving dangerous materials. I would often take off my badge, hide it behind a potted plant, then climb the ladder to the top of the biggest reactor. There would often be a white-suited specialist up there giving folks a lesson about atomic energy, while filing them quickly past the reactor's open core. When it was my turn, I put my face in the opening as far as I could before the operator panicked and told me to move along with the others. I studied this tour arrangement, searching for a way I could beat the system. Found it. Operators were only on duty for short periods. With each change they made, I'd be back in another line, looking down the core, loving how it felt. At the end of the day when I had to leave, I'd reattach my badge and pass through the door frame. I did this for several years, whenever the place opened for visitors, without any problems. I loved those reactors, that energy, and never got enough of it.

I do not mean to imply here that nuclear energy or its radiation is harmless because I suffered no ill effects—but I do mean to imply that the ecstasy I experienced there opened a door inside my heart that never closed.

Chapter 5

Be Here Now

"The most exquisite paradox . . . as soon as you give it all up, you can have it all."
—Ram Dass

A great pick, Boise. We caught on quickly that the main part of the city was located at the bottom of a "cup" ringed by two levels of higher land masses called "benches." We bought a house on the second bench because it's closer to the airport and farther away from the Capitol, which is central at the cup's bottom. A large river was close by, as well "steps" to high mountain ranges, desert spreads, extinct volcanic cones, and rich farmland. My apologies if this sounds like a tourist bureau ad, but the place really did look like heaven to us.

The nearby airport pleased my husband. Large schools were close. Our new home had a closed-in garage and tall fence around the back yard—enough room for some gardening and flowers, along with a for-real-pioneer-wagon-wheel-display. We were very happy there . . . for a while.

With my husband now involved in business matters and selling insurance, we often took off on weekends for family adventures like exploring ghost towns and hunting special rocks—among them

Bruneau Jasper, my favorite. Even just picnics at Julia Davis Park were a treat, what with the museum, zoo, paddle-boat pond, picnic tables, and critters to feed.

On a particular Saturday, with the family far ahead searching for picnic space and me lugging a large picnic basket full of goodies, I suddenly stopped short. A slender man dressed in white sat in a lotus position on the band stage talking about the inner path to true enlightenment, describing what you could see and know once you "let go." Ram Dass. Drugs were his eye-opener. A little old lady sitting up front walked to the stage, hardly tall enough to be seen, and shouted "I see all of that every time I crochet." I wanted to yell "me too," but didn't. I could see and do everything Ram Dass talked about without any need for drugs. Before I could pan his drug use, the life I was living suddenly did a complete 180. Ram Dass opened up a heaven I had no idea even existed. That spark had to wait, though. Kids and work came first.

Our son joined a dojo to learn about judo with the aim of someday earning his black belt. Good thing, because diagonal spacing/curving designs easily challenged him (like with some flooring patterns). While he busied himself with tournaments, our oldest daughter joined a Scout troupe with me as the leader. I had to relearn sewing because I used my right hand to sew like a lefthanded person would. Neither my son nor I realized the full span of what being ambidextrous meant: decidedly left-handed for some things, right-handed for others.

Then there was my youngest. Every time she had an injury, skinned a knee, or cut herself, she'd say: "Am I going to die now, Mommy? Does this mean I'm going to die?" Actually, the very first sentence she ever uttered was that very same one. What kid does that? One day I'd had quite enough of this odd behavior. I made a bee-line from the kitchen to the living room, grabbed her off the sofa while she was still asking questions, then drove to the nearest cemetery. We spent several hours laying on graves, reading tombstones, imagining what it might have been like when that person died and where they might be now. She never mentioned death again.

I worked in the office of a car dealer for a while, then at a bank doing mortgage loans. During breaks I played with pens and paperclips. I put them in the flat of my open palm, commanded them to roll over, and, surprise-surprise, they did just that. I felt a surge of heat when this occurred. Such doings got to be a sensation in the break room. My ego loved this until I recognized what was really happening and stopped short. I wanted to learn more about the world around me and who I really was, not be some coffee-break clown.

A job for accountants who handled needs for various large companies followed. They paid a much better salary. With every assignment timed, I worked high-speed every day, year after year. Coffee breaks were a requirement with this type of schedule. I was never one to gossip, and didn't even like coffee (I swear Norwegians wean their babies on coffee as I had so much by age five I couldn't stand the stuff anymore). I spent my break time either outside walking or inside some office reading a book. One in particular held my attention . . . about a psychic named Edgar Cayce.

Called the "Sleeping Prophet," Cayce learned (accidentally because of a health challenge), that he had the ability, while under deep self-hypnosis, to see, hear and know things nobody else did. Psychic? Such a word. I'd never heard it before. It took me a whole year to read that book. And that's because I had to test everything I read, do it myself, experiment, try again, and then see where things led. The biggie for me concerned ramifications. What was the point of ever doing this kind of thing to begin with?

At work I met a woman who practiced "automatic writing," where you let an entity (some source not of this world) use your hand to write messages on paper while you hold a pen. Exciting. Different. So I tried it. One night in the kitchen when everyone else was sound asleep, I began. It was easy to do. Someone or something quickly took over my hand. Words flowed effortlessly and fast—so fast I could not read what was said until I was finished. The entity, or whoever this force was, said good things about me, praised me, then invited me to join him. I found myself hanging on every word, craving the mysterious love he promised, when suddenly, flowers newly cut and sitting in a vase filled with fresh water collapsed and turned black. I tried to stop "whatever-it-was" or "whoever it was," but couldn't. Horrified and trembling, I called the woman and asked for help. "Never do it again," she cautioned. "I'll call back tomorrow."

She did, telling my husband she wanted to take me on a special trip that Saturday. This drive-a-way took us past Floating Feather Airport, far from the Capitol, to tucked-away places in the foothills. We stopped at a cozy house. I walked in the front door and everyone there could instantly see right through me. They knew everything about me since birth, including many things no one else knew. They said they could see my aura (body/mind/spirt energy). Because of that, they now knew more about me than even my own husband. Scary. My son's school teacher was there, of all people. Others included a school principal, the Governor's secretary, and an assistant to the Governor. The people there were true professionals. Most had college degrees. No flakes. No phonies. No money involved. These people simply wanted to help me. Totally overwhelmed by it all, I agreed to be the recipient of a forty-four-Breath Huna Healing Prayer. No guarantees: "Let the rains fall where they may."

How do you describe a lightning bolt? After the 44th breath, bolts flew into both palms, ran up my arms, spread throughout my body, and burst through the top of my head, sending showers of sparkling light everywhere. No exaggeration here. Instantly, the whole room was alive and everyone there was made new by helping me become new. I told these people I didn't know who they were or what they practiced but I wanted to be in their group and learn more. Can you believe it? They turned out to be an Edgar Cayce Study Group—who practiced Huna on the side. Blew me away. Their text: *A Search for God.*

Our group met weekly and there were always assignments. When we came to the chapter on Patience, I chose to make a simple weaver's loom of cardboard and pins so as to fashion a pillow—handwoven. Silly of me, really, since their was no way cardboard could provide loom strength. Still, I did it anyway: my patience pillow. One Saturday a month, our group took on special projects, and one of those turned out to be past lives and how to track your own. What fun that turned out to be. Meditation first, then prayer, then we played around with paper, large marking pens, pictures we cut out of magazines, whatever moved us. They were timed exercises. The faster the better. Forget thinking. Feel. I later framed a huge drawing I made of the energy forces I discovered that drove me in this life. I wanted to know what they were for and what I could learn from them.

Extras like this were put on hold when my son, who was in grade school at the time, got pushed off the top of a haystack by his cousin on Thanksgiving Day. Medics rushed him by helicopter to Boise, then to St. Luke's Hospital, which was close enough for me to walk to during my lunch hour. A compound fracture of his upper leg bone broke through the skin. It was a large cast. Elevated.

I could hardly hold in my grief. Yet conditions soon reversed. In trying to be strong for him, he bettered me. "Don't worry, Mom." He spoke with ease, somehow satisfied. "I always wondered what it would be like to break a leg. Now I know." He possessed a certain wisdom. All my kids did. I wondered sometimes who was the parent and who was the child.

Because of the Cayce group I attended (and other esoteric truths I studied), a unique invitation came my way to attend a special concert by a nationally-known visiting harpist. What a night. The man emphasized that he used only cat-gut strings for more direct effects at the soul level. The sounds he achieved vibrated every inch of me to a level I had not experienced before. During the break, I felt myself float to the kitchen, hardly aware that I still wore a body. Several people noted that I walked about three inches above the floor. Literally. How could this be true? What happened to me? No one could say.

By the end of the concert, not only did I continue to float—identities switched. My "me" no longer existed. Plus, I had absolutely no need for that "me." Fortunately, in one of those "extra" Cayce group sessions, we did an intensive study of color, exploring what it was, how it affected us the way it did, and why. From those studies, I knew the color red could mean caution—and that knowledge, only that particular knowledge, enabled me to safely slow my car down on the way home and stop at traffic lights. Once home, I floated into the kitchen (at least it felt as if I floated), and saw through the window scenes of ancient Egypt. I could see myself there, where I lived, and my life then as daughter to one of the architects who designed great temples. Totally there. For hours. Finally, after gulping down glass after glass of water to break the spell, my feet were back on the floor and I tip-toed to bed. I could no longer accept the history of who I thought I was after that. I'd had a full, deep kundalini breakthrough that night: kundalini—that ball of energy said to exist at the base of the spine, which, when roused, would shoot up the spine and awaken all the energy centers of the body as it rose until it broke through one's crown chakra (the top of the head). This experience so changed me that I had to pretend to be the same person as before, so as not to alarm my family.

Three days later, after the harpist performed at a large advertised event, we met, at his request, in a private room. He wanted this, as he also had memories once he laid eyes on me. Our memories of each other were nearly identical. We cried, hugged each other, kissed, and cried some more. He was married. I was married. We agreed to go our separate ways, blessed with memories. We never contacted each other again.

Several years later, I packed up the kids and drove to Asilomar, California, for a ten-day workshop on the many forms spirituality can take. I also signed up for classes on Huna, the spiritual tradition of Hawaii and the Island Nations of Polynesia. I soon found myself deeply involved in what is called "The Ancient Mysteries" of the British Isles, Scotland, and France. I also found myself following "hooded ones" both in dreams and while fully awake, in time tracks crossing scratches of earth, leaving humanness behind. I participated in just about every esoteric tradition you can name, plus others you can't . . . all of them in addition to what I learned as a youth from the Spirit Keepers, voices of sage brush, desert land, mountain peaks, and black-sharp lava flows. I found wisdom voices everywhere.

An offer came to attend a three-day intensive on out-of-body-traveling. Of course I said yes. An accomplished psychic attended who could see whether or not someone really did anything at all. He graded us. I nearly flunked my first try. I could only raise the spirit component of my "torso" up from my prone body. Nothing else. This was so embarrassing. I knew I could travel without my body in spirit form, but? Finally, I did it. Prearranged tests: people in far-away places agreed to be at home at certain times. Our job was to leave our body, go to each home in spirit form, look everything over, then return, re-enter our body, and write on a piece of paper everything we saw in detail. Stunning results. Most people got everything right: furniture, colors, what, where. Several of us saw a guy present at a certain place and described him; two more at another place. A mic by the phone receiver enabled all of us to hear final tallies: everything we wrote was either corrected or challenged, especially whatever was unplanned.

A secretary to one of the attorneys on my floor came up to me soon after and spoke of a very interesting offer. A sheriff's deputy needed handwriting samples so he could complete an assignment about testifying at court trials. He had plenty from criminals, and needed more from "regular" folk. The only catch: I would have to write back after receiving his interpretation to let him know what he got right and what he missed. No costs or fees involved. Well, this was something new and different so I said yes, copied a few paragraphs from the front part of a phone book, and sent them to him. I heard nothing for months. Around the time I gave up on the whole thing, I received his interpretation: a whole page, small type, hardly any margins. As an example of that man's genius, he could even tell the type of food I liked to eat—just from my handwriting. Unbelievable! Then, to my utter and complete surprise, he wrote: "You're in the wrong job. You should be a writer." I wrote back, praising him for his accuracy, except for that part about being a writer. I had completely forgotten about the experience I'd had in that tiny high school library—"seeing" a book I wrote on the library shelf. Nonsense. Not for me.

I set aside the whole thing, letter and all, what with the new busyness in my life and opportunities to "see beyond sight." As if on cue, my workload became obsessively cruel. Plus I had three kids in the hospital at different times—one in twice. Just to survive each day with a head on my shoulders proved to be my number one goal. Prayer and meditation made the difference. Kept me sane.

After a while, I got to thinking: Why not? That sheriff's deputy might be right. Truly, the job I had no longer satisfied me. The money I made paid the bills, but that's about it. Still, I knew nothing about writing, how to start, or what to do. So I picked up the Bible, prayed for an answer, shut my eyes, opened it to a random page, pointed a finger, then opened my eyes. It read: *Seek and ye shall find; Knock and the door will be opened unto you.* That's it. The advice I needed. Right away I started asking people, even complete strangers I met while walking uptown: do you know anything about writing? Do you know anyone who writes? The third person I stopped said yes. He knew the President of the Boise Chapter of the Idaho Writers League. He gave me a name. I called. The woman who answered said I should come to the next meeting in order to find out more about them.

When I first walked into the room where members met, I felt as if I had left the planet. People of all ages were there—male and female in nearly equal numbers. They were alive, creative: living sparks of an energy I had not encountered before, oozing with ideas, writing things, selling their work, encouraging each other, happy. Afterwards I asked what it would take to become a member. Answer: create three works and hand them in. They would be read by the membership committee, then one would be chosen to read to the whole group, who would vote yea or nay. There was a yearly fee. You couldn't just join. You had to have talent.

I used my so-called coffee breaks to create those three works. But what should I write about? Then I remembered a favorite English teacher who always said . . . write what you know. Well, my oldest daughter was born with a hip joint deformity that required surgery to fix. We couldn't afford it, so we chose a split-leg brace instead. I could write about that. Other ideas sparked, and I handed in all three. On that "more-than-eerie" night, a man who wrote professionally for the *Saturday Evening Post* read one of my submissions. I bowed my head, wanting to leave, feeling so embarrassed, so small. When he recommended me, saying I was a natural, I couldn't believe it. My face turned red with embarrassment.

I attended every meeting after that, entered every contest, tried every idea—mine and theirs. I submitted articles whenever I could. I told my mother about my goal—to become a full-time writer within two years. She went off. "Don't you understand what it takes to become a full-time writer, what you need to know about words and how to use them, the experience required?" No, I answered. That's why I'm going to do it. Six months later, The Idaho Statesman accepted a story I wrote about tombstone rubbing (where you take heel-bar wax and parchment paper to rub pictures from carvings on tombstones). They gave me three-quarters of a page and assigned a photographer to follow me and my kids to a graveyard where we made actual tombstone rubbings. He took a lot of pictures, and they're all still hanging in the room behind me as I write this book. The public went wild about the story. Some widows warned me to never step on their husband's graves, but most raved, including the head writer for the Idaho Department of Commerce and Development. She offered me a position: full-time writer, great job, great paycheck.

See Mother? I did it in six months!

Chapter 6

Doors Wide Open

"Vision is not enough, it must be combined with venture. It is not enough to stare up the steps, we must step up the stairs."

—Vά clav Havel

Totally awestruck. *Me* working in the State Capitol.

Staff: Executive Secretary, Assistant to the Executive Secretary, head writer, secretaries, an accountant, and now me. All kinds of assignments: columns and stories for newspapers, magazines, ads, tours, campaigns, large conferences, and meetings of every kind imaginable. Oh, and on occasion, schmoozing with politicians.

Everything the head writer told me to do garnered a blank stare. What on Earth did this woman want and how could I do it? She might as well have been speaking Icelandic. Mercy was needed. She must have had some, because she finally slipped into training mode and showed me some things—all the while expecting me to know more than I did. Her speech was clipped, demanding. I crashed daily until I caught on. My real job was to sell my state, its people, their history, and their projects to a hungry and curious public. Writing wasn't the key. Selling was . . . ideas: when created, where used, who profited (maybe not deep pockets all the time, but certainly as per political coattails and campaign promises).

Didn't matter how gifted I was. The real question was: how clever?

Being a member of the writers group actually became a decided advantage, as I knew who to contact for what. I could experiment in group meetings with what I needed to tackle at work. Because of this connection, the department paid me to attend statewide meetings of the Idaho Writers League, especially when a famous author headed the programs. It's no exaggeration for me to say that I literally sat at the feet of many celebrities, hanging on every word said, asking if they would be kind enough to comment on ideas I had (and a few times even about works of mine that were in progress).

One assignment: develop a newspaper column that advertised the unique beauty of our state, while also promoting places to stay and things to buy during celebrations and special events. I had help. I met or corresponded with newspaper and magazine editors, and some even became special friends. I won statewide recognition for what I developed, as well as a Press ID card. I found out later (to my amazement), that, after hours, some of my colleagues secretly practiced meditation and pursued material on reincarnation and spiritual development. Who knew? This was very risky at the time. A professional secret. Yet, their Halloween parties were always themed: *Come As You Were*.

I shared everything I learned on the job with my writers group, and more. Within one year, they elected me President of that Boise chapter. My goal: to get everyone writing and publishing their work. I did this by staging unusual settings in the room. Once I had a huge tower of buckets spread out on tables surrounded by wire. Another time I had actors run through the room, yelling loudly and for no apparent reason. After each shakeup, I'd always tell people to write about what they saw. Members would moan and groan saying they had to think about such things, get in the mood. "No," I countered.

Be spontaneous. Anyone can. Give it a try, see what happens. I'll never forget one particular night when everyone (well over twenty people), told about a sale or special recognition they received because of something they'd been inspired to write. I was so proud. The way I saw it, the President's job was to help everyone succeed. The next year I won Presidency of the entire state organization. I only held that spot for one year though, because I often "butted heads" with entrenched do's and don'ts. My motto was: if you can't make changes for the good, get out of the way of those who can.

Department work quickly mushroomed. No matter the job I was given, I found a way to do it. For instance, one afternoon I was asked to stand-in for the Governor because he would be arriving late to a special meeting at the Capitol for business leaders. What? Me? Instant fear. How could I possibly "entertain" business leaders who were anxious to face the Governor with their complaints? Impossible. My boss begged. Apparently no one else could be found to do the job at such quick notice. My panic faded when I remembered "who" was really in charge. I gave it all to God, then walked into that special room and straight up to the podium. With great energy, I bragged about our Capitol Building and the tourist attractions it offered. I then proceeded to tell the crowd every "gem" I'd been teaching young people to say in a program I'd developed with the Boy/Girl Scouts. This program (which ran for a number of years), enabled hundreds of young people to come to Boise and earn special badges for service to their state. Surprise! The gathered crowd loved my talk and laughed openly. When the Governor arrived, I introduced him, and then quickly disappeared. Afterward, my boss celebrated my success and bragged profusely that our department "won the day" for the Governor. He gave me a raise, and I turned down several other job offers.

Our head writer turned to me in panic one afternoon: "I need an article about Grand Targhee Ski Resort on my desk by five. It's for our state magazine *Incredible Idaho.*" I had done biggies like this before, but always had enough time for research first. This time, she tossed me a brochure of the place and left. That's it. Time: 2 pm. I called the State Library. Because Grand Targhee was so new, nobody had anything on them. Time for desperate measures. I asked the department secretary to hold all my calls. I shut the door to my office, sat down, "zapped" my soul out of my body, was instantly there, and used the brochure to zero in on exact locations. It happened. Totally. I walked everywhere, looked around, skied a few slopes, inhaled bites of mountain air, came back to my body, re-entered, gave myself time to re-integrate, grabbed paper, put it in my typewriter, and wrote down every little thing I saw, smelled, and did. Using that material, I wrote the article, "At the Base of Heaven," which was featured in the magazine. No questions asked. Later, after the magazine came out, the manager of the resort and one of the owners came to our department bragging about all the hype they were getting from that story. Sensational. Incredible. Nothing like it before. Totally accurate. Their joy translated into a special offer handed to me: "The next time you come up to ski the place, it's on the house." It took all the strength I had to keep from saying: "Should I bring my body too?"

Opportunities like this came often—like doing "stringer" work for the Western edition of *Sunset Magazine*. Stringers work only at the last moment when something special needs to be done outside of regular employment. This wonderful extra was a guarantee given to me by my boss during my early days at work—a special kudos.

Things suddenly started getting dicey. My second year had come and gone. Our head writer still refused to have me mentioned on the masthead for the articles I wrote for the magazine. Correction: she did allow me to be mentioned once. The more I did, the madder she got, until the day came when she ordered me into her office. Door shut, she stared at her desktop, lit a cigarette (she always smoked), and muttered: "No matter what I tell you to do, you do it. I can't get you mad. No matter how I insult you, nothing budges you. I can't stand this anymore." With that, she stood up and started throwing books at me, forcing a run for the door. I couldn't help but smile though, as this was the first real-life event I ever had that proved: when in conflict, "turning the other cheek" wins. I came to find out she had previously driven out all former writers in the department with this same routine. One quit after six months, others in about a year. I had been there for over two years. Her shenanigans hadn't worked on me. I saw a loaded gun in her purse right off and knew that, with her, only kindness could guarantee any length of employment.

During my stay, lots happened. A few times my family went with me when I was given stringer assignments to investigate tourist attractions. This extra activity gave me a better angle in writing my material. I started taking astrology classes around that time, and found the spiritual science so helpful that I continued to study it for many years. I also studied numerology, the spiritual truth behind numbers. I blended three other methods with the ones I discovered, and wound up training over a hundred people to practice and teach what I came to call "The Number Bounce." De-haunting houses turned out to be an easy task, at least most of the time. Still, there were occasions when ghosts seemed to gain the upper hand no matter what I did. One such event concerned the early family home of a famous senator. His little brother died there, a well-kept secret. Several attended, including a reporter. It made the paper, complete with photos. The woman who rented the place and lived there with her son had to move out shortly after this, as the resident ghost, resenting all the attention, set the place on fire. There were lots of theories as to what and why, but no solid answers.

I once marched in the streets downtown, declaring women had the same rights as men and that the Constitution of our country must be amended to reflect this. As I walked, I noticed a news cameraman setting up dramatic scenes by himself. No women. His prize-winning photos were all phony. This made me re-think all the hysteria about parades.

Yoga entered my life, both as a science of how the body operates and why, and as an exercise in working with one's own body (and its agility) in order to improve health and attain spiritual truth. I began first with 3HO, a very rigid system that demanded strict protocols, then switched to Hatha Yoga under the tutelage of Rukhmani Devi, student of Dr. Swami Gitananda of Pondicherry, South India. The Swami, once a heart surgeon in Canada, felt called to leave his practice and return to India. His background in heart surgery enabled me to respect the broadness, depth and worth of what he taught.

I met Clara Ross, later to be known as Rukhmani Devi. She became a widow after her husband was killed by secret police in Europe while he worked for the Pentagon. What she went through to raise her daughters without receiving compensation for her husband's death is the stuff of legends. Going to India and being trained by Swami gave her the ability to turn her life around and find a peace she could find nowhere else. Living in Portland, Oregon at the time, she moved to Boise to be near me because she felt I could design and publish several books on Yoga she was working on. I did not share her faith, yet my designs worked and her books saw "light." Coming to know Clara and taking her classes led to the miracle of Swami himself coming to Boise. For several weeks, about a hundred people attended his Yoga program in order to learn about and practice the power of Kundalini. Daily classes were a must. Yes, I managed to squeeze out enough time to attend most of the events. Twice more, the thrust of a power greater than one can describe rushed through me, lifting me higher and higher, bursting out beyond any sense of self or time. Swami looked through me and smiled. Words vanished.

The dowser's group I later joined actively put principles to practice. If weather allowed, we'd meet at differing locations to search for whatever object had been hidden, carefully mapping what route we took and what we encountered. Be it coat hanger or dowsing rod or pendulum, whatever tool used became your partner in seeking out water veins, hidden objects, buried treasure of any type, and answers to questions. Our written reports, to the best of our ability, showed the what and why of things. Sometimes we went on pilgrimages to unusual sites where we could test, measure, and explore differing types of energy and historical claims. Finding water always came first. Several in our group had 100% success in not only locating water for a given well, but in finding the right amount of flow for long-term needs. Well-diggers seldom liked dowsers, and even resented their presence and successes. Dowsers made well diggers look foolish, I suppose. Witchcraft they'd say. Nonsense. Considering the thousands of dowsers just in this country alone, not to mention throughout the world, results have consistently shown that dowsing is a healthy and practical skill. For some it's a good career. It personally gave me an edge on explorations and taught me that taking notes is extremely helpful when you're trying to recall, understand, and process information.

The dowsing group I joined already had a side project going before I came: to see if there is a difference in brain patterns of dowsers when they are "locked in" on a target. To measure brainwaves, they used a Mind Mirror EEG biofeedback machine that tracks and measures the rhythms and frequencies of both sides of the brain. Although not a participant, I did watch actual field tests when individuals were in the dowsing mode, versus when they meditated or engaged in other forms of thought. Consistently, a dowser in the dowsing mode (actively searching for a target) always exhibited a pattern of "active rest," where the subject is hyper-focused, hyper-aware, hyper-sensitive (while at the same time exquisitely at peace and comfortable). This "feel of mind" can lock into "spots of knowing," very different from the usual pattern of brainwave function. What I saw, and later did myself, proved that we truly are, all of us, unlimited in what we can conceive of and do.

It didn't take long before I discovered the work of Dr. Wilhelm Reich, a prominent Austrian psychiatrist, who went deeply into the causes of disease and environmental distress. I found his work with orgone energy (the basis of life energy) enthralling—so much so that I began working with a group of others to conduct our own tests of Reich's work.

The deeper I searched, the more intently I became engaged with other explorers in testing the range of human thought and motion. It's like I couldn't learn enough fast enough.

For the second time in my life I went begging—first to my Dad after I graduated from high school—now to my husband during a deeply sincere discussion: I wanted to go to college. Dad said no because he couldn't afford to send me, and he truly believed that the only reason a woman goes to college is to find a man—and I would have to find mine locally. This time I was prepared for such an argument. I'd gone to Boise State to check on admissions and financial assistance, and found out that I could qualify for a loan that would cover most costs until I earned my degree. My husband pounded the table just like Dad did, only this time the answer was, "No, we need your full salary to pay bills." What truly shocked me about both my dad and my husband is how they were so convinced that women had no business getting a college degree. And how identical their body language was to back up what they said.

Election time. Democrats won. Everything at work suddenly turned upside down, with fear being the driver. The head guy of our department was gone. His assistant took over, a man deeply suspicious of every little thing and very nervous about anything said. I didn't know it then, but he was looking for a way to get rid of me. Our new Democratic Governor offered me a job as speech writer. I turned him down because I didn't trust him. I saw the way he worked and heard what he told people, and this only added to my distrust. Our Republican Governor (who was a little quirky sometimes and overly self-conscious of how he looked when he wore glasses), always went the extra mile for anything that would improve projects and help people. The man was awesome. I missed him already.

Before any of this happened, I put my name in for a newly "minted" job as Manager of the Public Information Center for the State Legislature. Nothing like this existed before, ever. To have a direct and daily way to inform all newspapers and school teachers in the entire state as to what occurred every day in the making of law was simply unheard of and had never been tried before.

As fate would have it, our new department head used the fact that I worked as a stringer for *Sunset Magazine* as fodder to fire me. Never mind the truth of how I got that extra job. What mattered to him is that no such "extra" appeared in state code for the position I held.

Fired.

I walked from one floor in the Capitol to another to begin my next position. I had about ten minutes to read through applications and pick out who would be message carriers and who would be message takers in this brand-new experiment to reach and inform the masses. Pushed into such a high-stakes decision, I used numerology to pick my people (the number value of first and last letters of each name are the visible upfront energy patterns each of us have). I couldn't have picked better had I seen their resumes. No one, however, offered to back me up or even explain what I was expected to do or how. I designed what I thought would work and took it to the House Speaker's assistant for comment. They'd never heard of such a thing. I went again, and even begged for advice. Nothing. Went a third time. It was as if I didn't exist. This big test run, what committees had been working on for years, didn't provide a single soul I could check in with or discuss ideas with. The whole experiment rested on my shoulders—a woman with limited experience in politics and constitutional policies.

I executed my plan and trained Message Takers on how to greet the public, take phone messages, handle questions and arguments, and provide information. I trained Message Carriers on the protocol of delivering things to a Senator or Representative, especially if that particular House was in session. Flirting became a big issue . . . between certain Message Carrier females and male Legislators who just wanted to party. Reporters looking for a hot story popped up when least expected—an equally big issue.

Then I executed the rest of my plan: daily reports of everything that occurred were sent directly to every school teacher in the state who wanted them, every newspaper or bulletin that showed any interest, and to public officials. I stayed late every afternoon the Legislature was in session to make certain those reports got out. No exceptions accepted. I worked my tail off.

At sine die, when the legislative session ended for that term, I prepared my report and sent it to the heads of both the Senate and the House, along with various other top officials. In that report I not only presented what we accomplished, but made various recommendations for the future. My mistake: I noted some of the downfalls found in trying to deal with certain officials.

Did I ever get creamed. I made the front page of the paper, bottom left, in a small article branding me incompetent.

True, I did not follow protocol (whatever that was), nor did I honor the sensibilities of elected officials who regularly ignored the people who elected them. My report simply told the truth of what I believed to be an exciting new way the public could be involved in the legislative process.

Ha! Get this: an investigative committee from the State Legislature of Oregon paid my way to fly there and testify about what happened in Idaho. I came to find out they had been following the whole scenario from start to finish. They lavished me with praise for being "ahead of my time," then told me that they would take what I did for my state and use it in theirs. Tears fell.

Strange miracles can sometimes heal what supposed friends ignore. I flew home ready to begin again . . . somehow, some way.

Chapter 7

Exploring What's Possible

"When you have exhausted all possibilities,
remember this—you haven't."
—Thomas Edison

One sunshiney day, my son hurried home from school on his bike, shaken. As he described, a carload of people in front of him turned to the right, drove halfway up the hill near his school, then disappeared. Car and all. Gone. He got off his bike and stared. Where did they go? What happened? He was scared and thought something might be wrong with him. People just don't disappear like that.

We sat down together. I smiled and told him they were walk-ins—those who walk in or enter this dimension from another for whatever reason, then walk back (disappear). I'd seen several myself. Once around lunch hour, while hurrying back to work, a woman maybe ten feet in front of me vanished. I mean she just went "poof"—gone. Total surprise. The idea of walk-ins brought to mind what Clara once told me happened when she trekked the lower reaches of the Himalayas. She accidently lost her balance and began to fall when a young girl manifested in front of her, grabbed her by the hand, led her to safety, then disappeared. Swami spoke of this and so have others. I don't know the all of it, but I do know that such things are okay. They serve a purpose in the overall scheme of things.

Relief showed all over my son's face as his mind processed what I shared. He now felt at ease about the whole thing. Nothing to worry about. I remember feeling so grateful that, in our house, children could discuss anything without embarrassment or fear. Yes, we had some strange zingers occur, like when our youngest levitated a carton of cigarettes to impress her friends. Not allowed! Psychic abilities were an extra to be used only when extras were appropriate.

Pyramids were all the rage then. If you made a closed pyramid (sides in place), you never entered or meditated in one right after eating. It's the same as taking a dive in water after eating—you wait about a half hour, then all is well. 'Tis true that pyramids do indeed enhance dream states, meditation, prayers—anything psychic. Those who dangle a small open frame over their head often pay dearly in the form of headaches or egotism gone wild. There's real power in pyramid shapes, especially open frames. We found that if we placed a large open frame over a garden with exact points for directions (like true north), bugs or blights disappeared, and crops were more healthy and abundant. I still use grids (a plate of numerous small pyramids) to keep food from spoiling for several days if left out on the kitchen counter.

Another group I participated in experimented with trying out different ways of using rows in gardens. Certainly straight up and down rows are standard, and work well. But in other countries rows in circles or various curving designs are used too, as well as raised beds in rectangular shapes. What we found is that straight up and down rows produced quantities—but special shapes, especially curves, gave us better quality. There's something about curves that enhance taste.

I quickly jumped at the chance to be in a group that experimented with some of Wilhelm Reich's work and his theories about orgone/life energy. He found that organic material would attract and collect life energy, while metallic, inorganic material would both attract and repel such orgone. He theorized that he could build box-like structures with inner walls of metal to attract orgone and outer walls of an organic nature to hold the energy inside to help heal physical ailments. The full theory Reich developed made perfect sense to me even though I didn't fully understand the ins and outs of how it might work (neither did anyone else in our group, by the way). Regardless, we made such a box, then the thing blew up in front of us, scattering blue sparkles everywhere. Over the years I've asked what those blue sparkles were. Are they the basic energetic makeup of life itself? No one knows.

Once, while using a kettle to make a fifteen-day batch of sweet pickles, I busied myself by reading the various discourses of Edgar Cayce. He said there were three dimensions to existence: time, space, and patience. What? Patience? While arguing with myself about this, the thick, bubbly-hot liquid in the kettle started boiling over. All over. That sugary goo not only spread out to cover the entire stove top—it quickly coated the inside surfaces of the burners, drip pans, oven, inner framework, large drawer beneath the oven, and the sides of nearby cupboards, until finally puddling underneath and to one side of the stove.

Instead of screaming in horror (which would have been normal for me), I calmly stepped forward into what seemed to be a resplendent, gauzelike, misty netting. As I did this, time and space seemed to overlap, fold, then converge into each other, while my movements slowed tremendously. The integrity of my kitchen as it existed, even the very fabric of the air, shifted. Dimensions switched.

When I reached for the kettle, it was as though my arm glided through the bright gauze, which I experienced as threaded strands of tiny, sparkling bubbles—microscopic, but clearly visible. My face—my entire body—registered sensations of touching and being touched by this stringy fabric netting. There was a smell present that was similar to what one encounters in heavy traffic—a type of ozone.

Without thought or effort, I slowly, gently, and ever so easily removed the kettle and put it in one section of my divided sink, turned off the stove, filled the other section of the sink with hot sudsy water, then proceeded to wash every single inch of every single thing. I unplugged the stove from the wall and pulled it out to the middle of the kitchen, mopped the floor, pushed the stove back, and plugged it back in. Not just once did I scrub and mop, but three times. Sugar syrup is quite sticky.

When the job was completed I looked at the clock. Six minutes had passed. *Only six minutes!*

The surprise of seeing the clock snapped me out of the state I was in. Dimensions re-adjusted, while time, space, and motion resumed their regular speed and proportions. There was enough syrup left that, with added sugar and water, I went ahead and completed the job. When I had first stepped forward, it truly seemed as if I had stepped from one dimension into another. Even the composition of the air had changed to that of a buoyantly touchable, completely visible substance of a string-like netting. Colors, sounds, sight, sensations, even smells, had somehow been enhanced and altered—with everything operating in slow motion. Was this what Cayce meant? Had I accidentally discovered the dimension of patience . . . where stress was non-existent and energy was unlimited and readily available? A place where time and space seemed like nothing at all?

Later on I tried a version of this experiment with my family. I always baked my own bread. This time, with the bread dough in my hands, I prayed that anyone who ate of it would be blessed and feel loved. Honest to goodness, I felt a surge of energy move out from my heart when I did this. It traveled down my arms to the center of the dough I held in my hands. Again and again I felt that energy move. Then I plopped the whole of it into a dish as I fashioned loaves from the dough, put each into separate pans, and covered them with cloth to rise again before baking. At supper time, you can always depend on kids to part the air. The youngest first. "Hey, Mom, look at this bread. It's whiter and I can bounce it all over the place." And she did indeed bounce that bread around the table. Another affirmed. My husband asked if I had used another recipe, as this one was a big improvement over previous batches. I never revealed my secret. I just smiled, affirming in my heart of hearts that from now on I would use prayer more often in cooking as a physical and very present "ingredient."

Dream work became a bonanza. I kept paper and pen handy each night, and trained myself to grab my dreams once I woke up. I wrote down everything I could remember, then learned how to interpret it. I kept a dream journal for years and taught others how to do the same. Of all the surprises, a professional hypnotherapist came to town and offered me an opportunity to become one of his students. Double yes. Although the Edgar Cayce group I attended had already explored hypnosis as a way to better understand our dreams and the way we lived our lives, this visiting pro was a dream come true. I paid for my class by doing the advertising and making business arrangements for him.

Words cannot explain the depths of life one can encounter via hypnosis. Sometimes a past life regression only takes people back to their current life's childhood and helps them relive and understand the right-now of things. This was especially helpful with teenagers. But lives before this one? Always chancy. Success or failure often depends on how a hypnotist uses words and "watches." Yes, watches. This pro insisted that we learn how to follow our clients, literally take the "trip" with him or her, so as to better protect the individual and guide the process. I was such a natural in doing this that my teacher insisted I participate in all the stage work he did. Advertised events were always packed.

At one such event, as he took a woman back through several lives, her skin began to look red and feel hot to the touch. She screamed—condemned to burn at the stake for witchcraft—back in Europe, Medieval times. No joke, her skin really turned red and looked like it was burning. He immediately took evasive action and brought her out of that time-frame, explaining softly, gently as he did, what had happened and that she had nothing to fear. This event became seared in my consciousness. If I was going to become a true professional, I had a great deal to learn about how to talk and how to recognize when intervention is necessary. He loved stage work because picking the right participant was easy—you just look for people who follow your eyes when you're talking. Always allow the individual to be the explorer. Your job is to encourage slightly, protect always. You run into multiples from time to time—like a dozen Thomas Jeffersons. Again, your job is to help your client find meaning, not necessarily "proof."

I earned my shingle: professional hypnotherapist, specializing in personality problems and past lives. Years went by. My practice flourished whenever I had the extra time for scheduling appointments. Two special sessions changed everything for me, however.

The daughter of a friend came to me with no special agenda. She just wanted to give hypnosis a try. To my surprise she went under deep and fast. No longer the young woman I knew, she was now an Englishman, older in years, obsessed with moving from his flat overlooking the Thames to a dreary cottage in Ireland. He had once been a successful barrister who became a judge, then promptly retired. Unmarried, he engaged his housekeeper in sorting through a library of books and papers, fine paintings, and other riches, selling all but a small pile he saved for himself to take to Ireland. In the center of the tiny house he had purchased, he placed a rocking chair and spent the rest of his days in that chair reading his favorite books until he died of cancer. Suddenly the man manifested on my couch as a distinct energy form apart from my client. A second energy form took shape and the two began yelling at each other. I could plainly see and hear both forms; neither were picked up by the recorder. That second form turned out to be the man's mother. She had been waiting for this moment, any moment, to explain to her son why she gave him away after his birth. His hatred for her was so vile, his opposition to her sobbing pleas so unreasonable, that I forced the issue by becoming a mediator so each could present their case.

The story that tumbled out was very sad. She was a poor bar maid in Ireland who had been raped by a customer and then shunned, so she left her baby in a basket at an orphanage in a nearby town. She died of starvation soon after. The orphanage turned out to be a cruel place. He ran away as soon as he was strong enough, stole aboard a boat, and landed in England. Resourcefulness won him a series of jobs and enough schooling to apprentice at a law firm. A talent with debates and clever political posturing helped him attain a lucrative career. There was no time for women, which suited him just fine.

Once both entities had a chance to speak, a profound reconciliation and healing took place. Both energy forms quickly disappeared when my client regained consciousness. Her eyes seemed as big as saucers as she launched into a volley of "oh-my-goshes." She'd hated her mother since childhood with no reason for that hatred. She had been drawn to law in college, won many debate-team contests, and never had a love affair. The next morning she and her mother listened to everything that made it onto the tape. Through tears, the two finally understood each other and hugged.

Not long after, a young man from northern California made an appointment with me. He too was curious about the notion of past lives and wanted to be hypnotized to see if there was anything to it. He quickly slipped into deep trance, shifting to a life in ancient Greece where he captained a large army. A patriot, he relished all aspects of war and soldiering, from torturing spies to killing hordes. He also took great pride in his wife and four children, remaining as faithful to them as he was to his calling. He died in, what for him, was the glory of battle after thirty years of defending his sovereign.

Next, the young man moved in consciousness to a life at the foot of the high Himalayas, where, as an itinerant healer, he roamed from village to village with little but a beggar's bowl and the rags on his "toothpick" of a body. He never had a love affair or fathered children, but delighted instead in the opportunity to help others, which he did for thirty years. No one offered him a hand. He died as if he were but a wad of dust hardly distinguishable from the dirt under foot and sandal.

Completely aghast at what I just heard, my first impulse was to see if I could reach his soul and find out the why of such an unusual turn of events during two life spans. Success. A voice spoke to me through the man's mouth, but, clearly, it wasn't him. I asked for permission to do this, unsure of who or what might answer. Immediately the room became incredibly hot, and everything in it began glowing with a light far brighter than any of the lamps. A voice spoke, not from the man as his lips never moved. "What do you want?" it boomed. Gathering my strength, I asked, "The two lives just described to me, what do they mean?" The voice roared so loud it seemed to shake the walls. "Thirty years of killing. Thirty years of healing. Now, all is well." With that the session ended and the man woke up. His life changed because of this, and so did mine.

These two sessions touched my heart. All that I had learned from childhood up to this moment, including from the three kundalini breakthroughs that I had undergone, showed me front and center that what I knew—all that I had ever learned—was simply a beginning. Step one. Time now for the spiritual, for going beyond what seemed real to the really real and beyond even that.

I just had a couple of things I needed to clean up first.

Our Attorney General decided for reasons nobody understood (except maybe he might have been trying to garner political points for himself), to raid, close down and even sometimes arrest any naturopaths practicing in Idaho. I knew one of them. Patients were alarmed, speaking out, and grouping together to find a solution. Although I'd never been a patient, I knew a phony setup when I saw one—so I asked one of the patients to gather all who would come to attend a meeting. Fear everywhere. I recommended that we begin a writing campaign informing the public what naturopathy is, what such doctors do and why, and why the Attorney General has no place—no right—to shut down such a beneficial form of healing practiced by college-trained professionals. After we spread out, we aimed directly at the Attorney General himself like political operatives, writing article after article for the newspapers. I encouraged others besides myself to lead, while asking for more input, more ideas. Yes, I made the papers again, this time with a larger space for a bigger story (appearing on the second or third page, I don't remember exactly). We won. The Attorney General had to back down, withdraw all charges made against the doctors, and return to each what was confiscated.

Not long after this, a large firm of shopping center builders wanted to hire me for my expertise in setting up promotions. This came about because of a big promotion I did for a shopping center just outside of town. The biggest ever. I had drill teams and bands from schools there to parade from one end of the center to the other. All stores agreed to have special sales, with lots of splashy decorations. Advertising was heavy. People came in droves. When the entertainment ended, some began to leave. Big oops. I forgot to arrange police help with traffic. That meant yours truly stood out in the middle of a busy highway waving to stop highway traffic so those from the shopping center could ease out and leave without incident. Dicey, but it worked. No accidents. My firm was so impressed with how I handled everything, they encouraged me to submit the details to a national "shopping center promotions contest." I won honorable mention. My boss's offer: join the firm, and they'd pay all my expenses to move to Salt Lake City and do big-time promos at shopping centers there. Their offer was huge, yet I knew if I said yes it would mean a divorce. My husband would never agree for me to advance in that manner, plus our kids might not like living there. I said no, finding instead what jobs I could in order to remain in Boise.

Chapter 8

Inner Forum

"The center point of the world, the axis mundi, is the point where stillness and movement are together. Movement is time. Stillness is eternity . . . Realizing how this moment in your life is actually a moment of eternity as you are experiencing it within the temporal is the mythological experience."

—Joseph Campbell

We met as a family, usually once a month, to discuss whatever. No agenda. No demands. Simply "what's up." Our kids really loved this and so did we. It was open vent-time. At one of these meetings, church became the topic. Why were we attending the Methodist Cathedral? We each gave our reasons. None of them had anything to do with God: bell ringers, fun with other kids, adult Sunday School that featured head-trip discussions. No one, not one of us, went to church to learn more about the power of prayer. What a surprise. So we stopped. We decided as a family that we should go the way that felt best for each of us.

It's interesting how that evolved. My husband, a former Mor-man, eventually became a Catholic. My son was drawn to Daoism, my oldest daughter to Science of Mind, then back again to Methodist churches. My youngest daughter gravitated towards Congregational and Brethren faiths. I started out with Unity Churches, then much later Science of Mind—both being metaphysical churches founded on spiritual principles. Prayer was dominant wherever we went.

Study group work and larger workshops with the Edgar Cayce material involved all of us. Topics wrapped around whatever it might take to encourage each person to explore the inner self; what moved us at a deeper level and why. This type of active format put Truth with a capital "T" front and center. Our "Study Group Two" often set up weekend projects which we advertised. Occasionally we designed family get-togethers, with emphasis on the dreams and desires of each child.

To me, this kind of freedom opened wide yet another door to the celestial, to a universe teeming with life, unending and forever, available just for the asking. Sounds grandiose? Yes. That's why I grabbed on and ran with it. What is *real* truth? What *really* is behind life's mysteries? During this stage of my life I met Art Yensen, and at a large standing-room-only affair, a crowd gathered to meet Edgar Cayce's son Hugh Lynn. They wanted to learn more about the Association for Research and Enlightenment (a place where anyone can go to explore reincarnation, the inner self, psychic abilities, and the power of prayer). Art and I became like best buds in the years that followed.

Afterward, nothing seemed impossible. All that I had previously learned seemed as if little more than frosting on a much larger cake. My work life shifted back to banking, but this time as a writer—of technical manuals. Don't laugh. It's a living. Local study groups began to shift from just Cayce material to more open-ended explorations of meditation and the spiritual. For me, India-born Eknath Easwaran's LP-record on how to meditate proved to be exactly what I needed.

Margaret Matthews, a friend of mine, decided she would save the Cayce groups and I would help her do it. Tilt. This was not my intent, but who says no to Margaret? Older than I, she had the gift of being able to see through people. She gained this gift from the nightmare of dealing with a father and husband who both kept their alcoholism a secret, while at the same time declaring Margaret was the one with a problem—not them. They had her declared mentally incompetent. She had no defense. Treatment: electric shocks. Her father died. Her husband, a successful and well-loved businessman, invented excuses about family doings as he kept on drinking.

Those "treatments" made her realize what was really going on in her life: how she had allowed others to use her whenever they needed a foil. What helped her the most? The teachings of Ernest Holmes contained in the book *Science of Mind*. She loved her husband and father—her whole family—but never again would she allow anyone to trick her or treat her with a lack of respect. I wish I had a photo of Margaret I could show you. That woman shined.

We held Cayce group meetings in her home. My husband and I worked as a team with most of them. Margaret even "drummed the bushes," enticing others to attend until we had quite a large number coming each week. I was visiting with her one afternoon when a neighbor lady, the one who lived just across the street, came calling to ask Margaret a bunch of questions about life, psychic abilities, and life after death. Begging (I guess to God), she said she'd never had a miracle in her life. Clearly she wanted one now. Margaret smiled, "You'll soon get what you want." Satisfied with that answer, the lady left.

Maybe a couple of weeks later, on a Friday night, my husband and I were at her house leading a group who wanted to learn more about healing prayer. Margaret arranged this so she and her husband could take some time off with their grandson and tour Yellowstone Park. The phone in her dining room rang. I answered. Her son, surprised that anyone answered, exploded with grief. We knew each other so he held nothing back. It's as if he needed us to be there so he could talk and scream and cry. That afternoon, there was an accident. Some doctor's son trying to impress his date raced across the Park's tourist bridge in a new pickup and slammed right into the Matthews' car, decapitating Margaret on impact. The steering wheel gored her husband, and their grandson broke his pelvis. The grandfather stayed alive long enough to make certain his grandson would be found and rushed to a hospital—then he too died.

Two dead. Grandson injured. Our healing group was present and ready to invoke prayer at the instant of need. Everyone was deeply affected.

The following day, doing what I could to help Margaret's family prepare for the funeral, the neighbor lady across the street rang the doorbell. All color was gone from her face. She'd heard the announcement over the radio about the accident. "Not possible," she insisted. Yesterday, she had been outside sweeping off her front sidewalk when she saw Margaret walk out her front door, down the steps, then across the sidewalk. The neighbor lady greeted her and asked how she was doing. "Just fine," Margaret replied. Then she turned around, went back inside her house, and shut the door. The neighbor lady insisted that all of this was real—physical. Sounds and all.

When the neighbor lady heard the afternoon newscast, she called the Sheriff's office immediately, insisting that she had just seen Margaret and talked to her. The Sheriff's deputy emphasized how that was not possible, as both she and her husband had been killed. "What time did this happen?" she asked. The time the deputy gave . . . *was the exact moment Margaret had been decapitated.*

Silence. Finally I spoke. "You wanted a miracle. Margaret gave you one."

Boise burst its psychic seams. Suddenly people wanted to know more about visions, ghosts, reincarnation, past lives, anything different or spooky. Between the latest article in the latest magazine and fortune tellers galore, I became edgy. Surely there must be a way to bring experts to town at a price anyone can afford in order to pass along the best information "out there" concerning esoteric, psychic, metaphysical, and holistic realities. Taking a look at real research, seeing what passes the "smell" test, can make a huge difference in people's lives . . . for the better.

A woman on a short stay in town called me on the phone. "You need something like a forum here," she said, "where actual practitioners of the healing and psychic arts can give talks and demonstrations, handle questions." After she'd made her point, she disappeared. I never knew her and don't know how she got my phone number. Shortly after her call, while I was exercising in a swimming pool, Margaret walked toward me. Now hear this: *she walked atop the water, fully there, walking normally, looking good*. When she reached me, I was so flabbergasted I could say nothing. "Call it Inner Forum," she advised, as she laid out the basics of such an organization and how it might function. I just stood there in the water . . . looking up at Margaret . . . feeling both joy and utter disbelief. No way could I deny what my eyes saw and my heart felt. Real. Right now real. Margaret. Inner Forum. A miracle birthing.

How to start? With what bothers me the most: all the psychics in town. Me too, I suppose. Some were good, some pretty good, and some were downright charlatans. Aha! I had the idea to hold a psychic fair—a really big one—and invite everyone to come. It wouldn't be up to me to decide who's who. We'd let the public decide by trying them out. I got together with friends who had ideas of how-to, rented the big room at the Y.W.C.A., charged fees for table size/space, used that money to pay expenses including advertising, and away we went. What happened next? A huge turnout of people and laughter and music and games and contests and costumes. Unbelievable! The public did indeed critique readers and booths. It didn't take much time at all to manifest the discernment I wanted to see.

After that my head buzzed with ideas. How about a newsletter, like a mini-magazine, that carried all kinds of news, invites, cartoons, truisms, with enough advertising to cover paper and stamp costs? The newsletter's title: *Inner Forum*. Of course. So I mailed invitations to every group or person or practitioner I could think of. Then I personally went to the largest churches in town, sat down with the ministers, and explained to each what *Inner Forum* was—a way to bring the best of the spiritual-wellness-psychic worlds to the general public for their edification and enjoyment. What is real. What isn't. Truth. No sensationalism. The ministers listened and asked questions. Not one objected. *Inner Forum* took off, with me finding a place in my kitchen where I could put file boxes, my typewriter, artwork, and stacks of ideas. I did it all—arranging activities, finding space, contacting people, checking protocols. It didn't take long before the whole project mushroomed into a very large organization that attracted a host of talented people who recommended exciting programs and special research projects.

What put *Inner Forum* "on the map," though, was a singular event held at the largest hotel ballroom in town—the appearance of a famous medium who had enabled the dead son of a more-than-famous Bishop to speak live on national television. The show was seen by millions and caused a national stir. That medium was here now, with us, sharing the fuller story of suicide, religion, and forgiveness. Also present, Sun Valley's best pianist/astrologer—the one who actually made all of this possible. Double wow!

This event came together at the last minute, so the kind of interviews and advertising that had made such a difference in the past was impossible to do. I breathed a sigh of relief when the newspaper agreed to do a big story. So there we were, on the day of, teams of people, the ballroom set up for a large crowd, more reporters at the ready, the newspaper article just out . . . *without any mention of where*. Absolutely nothing, not even a clue. I phoned the newspaper in utter panic. Apologies. I knew about "Mercury Retrograde," one of three times per year when the planet Mercury appears to be going backward when it isn't. This optical illusion tends to "fool" people. And me the fool 'cause I forgot. The one saving grace I could lean on: things spiritual often operate under a different timing. You bet I prayed. Half-hour before start, still quiet. I did meet the speaker, a fabulous man. Now, fifteen minutes before. Suddenly the hotel staff ran outside. A rush of cars. Too few parking spaces. People were flooding in. So many, the ballroom nearly filled. The hotel staff went nuts. I nearly cried. Hardly anyone called the newspaper or hotel office. So how did all these people find out where to go? A miracle!

I stood in the back during the program, watching the audience and the speaker. The most beautiful blue, like a halo, hovered above every head. For the first time in my life I saw another entity take over someone else's body, use it, and speak through it as if trance work could be as natural and normal as everyday speech. Watching this miracle occur showed me that *Inner Forum* could be the best possible way for the general public to explore the mysterious. I thanked Margaret. Her idea had proven itself.

The medium and I became good friends afterwards. I brought him back to Boise numerous times, along with the help of my favorite astrologer, to give readings for a host of folks who wanted to know more about those who had passed on. He always treated me as an equal. For instance, any time he wanted something checked, he'd ask questions like "Did I turn the stove burners off when I left my apartment?" I never missed, though I wondered sometimes about the how of it. Like, how could I know things like he did?

Inner Forum was never just a magazine-type newsletter or a sponsor of talented speakers. I enlisted a group to hold regular biorhythm studies: how we each move from the busy-i-ness of activity to slowing down when we need more rest. These are natural rhythms that are wise to know when planning trips, jobs, and activities that demand more from us than the normal routines of everyday life. Other teams formed to explore the kundalini factor, night and day cycles, foods and their affect on us, what it feels like being near or far away from someone we are unsure of, and intuitive factors versus psychic ones.

I also tried every way I knew to contact knowledgeable speakers and offer them speaker fees for coming to Boise under the auspices of *Inner Forum*. The famous writer Brad Steiger sent his assistant. One of the best names in holistic health from Boston came. In the beginning, *Inner Forum* hosted meetings twice a month with plenty of people volunteering to help out. Soon meetings switched to once a month. Finding great speakers never a problem. People valued the organization. Later some questioned who was really running the show. How could an organization like *Inner Forum* just happen? When I claimed to be the core muscle behind the organization, nobody believed me. That's when it hit—I'd better incorporate *Inner Forum* and have it operate under a Board of Directors. I knew someone in the Attorney General's office. Under her guidance, *Inner Forum* became Idaho's first non-profit metaphysical corporation. Volunteers packed the Board. Now, no one could complain about the "me" factor, that one person really could do everything. Any desire to spread to other states was squelched by the simple fact that no one wanted to do the work necessary to make such an expansion possible.

During the seven years *Inner Forum* existed, we had plenty of newspaper coverage for our numerous activities. I loved doing the newsletter and people loved getting it, so I carried on. Even my kids had fun with some of the subjects tackled. I gratefully accepted any opportunities to give talks elsewhere and attend psychic fairs and various other types of large events. During a trip to New York City where I was asked to be a speaker, I met Brad Steiger and his wife. Immediate bonding. It felt as if we had known each other forever. Because of this, I became one of Brad's assistants in finding and verifying various topics. He even devoted one chapter in a particular book of his about my husband and myself and all that we were doing with *Inner Forum*. This friendship, and trades on research materials, lasted for decades—until he passed away after writing well over a hundred and twenty books. He never stopped asking questions or searching for answers. I cherish the friendship we had, even now.

It is impossible for me to explain the impact *Inner Forum* had. An estimate of three-thousand hardly covers the steady stream of people who regularly came to events, participated in experiments, and searched their very souls for truths beyond life, beyond death, beyond each word we say. Easily two or three times that estimate would be more correct.

During this crazy busy time, I spent as much time as possible with the kids and my husband. Cleaning activities were divided betwixt, but cooking was pretty much mine to do. And canning peaches, for heaven's sake. We had a peach tree on our lawn that loved to over-produce, which meant canned peaches for breakfast year-round, peach jelly, peach syrup. It got to the point where I could hardly look a peach in the face. Same with grapes and grape juice. Many decades later, I still can hardly eat or drink either.

Chapter 9

Who's Fooling Who

"It takes courage to grow up and turn out to be who you really are."
—E. E. Cummings

Times changed. People were now more interested in holistic health and transpersonal psychology. I tried to get the Board to alter the focus of *Inner Forum*, and move along with the changing tide. They wouldn't budge. Not a single member seemed able to either see or sense how people's likes and dislikes had altered. They expected *Inner Forum*'s track record to continue forever. Life doesn't work that way. I resigned from the Board. Sure enough, another group did indeed emerge—very much in line with new interests, and drawing a bigger crowd. The proverbial handwriting was on the wall.

During her last year of grade school, our youngest daughter was kidnapped from a park by a man with rape on his mind. Several of her friends called me on the phone, told me everything, and even provided tips on where they thought the man might take her. I have no idea how they knew such things, but they did. I informed the police. They picked me up and a bunch of us followed the clues. Darkness had descended by the time we closed in on the house where we thought they were. Police entered first, then me. We all stormed into the back bedroom and found them both nude, with the man about to penetrate. I grabbed her. She started crying as I helped her dress. When we were about to leave, the police asked if I wanted to speak to the would-be-rapist. Yes. I scolded him as any mother would, making him feel ashamed for even trying such a thing, then I marched out with my daughter in tow. Cussing wasn't necessary. What I said was strong enough.

Two months later the judge asked me to send in a statement that he could read to the court. The event shook up our daughter and opened her eyes. After that night, she started to excel at school. Where uninterested before, she now did extra work during class, studied more, got better grades, and had more friends. Literally, she had become a better person. I noted that the young man who wanted to rape her left clues that were easy to follow, as if he wanted someone to stop him. He hung his head in shame when I aimed one volley of disgust after another right at his face. My recommendation: send the man to school, give him the help he needs. Somehow, some way, what he almost did was, in my eyes, a cry for help. My daughter had learned a great deal from the escapade. It was time to give him a chance for a "course-correction" too. The judge thanked me for my letter. The man's sentence? A full educational/training program. Justice done.

My husband left. He knew about what had just happened to our youngest, but he walked out anyway. Talk of going to a marriage counselor was like pie in the sky. Two kids were in high school, the other was in the sixth grade. No way I could make enough money to support the family without his help. He mumbled something about finding work elsewhere and sending me something. His body sagged, face down. The man I married had somehow disappeared. Our youngest saw and heard everything, and ran to her room crying, blaming herself for his decision. The older kids were sullen.

Darkness descended on us all. I didn't cry. I just stood there, maybe waiting for a miracle—not sure. I had heard something in the news about food stamps. I applied for them the next day.

This wasn't the first time disaster struck in our marriage. While a young wife, I had a nervous breakdown from working too hard and having too many responsibilities. I drove around town in a stupor. Couldn't think. Hardly knew anything. I was taken to a doctor. He gave me a blue pill, triangle-shaped. Take three a day, he said. Big joke. I couldn't handle that pill. So the doctor reduced and reduced until, with my taking only one-half of one pill per day, I was a raving drunk. An example of how ridiculous things got: I had just returned from getting groceries, and everything was put away except for the eggs. In transferring each to a tray in the refrigerator, I dropped one. Looking down at the floor, I felt so sorry for that lone egg all by itself that I dropped another one so it wouldn't feel lonely. I laughed gleefully. Such a funny scene.

When the doctor learned of what happened to the eggs, he and I had a long talk. He noted that I had the most sensitive body of anyone he'd ever seen. He emphasized that, with my sensitivity, I never could have acted out like most kids do in school—things like heavy drinking, smoking, etc. "Why were you so different?" he asked. I told him about what happened on a particular Sunday morning in kids' church when I was nine years old. I hid in a supply closet until all the lights were out, then ever-so-gingerly tip-toed to the altar, which was adorned with red velvet, candles, and a huge portrait of Jesus. Powerful place. Down on my hands and knees, I promised God I would never smoke, never drink, and never use God's name in vain. I tried smoking once when I was much older. I coughed so hard it nearly killed me. I once tried to drink a "Grass-hopper" martini. Thought I would die for sure with that. Then I sipped a Vodka Collins. Loved it. My promise was definitely in peril with this one, so I never drank anything alcoholic again. Never ever.

The doctor thought about what I revealed as he studied my test results. “When you go home, I want you to get down on your hands and knees again and thank God you made that promise when you were nine. It’s all that’s kept you alive. Had you taken up either habit you would have died, probably around your eighteenth birthday, judging at how stupid teens usually are.”

When I finally “woke up” to what was happening in my life, I asked my husband to leave, bag and baggage. He had preferred taking naps on the living room sofa to bringing home a paycheck. After we parted, maybe two weeks or so, the kids wanted him back and, I have to admit, so did I. I loved the man. Years went by like the ticking of a giant clock. He actively embraced *Inner Forum*, rising in his own career, or so it seemed, and loved to be with his family and me and all that we did. There was no reason, not even a hint, that any new or old problems were afoot. When *Inner Forum* folded, my life, my marriage, my home folded too.

In the bleakest of days, as my husband stood in front of me saying he had to go, it seemed as if a bomb exploded. What can I say? He walked out the door. Left. Twice he sent me some money. Three months later he returned. ‘Twas Christmas time and he wanted to be with his children. I found out he’d been living with several other women in another state. Several, mind you! He voiced something like maybe we could try counseling. No truth in his words. I went straight to a lawyer and sued for divorce.

Angry? Ha! I was livid.

The judge assessed child support for the three. I asked for nothing—just help the kids. The assessed amount would be enough with my salary to guarantee living expenses. Monies had to go through the court each month before I saw a penny. Twice I collected. That's it. When I went back to the judge to complain and ask for help, my former husband became so angry that he refused to pay another cent. How dare I embarrass him. The judge had a fit at his insolence and raised the amount. Yet for some reason, the court, believing him, turned their judgment around and washed their hands of the case. I was left with a "no-thing" that could not be collected. He claimed he paid what the court demanded. But I never saw a single penny.

Friends knew. Numerous times I'd put my hand in a coat pocket and—surprise, surprise—there'd be money there. Bills. One time over $50. How this happened I have no idea. Never caught anyone doing it. Once in a while there'd be a sack of groceries at the front door. Never learned who did that either.

Difficult days. No solutions. Nary a letter, or even a phone call for the kids. Folks, remembering "the good ole days of *Inner Forum*," wanted to meet again, even if just in my home, to talk, to experiment . . . such as imagining a wall in the middle of the floor that would prevent our pet cat from going to and fro. We each participated. One called for the cat to come. She tried again and again, but couldn't get past what was invisible to us, but very real to her. She became more confused and frustrated each time she tried. No one could see anything there. Still, something blocked her. This became such an issue that we all "dissolved" whatever thought-wall existed by seeing/thinking/declaring it gone. The minute we did this, the cat ran the full length of the room as if proving to herself the wall really was gone and all was well.

Conversing with the former wife of one of the "four amigos" (what the four guys called themselves as they grew up together in Sucker Flats—my former husband one of them), I got the surprise of my life. When I said I had just divorced my husband, she laughed uproariously. Then she said something that stopped me short. "Those four guys were spoiled sons of wealthy fathers. That's why they all pal'd around together. Drank together. Kept a list of all the gals they had sex with, traded partners. Had the best cars, best clothes, best line to handle any problem. You're the last to wake up. All the rest of us divorced long ago."

We talked at length. She had two children who looked good, happy. Her secret? After her divorce she became a secretary to a bank manager. She learned all she could from him about the banking business, taking on more and more responsibility, positioning herself so that when her boss moved up in rank, he would make certain she did too. That's how she became the new manager of a branch bank. She made a great salary and dated a great guy who loved her kids as much as she did. She advised me to wake up. "Get out of your rut. Look around. You deserve better than this. And so do your kids."

My love for him had blinded me to what was really going on. All those insurance sales he said he made? Well, it turned out his boss had kicked him off the sales team. There were no such meetings. His determination to exceed in sales was simply an outplay of his college days, where he preferred parties to study. What she said about spoiled sons of wealthy fathers hit hard. Why didn't I see it? Can love really be that blind? Or is there something in me? I had so many fathers. The mom and dad who raised me, loved me—not mine. Replaced by a mother burdened by my existence, uninterested really. Her final husband was a true saint though. My police officer father, the one who adopted me, was an angel in disguise.

Honestly, how can I speak ill of the man I married? Maybe it was me all along, looking for a father, not a husband. Maybe it was me who needed to grow up. I'd spent decades helping others, making a difference in thousands of lives, doing my best with the children. Clearly, it was time for me to finally help myself.

Chapter 10

On the Way to Becoming a Bank Manager

"If there aren't any obstacles along the way, the path probably doesn't lead anywhere."
—Unknown

To shift and re-focus my life, I asked myself: *why not become a bank manager like my friend had*? Intriguing thought. I already worked as a bank analyst, so, I began taking classes at the American Institute of Banking. Those classes tickled my fancy. I enjoyed every minute of them. To me the old adage, "When the student is ready a teacher will come," meant that the vast new world of finance and banking was a good choice. At work, I was given the opportunity to take drafting classes as well—college level. A gift.

Weekly crowds still came to my home. People had questions about the larger realities of life, altered states of consciousness, psychic and spiritual things, and what could be proven and what could not. Lively discussions always. Despite this, my interest began to wane. One evening a fellow who wanted to show everyone the new way he found to steep tea in a cup was absent. I was too tired to wait. Come morning I would take my very first test on drafting at the mathematical wing of Boise State College, where my oldest daughter also studied. Can you imagine that? Mother and daughter walking along the hallowed halls of academia together, arm in arm, and in the mathematics department of all places. What a thrill! Indeed my life was changing and in a very good way.

Later that night the fellow who was absent earlier finally showed up. My daughter shook me awake. He was at the front door, muttering something about a car accident and the police report he had to fill out. The energy around him, his aura, bounced wildly. The story he told was jumbled in his mouth. Since the house had empty bedrooms, I pointed to one and told him he could sleep off his traumas there, then leave come morning. He accepted the offer, shutting the door behind him. I returned to my room and quickly fell back to sleep. I'm a heavy sleeper. Tales of Dad and his fellow police officers using the field outside my bedroom window for a gunnery range when I was a kid were all too true. I never heard a single shot. I accused Dad of lying to me about the whole thing. He just snickered. I swear a bomb could go off while I'm asleep and I wouldn't hear it.

Not until the man reached climax, yelling for joy at his conquest of my body, did I become aware of what had happened. I couldn't scream. I couldn't move. The man never asked to be with me, never said a word. He just snuck into my room and took what he wanted. I didn't matter. When morning came, he left—just got up and left. I was still wide awake—all night wide awake. I wanted to scream, but couldn't. This man had raped me. Grasping the import of that, the hugeness of that, was beyond my ability to grasp . . . even if this represented the way things go now, the new dating scene—sex first, then get acquainted. Where was love? Where was respect? Where was permission?

As days passed, he returned again and again, as if he suddenly owned me. No matter the questions I asked and the demands I made of him, he ignored any topic but his own. It was as if I suddenly belonged to him. My mind seemed to go blank. I just couldn't understand my place in this drama and wished he would return to California where he came from. Finally he did. Then I found out I was pregnant. I was horrified at first, then felt a strange kind of wonder. I loved children. But having another at my age, facing my kids, my boss, the people where I worked, the utter embarrassment of it all, the horror and crime of it . . . nothing added up. I felt lost in a strange kind of stupor and couldn't find a way out.

When he learned of my condition, he sent money. "Get an abortion," he demanded. "Where's a discussion about this," I countered. "Where's my voice?" I kept trying to talk about the issue, work things out. He flew back to Boise and became even more belligerent. He paced the floor like a wild animal, yelling to himself, then he flew back to California. Nothing offered. No comment. Wasted trip.

That night I put both hands over my uterus and prayed. "Your will, not mine. If this child is to be, let it be so. If not, let it leave." I felt rushes of love. Truly another will was present. Not mine. Not his. Not even the child's. Something else.

There was nothing left of me.

Death came.

Chapter 11

Twice Dead

"What lies behind you and what lies in front of you, pales in comparison to what lies inside of you."
—Ralph Waldo Emerson

January 2, 1977

I made it to the bathroom. Blood everywhere. Cramps. I started screaming as I positioned myself on the toilet. My voice—ever so loud—seemed to hurdle through the walls, ceiling, roof, and a sky that echoed every sound I made.

A tiny sac floated in a bowl now filled with blood. Stabs of pain ended things as I floated upward. Bathtub and sink, everything, suddenly far below. Me? I kept bumping into the light fixture on the ceiling, drawn to it like a moth to a flame. Again and again I kept bumping into that fixture. Its light was on.

Blobs formed in the air around me. Yes, blobs—like fully dimensional ink blots capable of movement. Strange shapes. They were gray and dark and I didn't like them. The more I questioned what was going on . . . what had happened to me, why my body was on the floor, yet I was next to the light fixture on the ceiling . . . the more blobs there were. Soon the air was filled with them. I finally caught on. My thoughts created them. The more I thought (didn't matter about what), the more blobs there were. How could this happen? Why?

Without warning there was a loud snap and I was jerked back into my body as if I had been nothing more than an over-stretched rubber band, entering through what had once been the soft spot in the middle of my head as an infant and feeling the need to shrink back down to size—since I was larger outside my body than inside. I was pulled right down to the tip of my toes. I don't know what/who did the pulling.

Back to the pain. Back to the mess.

I'm a neat-nick by nature and can see a dirt ball at fifty paces. Quite naturally then, my first thought was to clean up the blood splattered everywhere. What had just happened could be puzzled later. How I cleaned up the place I don't recall. What sticks in my mind is grabbing every pillow I could find, piling them at the foot on my bed, and stuffing towels between my legs as I raised them atop the pillows. Sleep. Calling for an ambulance or help of some kind wasn't something I would do. Since childhood, I had been taught to take care of any problem myself. And this I had always done.

A vague memory of my daughters shaking me and asking what was wrong remains. I feigned illness and asked that they busy themselves fixing their own supper. In an odd kind of way, I felt a sense of relief. The miscarriage guaranteed that no one need know about any of this. My foolishness would be my own affair, my life my own. Even the nightmare of being raped was over as well. Whatever else happened in that bathroom, I could forget. Perhaps what occurred was no more than a trick of mind.

January 3, 1977

Towels were not enough. Come Monday morning I was still bleeding, and profusely. My oldest daughter called my boss, saying I was ill. Both left for school. I was alone. Whether I understood what was happening or not, one message got through my fog: Go to the doctor!

I have no idea how I managed to dress, get in the car, and drive. The office of our family physician was maybe five blocks and one turn away, yet it took me nearly half-an-hour to get there. The road seemed to undulate, rolling up and down as if it were more ribbon than asphalt. Streaks like lightning bolts scratched at my windshield. Homes and trees on either side of the road kept changing shape. When I finally arrived, the pain was so great I could hardly park the car and turn off the key.

The head nurse saw me stumble in and cried out that I looked half dead. Immediately she rushed me into the examination room, the doctor right behind. I told all. His examination seemed thorough. He read my file then started laughing. His comment: "All this pain for one night of sex." I just stared at him. What? Did I hear this man right? I kept asking why my legs hurt so much, especially the right leg. He'd look at me and laugh again. Neither he nor his nurse responded to any of my questions, He made no recommendation for a hospital stay, as he felt the worst was over. He said I could heal just fine at home. He did give me a shot about mid-way in the side of my right thigh, but that's it. I never thought to ask about the "lightning bolts" and "zig-zags" on my drive over or why it took me so long to get there in the first place.

It took as long to get home as it did to drive there. The minute I turned the knob of my front door and walked inside, the bleeding stopped. That quickly—as if a faucet had been turned off. And just as quickly my leg pain increased, especially in the right leg (the right thigh to be exact)—where he had given me the shot. I went straight to bed, propping up my legs on that same tower of pillows from the night before, and went to sleep.

January 4, 1977

Again, my oldest daughter called the bank where I worked and reported me ill. She and my youngest left for school. That morning my right leg hurt so much I would have hacked it off if I had a knife. Never before had I felt the likes of this. I threw off my covers and stared in disbelief at what I saw. My entire right thigh, from my knee to almost my crotch, was now covered with a band of crimson, red-hot skin—and growing out the side of it was a huge fiery lump. My thigh was hot and burning. The lump, an angry volcano about to erupt. My only thought . . . get help!

Our only phone in the entire house was in the kitchen, some distance from me. Trying to get there involved as much falling as stumbling. I wound up dragging my legs as I fought for each inch of carpet, each pull of thread getting me closer. I made it to the dining room. The pain at that point was more than horrific. It obliterated any sense of reason or logic. Only me and the pain existed. That lump had become my enemy. It was killing me. It had to go. Instinctively I attacked the lump. This was the worst thing I could have done, since the lump was a blood clot, a giant one. I hit it hard, shoved, pushed, screamed, and hit it again and again. We fought. The lump won.

My body lay prone on the floor, face up. The me I was floated out and upward, passing through waves of pain, looking almost like the mirage one sees on a hot day when sidewalks and driveways shimmer like water. These waves were outside my body. I floated through them, past any semblance of pain, steadily upwards, until I bumped into the light fixture. Light fixture? This was funny to me. Another light fixture! I laughed and laughed.

I hovered around that light fixture for what seemed like long passages of time, often looking at my body far below and trying to find any sign of movement—a twitch, the passage of air, chest rising/falling, eyes—open or shut: anything that might indicate life existed in some form in any part of my body.

Nothing moved. I waited longer. Still nothing. Then I floated back down for a closer view. When there was absolutely, positively no life in me that I could discern, I felt a surge of utter freedom. Freedom! No heavy burdensome mass for me to lug around. No hair to comb. Nothing to scrub, primp, clothe, or feed. I felt as if I had just been released from prison. My body was not me. *I* was me. My body was something I had once worn, like someone wears a jacket or an old coat— the life in it now gone—and I was free. I shouted for joy, "I'm dead. Thank God I'm dead."

I felt no sorrow or remorse, not even the slightest regret or concern about anyone or anything, including my children and their welfare. I knew they would be okay. No unfinished business lingered, no anger or pain. It felt completely natural and comfortable not to breathe. I could still hear, feel, move around, smell, think, remember, reason, experience emotions—only it was different because I no longer had a body to filter and amplify sensations. I did not need that body anymore.

I was free! I was free!

In my new-found freedom I twirled around the light fixture as if it were a May Pole. Around and around. I did not miss my life nor did I regret my death. So filled with joy was I, that the life I'd just left seemed like nothing more than a dream. How could that have been life? *This* was life. This was real. I waited for confirmation—as if someone or something would agree. Maybe a visual. A voice. Something.

Blobs started to appear, popping up all over the place. Not the bathroom variety. These blobs flashed in gorgeous pastels—transparent, translucent, fully pliable. They were pretty and I liked them. My thoughts (the energy they consisted of) took on no specifics as they jelled into the blobs I saw. Intrigued by this, I began to play with them to see if I could direct or guide what happened. If I concentrated deeply enough, brought them into one single focus, then directed that focus and aimed it forward like a laser beam to a specific spot in front of me . . . could I do it? Could I take the energy of my thoughts alone and create something? Could such a creation continue to exist or would it simply evaporate when I was done?

When I was a very young child I once asked: what is this place where I have been born? Now as a grown woman I was asking the reverse . . . what is this place where I have died? Same question. Same dilemma.

As I busily fixed details in my mind of the experiment I was about to try, my environment switched. My dining room, where my body was, slowly merged into a nothing space coming down from above. I did not move. My dining room did not move. It's as though we were both absorbed into something else. Then my dining room faded away and I was alone.

How do I describe where I found myself? I was inside a nothing space—totally bright while totally dark, bereft of shape, form, sound, smell, color, mass, movement. It was aglow but without a light source. It was dark, a kind of blackness sans any sense of dark. Yet within this strange environment existed the presence of all shapes, all forms, all sound, all color, all odors, all mass, all movement. Everything that ever was or ever will be was there. Yet nothing was there at all. Everything and nothing. A feeling, a pulse, a sensation of something "winking" on and off filled the place—a sparkling potential which *shimmered* just as molded gelatin does when you extend a finger to test what you just popped onto a plate. In that tiniest slice of a moment, just before actual touch occurs, *shimmer* reigns. I called this space The Void because I didn't know what else to call it. And that sense of *shimmer* is what I came to recognize as The Void in continuous creative play.

I conducted my experiment here because it felt important that I did.

First, I decided to create and shape a house—a specific type of house. Exact details fixed in my mind—seeing each part, noting proportions, readying myself to project to what seemed like a definitive space in front of me. I then released that thought. I remember feeling some pain in doing this, a throbbing ache as if I were using muscles long dormant. This discomfort was similar to that of a new skier trying out winter slopes for the first time, pulling and stretching muscles in ways previously not done. I held true to my goal and there it was—the same house I had envisioned. I ran to it, at least it seemed as if I did. I kicked the foundation, opened and shut windows, stomped across the green floor of the front porch, fingered the brass doorknob, and gave a slap to each of the three porch pillars. As near as I could tell, this was the four-square white house with steeply pitched roof that I had envisioned. Right here. Right in front of me. Real!

For something animate, I chose to create a large oak tree complete with huge gnarled roots, a canopy of limbs, leaves and birds and fliers of all types. I pictured each detail in my mind, then aimed for a particular spot some distance away. Presto! It happened! Not only was the tree beautiful, it was complete with individual leaves, textured bark, and insect holes. No pain this time, no discomfort, only joy.

I proved it! A human such as myself could create from scratch. I could bring together pre-matter and thought-energy to form specific objects, animate or inanimate. It didn't matter which, because thoughts really are things. I had experienced this in the bathroom when I died the first time and again during the moment at hand in what was once my dining room. Thoughts are things!

I suppose it would take someone who went through something similar to understand what happened next. I went nuts!

On a binge of non-stop creation, cities took form, along with people, dogs, cats, trash cans, alleys, telephone poles, schools, books, pencils, cars, roads, lawns, birds, flowers, shrubbery, rain, suns, clouds, and rivers. Everything moved on its own and had breath, noise, language. All manner of activity occurred aside and apart from anything I designed—then went about their own business according to their own pleasure and perception. Never did I think I was some kind of god. Rather, I felt as if I was doing something completely natural.

As I rested, I desired to see family members and loved ones who had long since passed away. The moment I had that thought, they were there: Mrs. Stinson, Daddy Sogn, and a whole host of people from my past, including a grandfather I'd never seen because he'd died from diabetes when his children were still young. Everyone looked as I had last seen them—only more vibrant and healthier than before. The grandfather I didn't know bore a striking resemblance to photographs I had once seen of my biological father's sister in Montana. He walked right up to me and introduced himself. We talked long enough for me to recognize some of my own traits (which must have come from him because they were traits no one else in the family had). The missing grandfather was now revealed.

And Jesus: I wanted so much to see him. I wanted to thank him for the role he played in history and the examples he gave for others to follow. His life and mastery of being had deeply affected me. Instantly he was there. No, there was no sense or need to bow down and worship him as if he were some kind of god. He was my elder brother whom I had not seen for a long, long time. The mood was joyous. We laughed and hugged. I expressed the thanks held deep within me. When he vanished, so did all my loved ones, leaving behind what I had created. I dissolved everything by thinking it so. It felt right for me to do this.

I was alone once more in this non-place. Only this time I took a look at myself to see what form or shape I might have. Ha! I had no shape or form at all— just a sparkle of consciousness, the tiniest miniscule spark of light imaginable. That's it. And that felt good, as I no longer had need of ego or identity.

Within the nothingness I had become, I simply existed, ecstatic in perfect bliss, perfect peace, perfect love. Everywhere around me, sparkles like myself, billions and trillions of them, were winking and blinking—like on/off lights pulsating from some unknown power source.

Into this state of bliss an irritation burst through, like an old sore deep down inside me. And from that sore, waves of the "me I had once been" played out—from the moment of my birth until the moment I died. It was presented not as a theatrical play or review of some kind . . . rather, a reliving—a reliving of every thought I'd ever had, every word I'd ever spoken, every deed I had ever done . . . plus the effect of each thought, word, and deed on everyone and anyone who had ever come within my environment or sphere of influence—whether I knew them or not—including unknown passersby on the street. I even relived the effect of each thought, word, and deed on weather, plants, animals, soil, trees, water, and air. It was the total gestalt of me having ever existed, complete with the consequences of ever having lived at all.

No detail was left out. No slip of the tongue or slur went unnoticed. No mistake or accident slipped by. Truly this was hell, because I had no idea at all—not even the slightest hint of an idea—that every thought, word, and deed was remembered, accounted for, and had a life of its own once expressed. Nor did I know that my energy affected all that it touched, even those who merely passed by. It's as though we all live in some kind of vast sea or soup of each other's residue and thought waves, and we are each held responsible for what we contribute to the whole; the quality of the "ingredients" we add.

This discovery overwhelmed me.

There wasn't any heavenly St. Peter in charge of an afterlife. Rather, a greater or more spiritual version of me judged who and what my personality-self had become, and that judgment was unsettling. Even so, one particular trait filled me with joy: the me I had become always did something. I never waited around for someone else to give me permission to do anything. If there was a need, I simply got up and did the job.

During this judgment process, my environment switched once more. The Void faded as my dining room re-emerged. I was still next to that light fixture, above the body I had once worn. As I looked down I was so filled with love and forgiveness for the "who" of me, that I floated ever so gently back to my body on what seemed like a carpet of bright sparklers. Back to life—feeling the need once again to shrink and squeeze to fit back in.

When consciousness returned, I was so shocked, so stunned, I was completely incapable of relating to anything. Instead of crawling the remaining four or five feet to the phone, I crawled all the way back to my bedroom, lifted myself onto the bed, and remained there in a kind of stupor for two days. I did not recognize anyone or anything. Everything around me—clothes, sheets, newspapers, lamps, windows, clocks, including my own daughters—were foreign to me. The girls weren't sure what was going on, so they gave me space.

The only logical thought that finally entered my mind was money. My job was my only source of income. I had to go to work. Don't ask how I dressed myself or drove the long distance across town, or parked my car, as I have no words to offer you. The executive branch of the bank where I worked was remodeling, so my department was assigned to an old building without an elevator. Climbing those stairs was like climbing a mountain. It took forever. When I reached my floor, my boss just happened to be walking by. She screamed when she saw me; said I looked half-dead—just as the doctor's nurse had. She whisked me away to a specialist. And that specialist, after a thorough examination (and in front of his nurse) said: "There's no way you can be alive." I blinked.

Again, I was sent home. This time with pills marked "dangerous. " I had to take one every four hours for seven days. The pharmacist warned: eat before you take them or you'll throw up. He advised spending my time on a sofa in front of a television set. Get up only for bathroom duties. I did. Never once did I turn on the TV, though. I didn't have to, because three peculiar things occurred.

First, I could hear thoughts at the same sound level as I could hear voices. Since few, if any, say what they mean, I became mute. Second, I wanted to apologize to all my body parts affected by what had happened. I felt guilty because if I had just continued crawling a few feet more I could have reached the phone and called for help. Suddenly, I could both see and hear all the cells involved. By apologizing, I developed the ability to converse with my body, an ability that remains. Lastly, as I lay on the sofa, a rainbow bridge formed across my chest. Like a hologram, I saw everyone I had ever walked by passing from left to right, going back in time thousands of years. Reincarnation? Not like anything I ever heard of.

After the drug, I was put on aspirin therapy for six weeks. Since aspirin makes me dizzy and half sick, the days that followed seemed like a mish-mash of contradictions: I worked in increments that changed as I did. The man who raped me offered money to help pay my medical bills. I was forced to find new lodging since my landlord suddenly raised the rent (I found a cheaper place in an area of town that neither daughter liked). The youngest revolted, started hanging out with troublemakers and was nearly raped again; police were helpful, school officials weren't. I finally found a counselor who taught my daughter and I how to speak in a way that allowed us to "hear" each other when we talked. Exercises that were supposed to repair my body and retrain my mind turned out to be useless, because how I saw the world did not match how the world saw me. And threats from my boss laid bare my predicament . . . either get well or be fired.

What I had experienced in dying was like a puff of air. Of what use is a miracle if it does not apply to the life you have?

Chapter 12

Cyclones of Death

"Just so far as we depend upon any condition, past, present or future, we are creating chaos, because we are then dealing with conditions (effects) and not with causes."

—Ernest Holmes

Sometimes I'd chant "God is" over and over again. Daily. Nightly. This truth I knew. Nothing else made sense.

I could not apply what I'd just experienced to the life I was living. My miracle of miracles both uplifted and crushed me, stripping logic from foundational truth, turning the act of death into a fairy tale.

Eating? I'd look at a can of food and wonder why I was looking at it, then habit would take over. *Open the can with a can opener, find a pan and put contents into pan, put pan down, turn on stove burner, put pan on burner, heat contents. When done—turn off burner, get a plate, pick up pan, empty contents on plate, put pan down.* I'd look at the food when finished and wonder why I had done this—what good were such motions when they produced something utterly meaningless to me?

Meaning? It took a while for me to realize that my habits were intact. What I had lost was the meaning undergirding them. Regaining such basics meant reidentifying everything. To do this I tossed soap, bed sheets, and objects of every stripe into the trash can. Until I could find out what each item consisted of, how it was made, what effect it had in use, and why I needed it, I wound up replacing a whole lot of stuff (including pots and pans after I had obtained manufacturing specs and metallurgical reports from major makers and tested what I could in a local lab). Discovery: stay away from anything with a copper bottom or Teflon coating.

Speaking? Feelings, smells, tastes, sensations, undefined shapes, contours—these became my new language. Not words. This meant I had to translate my new feeling-based languaging into some type of word-speak others could follow. Relearning the power of archetypes (symbolic traits/signs/models) made a huge difference for me in understanding the basics of thought itself.

Meditation? Every time I tried to meditate I'd fall over. I'd be on the floor, just sitting there, moving my mind beyond thought into a meditative state, when all-of-a-sudden my breathing would stop. My body fell over every time this happened, no matter what I did to prevent it. Eventually I quit even trying.

Routines? Even performing simple errands challenged any definition I once had for "normal." When I'd see someone I didn't know, invariably their past life would be superimposed over their present life. Which do you talk to? What do you say? One day, while delivering papers to an office located several floors up in an open-air building with glass-like walkways connecting offices to central elevators, I saw a fantastically beautiful woman walking towards where I was standing. Movie-star gorgeous! All around her though, I saw scenes of her bathroom, a filthy place. Without thinking, I walked right up to her and asked why she never cleaned her bathroom. Immediately she became quite huffy and snorted that she just didn't have time to clean it—and besides, what she did was none of my business anyway. She stomped off in the opposite direction, leaving me rolling with laughter.

Rational? Nothing was rational. I took beginner's classes in about everything one can imagine—from cooking to writing a check. I still dragged my right leg. Pain packed each moment in my determination to make sense of this new world, and me in it.

My son returned unexpectedly from his cruise school (which took place on a square-rigger off the coast of Portugal). It wound up being little more than a glorified high school that cost him dearly. It was evening, March 29th. Both girls were overnighting with friends and my son was at a local bar tossing back a few with his. Suddenly there was a knock on the door. I opened it and was completely surprised when I saw who was there. It was the man who had raped me. I wasn't sure if I should, but I let him in. Once inside, he went over to the sofa, sat down, and just glared at me. I made one request: for him to please just hold me and let me cry. I wanted to be a child again with no burdens, no pain. He jumped up, shouted NO, and stormed out the door. Then he promptly came right back. He had story to tell me—about his daughter being raped—and that his whole affair with me was an opportunity for him to learn how to forgive the man who raped his daughter—and forgive himself because of what he'd done to me. He stormed out a second time and disappeared.

What? This whole escapade was just an act? A game?

The waiting bomb inside me exploded, and I died.

Dead again, really dead. I knew the territory and welcomed it. My body fell across a large, overstuffed chair as I rose straight out of my skull, up through the ceiling, passing through each layer, then up through the attic and roof, out into the night sky. I rose far into that darkness, watching the Earth become smaller and smaller in my voyage to elsewhere. I spied a bright light in the shape of a "lip" ahead of me. When I neared, the lip opened, sucking me in. Brilliance! Everywhere brilliance! Light as I had never seen light before. Relief filled me. Finally, I was where I wanted to be . . . inside bliss, inside ecstasy!

I stopped short, completely overwhelmed by what loomed ahead: two gigantic, impossibly huge masses were spinning at great speed like cyclones, with one cyclonic vortex inverted over the other in an hourglass shape.

The cyclone on top spun clockwise. The inverted cyclone beneath spun counterclockwise. Where the two spouts should have touched, but didn't, there spewed forth piercing rays of radiant power and in all directions. Not light. POWER!

Both cyclones were fat and bulgy, not at all smooth-sided as one might think considering their tremendous rate of spin. Even though the one on top spun right to left and the one on the bottom left to right . . . inside each was the presence of the other's motion plus a separate inner convolution. This tri-directional force seemed to create the powerful spin, giving an impression of layering across the outer surface of both cyclones even though no rows or bands existed to indicate this. That tri-directional spin actually swallowed space as it rotated.

Inside the top cyclone and somewhat towards the upper left, I saw myself—hardly larger than a speck, yet recognizable. Superimposed over who I was were all my past lives and all my future lives happening at the same time and in the same space as my present life. Around me were other people I knew. The same thing was happening to them too. Around them were others and more others until I came to realize that this same pattern was happening to all life forms. What appeared to be movement—the life-forms acting out their given roles—was actually an optical/perceptual illusion, similar to a hologram, yet produced by what I recognized to be pulsed-wave oscillations activated by individual and collective forms of consciousness. If any life-form changed the overall pattern of a personal scenario, and some did, "past" as well as "future" altered for that individual and for others so affected. I saw that, while each life-form was truly its own self, each was also connected to all others by a fabric netting or web that consisted of bubbly bright threads of light (similar to what I had once seen years ago when my pickle syrup boiled over on my stove).

And what occurred inside the top cyclone also occurred inside the bottom cyclone. As above, so below. The bottom cyclone, then, was a mirror image of the one on top. The overall scene initially impressed me as if a giant echo filling the width of a massive canyon.

The sheer force of cyclonic spin created a counter-activity alongside each of the cyclone's outer edges, manifesting another construct altogether. This "extra" occupied space to the left and right, seemed to somehow originate darkness and light as by-products of its existence. Thus, darkness developed to the left as light emerged from the right. This sight showed me that darkness and light, by-products of the spinning cyclones, were opposite "signatures" of the same dynamic. They provided the necessary mechanism and contrast for manifestation to be experienced in a meaningful way. I came to understand that darkness and light were corollary reflections resulting from the act of creation continuously recreating and altering itself. I felt as if I were witnessing Creation at its Centerpoint—the gateway to both uncounted and unknown forevers.

This witnessing continued for what seemed like countless hours, maybe eons, as I gazed in transfixed rapture at how vast Creation was, what it consisted of, the secrets it held, the way it functioned, the how's and why's, and the truth about God. No vision here. Absolute reality. Right *now* real.

Those piercing rays continuously emanating from the middle—the Centerpoint—caught my attention. They seemed to be coming from an entry point to all that God is—so I resolved to go there, to head directly to the Centerpoint's core, where at last I could return to the God from whence I came. GOD!

Meanwhile, at the Black Angus bar, my son and his friends enjoyed drinking and laughing and talking about old times with each other. He had a mug of beer midair when suddenly he slammed it down, stood up, faced his buddies, and firmly said: "My mother needs me. I have to go help my mother." With that, he left, surprising himself as much as everyone else. A year later, when he and I spoke of that night, he described the bar scene and told how surprised everyone was at his behavior. He gave numerous details about the living room and finding my body splayed across a stuffed chair. He said it never occurred to him to call for help. After sizing up the situation as best he could, he listened to his inner voice which said: "Sit opposite the body and start talking. It doesn't matter what you say, just keep talking." This advice makes sense if you realize that science has shown that the last faculty lost in death is the ability to hear.

To understand why he would trust that intuitive voice, know that all three of my children were taught since infancy to have faith in their own inner promptings, question all authority, and think for themselves. Had he gone for the phone and called for help, the rescue squad would not have arrived in time. His voice and the unconditional love he freely gave is what brought me back. I knew that wondrous kind of love existed on The Other Side, but I didn't know I could find it here. My son proved otherwise. I came back to learn what he already knew.

Chapter 13

The Voice Like None Other

"Your work is to discover your work and then with all your heart to give yourself to it."
—Buddha

Before I left where I was, even before my son said anything, something else happened.

Utterly transfixed by the scene before me, I knew, instantly knew, I was witnessing Creation as it *actually* occurred. I saw the role of Consciousness in the process of Creation, as Creation continuously continued. I was at the Centerpoint and I knew what the Centerpoint was. I absolutely knew! I came to realize I didn't have to pass through the cyclone's middle in order to witness, connect with, and merge into the truth of all existence, of being—mine and everyone and everything else's. All I had to do was look *through* the inside of what happened in front of me. I could do that because nothing separated me from the clarity of this truth. Nothing!

I saw thought-waves *everywhere*. They were beautiful beyond beauty, lustrous, shimmering, gloriously luminous, radiant and musical. To hear the tones of their music was to forsake forever all else save the memory and reality of God, The One True Source. I saw Creation as the stirring of thought in The Mind of God.

This stirring creates the pulse that sets in motion and maintains the ongoing oscillation of time and space—the ongoing unfoldment of the thought which stirred. The makeup of this thought is Consciousness, and all that results from its stirring bears the mark of this Consciousness. Creation allows The One to become the many.

On and on this clarity continued, revealing every detail of Creation and Consciousness—how both worked, what they were, and the reality behind and beyond every single thing. More than I could ever have imagined flowed forth, overwhelming me again and again. When it seemed as though I could take no more, "something" spread itself across the scene—a feeling of presence—and it spoke. I heard this verbally, its sound fully alive within the physicality of being.

My previous experiences in deep meditation and with spiritual/mystical/metaphysical pursuits did not prepare me for the all-knowing, all-powerful, overwhelming force and impact of The Voice that spoke. It was as if every molecule, every cell, every subatomic speck of Creation "bowed" to this Voice. I called it The Voice Like None Other because I didn't know what else to call it.

And The Voice said: "Test revelation. You are to do the research. One book for each death." It showed me what that meant, then revealed the three specific books I was to write. Book One was not named. Over the years I have often thought that maybe Book One was actually my first major book—*Coming Back To Life*—but I have no way of knowing for sure. Books Two and Three were named *Future Memory* and *A Manual for Developing Humans*. Never was I told how to do this research or how long it might take. The moment I accepted the task—that very sliver of a second—was when I heard my son's voice and I flowed back into life on the power of his love.

This time my body did not respond. It felt somehow cooler than when I left, and a little stiff. I panicked.

Instantly I assumed the role of coach and cheerleader, speeding from cell to cell, shouting as loud as I could, apologizing for leaving as I had. Back to stay, I promised I would do whatever I could to regain my health and make life count. I kept shouting at my cells to wake up. We all had a job to do—all of us.

The lungs were the hardest to restart. The bellows wouldn't expand, so I puffed and puffed until a whoosh of air entered. When it did, my consciousness shifted to head level. I blinked for a moment, then tried to stand, just to make certain "everyone" had awakened and all cells were responsive.

But standing was a struggle. My son, being wiser at that moment, reached out to help. My vocal cords wouldn't work. I could not speak. He put his large arms around me and held me tight . . . my prayer answered. My son supplied what the man from California refused. Tears came and then a flood. I cried silently for what seemed hours and then my son spoke. He told me about a letter he'd received from me in late January—a letter handed to him after a gale had struck (while he was at ship's helm)—forcing the ship to port in northern Spain. It was a dark and dismal time in his life. He had become uncooperative in class, depressed at discovering that this so-called special school on board a square-rigger in the Atlantic was not as billed. The program saddled him with a debt he could not pay, for what seemed to be a waste of time.

In that letter I had described life as being an immense school, where we each study certain subjects in certain "grades" according to our level of understanding. There were recesses when we earned them, but for the most part the schooling was relentless as we moved up grade levels to higher and more difficult studies—until we graduated. Nothing was ever wasted, regardless of how it seemed, and we were all, for the most part, headed in the same direction: back to the God from whence we came. The letter gave him hope and showed him that there was purpose in everything, even darkness and despair.

As I stood cuddled in his arms, he returned my words to me — words sent in a letter halfway around the world, words that helped him in his darkest hour, now returning to help me in mine. I saw a "circle" close and I understood. I took this gesture to be confirmation that my choice to live was a good choice. It was okay to be back. I really could rebuild my life.

Chapter 14

Through the Looking Glass

"As Jonathan Livingston Seagull's teacher, Chiang, told him, "The trick is stop seeing yourself trapped inside a limited body with a 42-inch wingspan . . . The trick is to know that your true nature lives, as perfect as an unwritten number, everywhere at once across space and time."

—Richard Bach

My son put me to bed and I slept soundly.

By morning I could speak, so I phoned Dr. William G. Reimer, a naturopath/chiropractor proficient in a number of disciplines including live-cell analysis. Although some of my health problems had been alleviated by traditional medical procedures, the crisis the night before made it obvious that something was very, very wrong. I had to take a chance. I had to try something new. My choice to explore natural types of healing meant I would need to relearn the definition of health.

In natural healing, the patient is considered an active participant and all treatments are geared toward that individual's own inherent rhythms of self-healing. Root causes are dealt with rather than symptoms alone, and, since disorders are "backed" out of the body the way each entered, the patient sometimes gets worse before getting better. And that's what happened to me. Not only did I get worse, I plummeted farther and faster than the doctor expected. I seemed to be locked in a downward spiral which could only be slowed, not stopped. The biggest stumbling block to recovery, as it turned out, . . . was my own sense of self.

Who was I? What was I?

This person in front of the mirror, her habits, personality, clothing, possessions, and lifestyle were foreign and irritating to me; yet, when I looked in the mirror, there she would always be, looking back, all five feet seven, nearly two hundred pounds of her. She was shaped like a pudgy balloon with a deep sadness in her eyes and a washed-out face rimmed with short wavy brown hair. There was ample proof in her belongings that she had once been a bouncy, spontaneous woman with a love of song and a lust for adventure — be it exploring caves or ghost towns. And she adored rocks. Everywhere she turned there were rocks, even in her purse. Rocks in her head too, I mused.

The more I looked around, the more life I saw. Everything had life, not just me. Every spoon, every dish, every wall, every staircase, every vegetable, everything! The world and everything within it was alive, moving, breathing, feeling, exchanging energy with me, having its own voice. I could see through people, and even recognize tumors or health problems before such things were visible to others. I already had a broad background in spiritual truths and realities before I died—born that way really, but this overwhelm spooked me. So I enrolled in every class I could find. Formerly a teacher, now a student. Numerous new ways to practice the art of meditation became available, along with prayer, psychic realities, and sacred pathways. Beginner's cooking and home economics were important too, so I took classes in them as well.

Money became an issue because it had lost value to me. What I earned and what I spent meant nothing any more until I rediscovered the meaning of "investment." Buying and selling, working and playing, are really investments we all make to enliven life. How this actually works so excited me that I had a cutline printed over the signature line on all my checks. It read: *All my expenditures are my investment in life.* (I used this cutline for nearly three decades before banks refused to print it any longer. I now print it atop each page of the ledgers I keep.)

Falling in love with the world and everybody in it failed my children. They wanted exclusivity, to feel special to me and me alone. It took some time for me to learn "play acting" so I could genuinely show how special they each were to me without cutting off others, people down the block, the world at large.

My daughters tell of the time when the lining of my favorite coat could be relined no more. Of course I held a funeral service for it. Why wouldn't I? My coat was a dear friend and I wanted to honor its many years of service. Both girls caught me performing the ceremony and roared with laughter at how funny it all was. It took me two years to understand why they thought what I did was funny. My faculties went "off-line" at will, making life more, better, bigger, realer—an explosion of purpose and power. Anything electrical, well, that became crazy huge—beyond what could be explained at the time.

Three people entered this chaos, all strangers and younger than I was—astute, enthusiastic, and voraciously bent on learning all they could about life and the potential of "Self." These three people offered to help me, and together we formed a kind of "extended family" whereby we exchanged keys to each other's homes, shared our resources, and formed a mutual support pact. Two were married and had a young son. The other member of our group was the couple's friend. I dubbed us "cousins" as we began our year-and-a-half-long-journey together, probing the depths of life and its living.

We would hold sessions employing various types of confrontive therapy. Sometimes our sessions were spontaneous and sometimes they were planned in advance, occurring daily or only once in a while. We tried out any ideas that seemed reasonable, including psychological games utilizing symbols for deeper insight. Sometimes we just went about the business of everyday living, carefully listening to what the other said while observing physical mannerisms. If we detected anything negative or self-serving, we would challenge that person immediately, forcing him or her to confront the situation or habit, where it came from, why it was there, and what might be done about it. Often we would verbally battle each other and argue heatedly. Many of our sessions were painfully unmerciful as nothing was off-limits to debate—and the more painful a session, the more successful it was considered. Personal issues of every description surfaced.

As this was happening, the treatments with my doctor revealed a long list of problems I didn't know I had, such as dyslexia (which was later confirmed by a medical physician). When I was a third grader, as I alluded to earlier, I would often feign play, sneak out to the old cinder-block "milk house" and lock the door, prop up orange crates for a stage, stand on them, and read comic books and Sunday funnies out loud until I finally trained myself to read and speak correctly. This "secret training" I invented took several years. Dyslexia was unknown then. Special classes for children with learning disabilities didn't exist. My drive to coordinate eyes, mouth, and brain so I could read correctly and without embarrassment was intuitive.

More medical surprises popped up, collected from a lifetime of reactions to pharmaceutical medicines. To help correct dexterity and speech difficulties, plus extensive damage done from three bouts with death, the doctor had me relearn everything: crawling, standing, walking, climbing, running, telling left from right, seeing, hearing, and organizing thoughts. I performed these drills by the hour, daily. The more vigorous I became, the more energy flares would shoot out from all parts of my body in all directions. Yes, energy flares! From me. Honest to goodness, I became a freakin' fireworks show that only I could see. I'll never forget that one summer day when I could run a full city block without falling and there was no pain and my right leg no longer dragged and my energy flares faded and I felt almost "normal." Tears flowed, tears of joy.

By Fall I ventured out and put some money down on a house with a large garden in the back. This move put my youngest in the part of town she enjoyed most and close to where her childhood friends lived. At first this move seemed like a gift. Then, suddenly, she reverted back to her old rebellious ways and was kicked out of school—repeatedly. In desperation, I found a therapist who specialized in cases like this. He helped us both relearn how to communicate with each other in a way that respected both our needs.

My overall health deteriorated after my daughter recovered. Crashed, actually. Too much. Too much. I suffered three major relapses; the last adrenal failure. My blood pressure reading registered sixty over sixty when I collapsed.

Immediate emergency treatment required that my "cousins" take over my household and my life. When I broke down, my newly purchased house broke down too, flooding out the girls' basement bedrooms three times and leaking everywhere imaginable, including the roof and bathtub. I missed so much work from this second round of health reversals that I almost lost my job . . . again.

Reading two special series of books kept me going: *The Hobbit/The Lord of The Rings* by J. R. R. Tolkien, and *Dune* by Frank Herbert.

I entered the thought-streams of both series, became each character in each book. Good or bad didn't matter because each character was an aspect of me. Mentally, spiritually, emotionally, I lived their life, felt their feelings, dealt with their nightmares and their joy, fought in each battle, died each death, survived each crisis, and held each hope and dearness they had close to my heart. I was them—all of them—and they were me.

Losing myself in these books gave me the keys to healing. In *Dune*, there is a litany the convent sisters were taught about how to handle fear. I have no idea why I changed what Herbert wrote, but I did. Here's my version of the Litany of Fear:

Fear is the mind killer.
It is the little death.
I will face my fear.
It will go around me and through me,
And when it is gone—
I will remain.

This Litany enabled me to put one foot in front of the other with a determined smile on my face. It helped me to understand what fear is and how to handle it. A rare gift.

My "cousins" had a bright idea. They felt a change of scenery was what I needed and the best place to find it . . . Seattle, Washington. The "Mind Miraculous Symposium," scheduled for early November, would be held in the Opera House. Luminaries packed the program, especially people like Dr. Elisabeth Kübler Ross. My doctor said yes.

Can you imagine a doctor getting up at 5:00 am to give you a shot and a bag of medications as you lay snug in a van, about to be trucked up to meet a miracle?

Chapter 15

The Eternal Now

"The more real you get the more unreal the world gets."
—John Lennon

The auditorium was huge—filled to overflowing with several thousand people. I, reasonably human by then, sat in an aisle seat halfway down on the left. My "cousins," plus good friends who owned the van and traveled with us, sat in the next seats over.

The first speaker, Dr. William Tiller, a physicist at Stanford University, talked about "The Eternal Now." He spoke of energy masses and interpenetration, yet I only remember staring blankly at charts and drawings projected on a giant screen behind him. As his talk ended, he stated that, according the science he had explored, everything happened at the same time in the same space in an Eternal Now. He then flashed on the screen his rendition of what the physical dynamics of that phenomenon might look like. The image, a diagram, featured two spinning cyclones inverted over each other forming an hourglass shape where the spouts should have touched but didn't. A powerful force shot rays out in all directions.

I jumped from my seat. Fled the auditorium. Collapsed under a wall sconce in the hallway.

In muffled screams I cried: "He saw it. He saw it, too. I'm not crazy! The cyclones are real. It all really happened. It wasn't a dream or a hallucination or a fantasy or a projection from any kind of memory. It was real. I am real. I can be who I am because the me I am is okay." My heart practically pounded out of my chest.

Tiller's talk, that chart of his, was the miracle I needed.

A medical doctor happened by at that moment, returning from a call he had made to check on a patient. Supposedly impressed by the "glow" on my face (or so he said), he walked over and sat down beside me, then offered me a job should I ever move to Seattle. What? A job? Unbelievable. I said little except to confirm I would consider his offer. Several days later I phoned to say no.

Everything from before—every bit of it—now fit together as if they were pieces from some giant puzzle. I could trust myself and the world around me, and I could trust the process I found myself in. Beginning right then, my life began to remake itself. The past faded. The future slid into Now.

That shift, though, ran afoul of the time factor. I needed to catch up with myself. I needed time, more of it, lots of it, and the time I needed came . . . in the form of a time fan that created itself, by itself.

This happened when my job at the bank morphed into that of a Forms Analyst, researching the need for each bank form, then drawing to specs exactly what could be used. My desk became primarily a drafting table. On an exceptionally bright morning, I found myself concentrating harder than usual as I put finishing touches on a form headed for the printer. My eyes slipped for a moment past the edges of what I'd drawn and settled into a stare at the light blue measurement squares on the form paper I used. Without reason or warning, each square spread apart. Border lines elongated in size, buckled up from the paper, stood, stretched, and then shot into the air near my nose. I had to jerk back to avoid being hit. The very second I did this, the expanding squares spewed forth clouds of energy that formed a veritable fountain of surging, glistening, brilliance. No way could I blame this incident on medication because I hadn't taken any that day.

As my mouth widened in disbelief, a kind of vortex formed around the spraying fountain of energy, sucking in and pushing out masses of a mist-like, foamy plasma, until most of the board and the air in front of me filled with it. The misty plasma began to narrow into the shape of rays, then from a central point in the middle of my drafting board the rays spread open to form a fan. The glistening fan then divided itself into eight equal sections. It was as beautiful as it was awesome. Before I could question anything, I felt energy from my own body join the fan. This continued until I could feel parts of myself in each section—eight satellites of me plus another extension above and slightly to the rear of my head. Counting me sitting on the stool, there were now ten divisions of myself. Each satellite began to immediately perform specific tasks, without any effort or thought on my part. One meditated. One prayed. Another continued an exploration of The Void. Still another went off to visit a friend who was ill. The four remaining engaged in various projects, considering ideas that were important to me. The extension from my head acted as a supervisor to make certain no satellite got lost or had any problems. The original me remained in my body and looked the same as always. The others looked like sparkling masses of a mist-like energy . . . forming a time fan.

This situation went on non-stop for ten full days and nights. But there was a catch. As time contracted into space, space expanded into time, then both converged. This created a state quite workable for short-term activity but not for anything long-term. My physical body and all my physical movements slowed tremendously, like a 45 rpm record being played at 33⅓. This meant I could no longer walk, talk, or move in a normal manner—but I could think and hear at remarkable speeds, even multi-angled. I experienced myself as superhuman, while physically I appeared subhuman. A short conversation took forever. The process could be compared to several people attempting steady dialogue from opposite ends of an echo chamber. Driving, stepping up or down, lifting a knife to cut a potato, turning a dial, trying to squeeze toothpaste from a tube, tying shoelaces—each and every physical task required ridiculous lengths of time to perform. This caused all kinds of problems everywhere I went, especially at work—freaking out my co-workers and confusing my boss. “Stop this now,” she demanded. Prayer and determination restored my natural speeds. How time actually altered itself turned out to be as much a problem as a miracle.

Next, my weight. Seeing myself in a mirror became painful. I was so huge, more than 200 lbs. Diets didn’t work. Taping photos of slender gems on the fridge didn’t work either. It wasn’t until I stood naked in front of a full-length mirror as my period began, reached down to cup a handful of blood, that I felt power—me as a woman making new. With that sense of specialness, I began to eat only when I wanted to, and only as much as I felt was right, like grazing. I’d cook for others, but food for me became praise-bites. Gratitude replaced calories each day, every day.

My first big test of this new regimen came when my boss had a birthday. That meant a celebration potluck where everyone brought their best dish to work, combined with all the others to form a “groaning board.” Desserts first. As the line advanced, the woman in front of me spied a pecan pie and choked, “Oh, if I eat a single slice I'll gain 10 pounds." The woman following me readily agreed. Pause. No one moved or said one word, as if waiting. Immediately I recognized they were waiting for me—to do or say something—*because there exists a "social contract" between people . . . we acknowledge through response.* I'd insult them if I didn't do or say something. So, out loud, I praised whoever made that pie and applauded how beautiful it was. That satisfied the woman in front of me and the one behind me. The line then advanced, with me happily sans pie.

Hardly a week later, while waiting to see my doctor before lunch, I found myself fixating on a large photo of a chocolate torte in a better-living magazine. Saliva began rolling around each tooth as my stomach growled. I began pressing my fingers to that page as if caressing the torte. In a second, every aspect of my body/brain/emotions merged together—all of me together as one single focus of pure power! Again, I recognized the moment: when every aspect of being merges, a powerful focus is achieved. Whatever the focus, it comes together like magic. I acknowledged myself as slender, a focus I held as truth. Satisfaction replaced hunger and I felt fine. During the course of that month, a total of sixty pounds simply dissolved. It did not come back.

To top off what I had just learned, I tackled a mind-game. Choose a mantra (I chose "*Every day in every way I am getting better and better. I am becoming more and more*"). Write it by hand (no cheating) one hundred times a day for three weeks, stop for three weeks, start up again for another three weeks, stop. You can go another round of three if you feel the need, but that's it. No more. This activates the nerve endings in your hands, which directly feed the brain/mind assembly (a quick way to change deep-seated patterning). Another technique I involved myself in, as a follow-up, were classes in the art of affirmative prayer . . . an opportunity for me to relearn the basics of how to think and how to speak (Science of Mind class SOM-1, now taught at Centers for Spiritual Living across the country).

Life's basics were relearned this way, just in time for me to sell the home I'd bought several months before—a cash-out deal, that concluded the very day I returned from a trip to Chicago to visit a favorite aunt and uncle. That trip sealed my future . . . because on that trip, I met and visited with Elisabeth Kübler Ross at O'Hare Airport. We chatted like a couple of kids: me telling her about what I'd just been through and she telling me about the phenomenon called "near-death experiences." Never once did she call me an "experiencer." She used the term "survivor," and truly I felt like one. Our visit hummed in my head as if I'd been given "instructions" for the job I was about to do by the best teacher one could ever have.

My first Monday back I was to meet with my boss. Not only for a pay raise, but a bank title—me—a woman. In those days, this was a very big deal indeed. I had excelled as a bank analyst, a far cry from just working with forms or writing bank manuals. The time for our meeting was 9am, so I busied myself until then with pen in hand, flipping pages in a report. Without warning, everything around me froze in place, my body included. Gushes of heat rushed through my paralyzed frame from feet to head, overwhelming me with an ecstatic thrill. As this rush continued, my desk began to fade from view while a field of brilliant sparkles descended from the ceiling, spreading out to engulf the office. I was back in The Void. A swirling mass took shape—a veritable whirlpool of wave upon wave of energy, until it sucked me into its core like a helpless leaf. The core widened, then stopped spinning. When it did, I found myself living, in advance, the life I would come to live until the following spring.

Briefly, this pre-living covered . . . *renting an unfurnished room from a fellow analyst and sleeping on the floor in a sleeping bag now that my home had sold. For three weeks, I attended a party a night, saying goodbye to everyone I knew. I was given a set of casting runes by a Renaissance troupe that traced back to ancient Europe and areas of the Volga to help me balance what was true with what wasn't. I either stored, sold, or gave away everything I owned except what I could stuff into my Ford Pinto Hatchback. I crossed the United States, fulfilling all my childhood dreams and wishes, along with watching the sun set silver over the Pacific, taking a mule trip to the bottom of the Grand Canyon, touring New Mexico/Indiana/Kentucky, and resting four days in each of those states before reaching Virginia where I would first live with cousins near D.C., then move to Falls Church. Soon afterward, I would watch the sun rise golden over the Atlantic, find a job in D.C., and begin my near-death research, with another future memory episode to occur come Spring.*

Simultaneously, I both watched and lived this scenario in great detail, as if each physical motion was being performed in actuality—each thought, feeling, taste, touch, smell thoroughly experienced. When the future concluded itself, The Void and everything in it disappeared as it had come. I had just experienced the life I would live before it could happen, even though I had not moved in any manner—not an inch or a twitch. As near as I could tell, about ten minutes had lapsed in clock time. I felt somewhat cooler than before, my body a little stiff.

My mouth fell open. The episode unnerved me. I shook my head until it seemed as if my teeth rattled. The pen I had been holding dropped. I asked around the office but no one heard, saw, or felt anything unusual. Only me.

There had been a teaser. *After the coming of Spring I would move farther south in Virginia and meet the man I would marry while taking a walk with him on a day heavy with the coming of rain. He was taller than I, younger, with black curly hair and bronze skin; a conservative fellow, refined, well-traveled and well- educated, unique in his devotion to the spiritual path. He would recognize me instantly; it would take me three days to recognize him. In weeks we would marry. Twins would be in our lives along with nearly continuous writing, speaking, and traveling.*

That teaser rattled me even more. None of it made the slightest bit of sense. A hallucination maybe?

Still, another experience I had pre-lived was attending a Death & Dying Seminar with Elisabeth at her Shanti Nilaya Ranch in Escondido, California. Impossible! Previously I had tried to register for any type of activity with her. Hundreds always beat me to it, so I dismissed any such idea.

Knowing this, friends had recently given me the direct phone number to Shanti Nilaya. Scrunched up in my pocket, I pulled it out and called. Boots Martensen answered. I'll never forget her. After I danced around saying I just might be able to attend the Fall seminar because I might quit my job and move, she laughed: "Goodness, goodness, just get here. You're already registered." I slammed the phone down. No way. Next I called my cousins near D.C. and danced around some more.

My cousin's wife, whom I had never met, declared: "It's Providence, you know, Providence. You are supposed to come here and live with us until you find your own place." *I didn't know this woman. Never spoke to her. Hardly knew my cousin. I only had their phone number because my Uncle had given it to me while in Chicago.*

Silence reigned.

A coworker spoke. "It's 9 o'clock."

Out the door I scurried. Bursting into my boss's office I announced: "I'm quitting my job because it's time for me to chase rainbows." Her face paled. She motioned me to sit down and say nothing. "I had a vision this morning at 4:00 am. Mind you, I never have visions. I woke my husband and told him so I would have a witness. I dreamed that I went to the Head Cashier and told him you were quitting because you were going to chase rainbows. I had to replace you."

Now this was way too much. I stood straight, banged on her desk, and shouted: "That's not fair. You knew I was going to leave before I did!"

In days my son informed me he had joined the Coast Guard and would soon leave. My oldest daughter, facing major surgery on both legs just below her knees to correct birth deformities, grabbed my wrists from her hospital bed and spoke in a voice steady with wisdom: "Mother, you cannot stay here to help me. You have to go. It is your time. I'll be facing this kind of surgery again and again in my life. If I don't learn now how to take care of myself, when will I ever learn? Go. Go now. Friends will help me as long as I need them. You must live your life and I must be free to live mine." I cried uncontrollably once in my car. Then calm. My youngest, anxious to be heard, informed me she had called her father and she would now live with him in Spokane. Her news sliced what was left of my heart. Letting her go while still so young meant to me that I had failed her. She, though, was joyous and never once looked back as the train left the station. All three just up and gone. I loved my city. I loved my life. I loved my children. From that lofty hill above the city where the train depot stood, I said goodbye to memories I will forever cherish. Born in Twin Falls, Idaho, died in Boise, Idaho. A life lived as few ever do. Yes, time now for me to go.

In a flurry of activity I sold, gave away, or stored almost everything I owned, taking with me only what I could stuff into "Herbie," my Ford Pinto. Before driving off, a professor at Boise State said he wanted to see me. I never heard of the man, but went. For an entire hour he berated me, cursed me, made fun of me, attacked my claim to have died and had three near-death experiences. How dare I call myself a researcher. Where were my credentials? His attacks against me were so rapid-fire, so vicious, I could hardly stand my ground—but I did. When he finished, I demanded to know what was going on. I didn't know him and he didn't know me. So, why?

He smiled. "I just wanted to be certain you could do the job that lies ahead of you." Stunned, I walked out . . . on everything.

Chapter 16

Coast to Coast

"At the center of your being, you have the answer; you know who you are and you know what you want."

—Lao Tzu

I stopped at my parents' place outside Twin Falls before I left and walked straight inside. I grabbed my mother by the shoulders, told her I loved her, and hugged and kissed her. Dad watched the whole scene with a big grin on his face. She froze, mouth wide open, skin white, as if she had been assaulted. Dad was always loving. Mom was the opposite, at least to me. This moment opened a door between us, enabling love to find a heart place.

I cried most of the way through Nevada. The truths revealed to me during death poured over me non-stop, and I struggled to write down every word while also attempting to drive. The route I took hugged the flats. I stopped once just to test all those tales I had heard about the quicksand there. Hardly 20 feet from my car ground began to roll underfoot. "Okay," I yelled. "Stories true." With that, I tip-toed back to the car and didn't stop again until I reached Big Pine, California, and the Bristle Cone Pine Forest.

I felt pushed to reach the mountain top. Herbie made it most of the way. I climbed the rest. Somehow I knew the place, all of it. My search was for a particular tree—long dead yet waiting patiently for this day with me. Bristle Cones live the longest of all trees. I *knew* them, and I especially *knew* the one I searched for. Finding its gnarled limbs, I sensed a pulse we both shared and snuggled deep. We were the same. What enabled its life enabled mine. It's soul, my soul. Caressing the sum of what I could touch, my gaze meandered across mountain tops—higher than birds fly. We meditated together in a shared heaven. Don't know how many hours. The setting sun signaled that I must go. I made it to the highway and a cabin just as dark closed in.

Before pulling into Shanti Nilaya, I felt drawn to Mt. Palomar and the Observatory there. A friend of mine met me and we toured together. Looking through their giant telescope, walking the place, I felt as if I'd been there before, long before one counts time and in another kind of body very different from the one I was in now.

When I finally pulled into Shanti Nilaya, I went straight to see Boots Martensen. She laughed when she saw me. "I know what you want," she chortled. Out came the registration book. She flipped over to the current page. "See," she grinned, "there you are, typed in no less—though I must admit your name and address were not there the day before you called." The address used was on Marvin Street, where I lived for only a few months before I sold the place. Hardly anyone knew that address. Certainly not Elisabeth or Boots. Words escaped me.

The Death & Dying Seminar was a live-in. After meals, we would gather around a large mattress with Elisabeth at the head, assistants flanking her, the crowd of us seated on the floor. Only the handicapped sat on chairs. A tableau of pain, fear, regret, and anger crushed the hours of each day, with Elisabeth deftly helping anyone who came forward to work out their issues on the mattress. On the last day I sat against a side wall, waiting for whatever might occur. Nothing. Then I felt a boot come through the wall, giving me a decided kick in the seat of my pants. Now standing, I found myself sharing my stories of dying and coming back three times. Elisabeth looked relieved. What I described gave her the "stage" she had been waiting for—to talk about death and dying in a new way. That night at the bonfire, all of us gathered hand-in-hand, singing, as clouds formed a giant halo cupped gently over the top of us. A miracle. The next day I drove away, singing.

Soon I would be in Arizona staying at a grand hotel located near the edge of an even grander Canyon, brimming with history of times past. I emptied the bag of runes in my lap—runes that had been prepared for me several weeks before I left.

One of my "cousins" had held a potluck dinner at his home to welcome a Renaissance troupe he'd just met. A crowd came. A woman in the troupe offered to stage a "thank you" session by demonstrating what she called *The Runes of Njord*. I stood near the back wall, but was still able to see everything clearly. "I'll answer three questions," she offered. Small stones, each a different shape, flew from her hands with each cast she made, forming designs around a question stone. I found myself silently, in my mind, critiquing everything she said, as if I had cast these same runes for over a millennia. Before her second cast, she turned my way and said out loud, "You know more about these runes than I do." Embarrassed, I tried to shrink into the wall. After the party ended, I cornered her and asked what she meant by such a comment. She winked. "I know that you know." Puzzle. Before I left, I asked her if she would prepare a set for me. "Fifteen dollars, velvet pouch, hand-sewn, pebbles from a stream in Mexico." I accepted. At a full moon meditation held before I left, I "washed" them with the energy of prayer. Despite my respect for her, her way was not my way.

At that Grand Canyon Hotel, I greeted my new rune friends and welcomed them on this journey of mine into newness. A small instructions slip was stuffed into the bag, virtually useless as it made no sense to me. I would have to learn by doing. There were fourteen message stones (picture glyphs for viewing the territory) and two question stones (male/female) to represent the questioner. With each cast, I drew its design on paper and wrote down my interpretation so I could later check it for accuracy. I dedicated my set to The Allness God Is, and said prayers before each cast.

My trip across country was filled with this same magic. I kept a log of every penny I spent and for what (I still have that log). Each night Daddy Sogn was there. He had died many years before, but you could never tell that just by looking at him. He looked healthy and his presence was a gift. Sometimes I saw small balls of energy floating along in the air some distance from my car as I drove along. No reason for this ever revealed itself. At Grants, New Mexico, I had to stop. Clouds had gathered to form a halo over the area. I asked a highway patrolman about this. "Happens every afternoon, rain too." When I asked why, he couldn't think of any reason; then he started bragging about the huge uranium deposit nearby. Bingo!

As I neared Albuquerque, a heart tug kept pulling at me from my left, out into the desert. I could trace the feel of it to a large boulder inside an extinct volcano. That boulder was part of me, just like with the Bristle Cone Pine. As a youngster I had learned about things like this from the Spirit Keepers, those transparent energy beings that rose up "like a mountain builds" around pastures, cliffs, and the bottom lands of Rock Creek Canyon. Ofttimes on weekends I'd trek up to that log in the upper pasture and wait. No words can define them. Everyone thought I was only daydreaming on that log. Not once. After I died, I saw the truth of this—that Spirit

Keepers literally are the "glue" that holds every molecule of our planet together: our consciousness in partnership with theirs. What had once been "teachings" and "revelations" from my youth were now becoming everyday fact.

My cousin's house was in Reston, nestled near a whirl of circles and roads with crazy signs pointing in directions that made no sense to anyone with a lick of logic. I got lost so often it became a standing joke. Every gutter and building seemed to call me. History was everywhere. My cousin's wife was spooked when she learned how huge the bigness of God was to me. She grabbed a Bible and demanded that my cousin ask me to leave. He gave me a time limit. I panicked. Prices were sky high in the area, so I opted for cheap housing in McLean. That lasted one week. A hungry cockroach attacked me while I ate supper one evening, sending me screaming into the hallway. How I managed to cancel my renter's agreement in four days and get my deposit back is a mystery. What remains fixed in my mind, though, is how quickly I found an apartment in Falls Church where I was supposed to go in the first place.

I met a couple from Boise, who lived on the floor below me. We shared meals and visited often. This paved the way for me to find an employment agency, who sent me out that very day for an interview. Well, you could call it an interview. I actually have no idea what to call it because when I arrived at the place, I saw myself already there. Seriously. The me I knew myself to be worked busily at the desk, got up to file papers, walked to the boss's office for an assignment, went back to the desk, and answered the phone. Me! Already there. Already employed. I froze in place. Couldn't move. All I could do was watch what played out in front of me and smile. A second boss peered from his office, saw me, and invited me in for my interview. He acted as if he knew me, and said he would call the agency later with his decision. Once out of there I started laughing, went straight to the first park I could find (in the middle of a downtown traffic circle), laid down, crossed my hands over my purse (which was laying on my chest), and went to sleep. When I woke up, I found a pay phone and called the agency. Apparently they were in a panic to find me, because the job was mine. I then called my new boss and said I would see him at 9 am. There is no explanation for any of this.

Folks said I developed "Potomac Fever" (fell in love with the place). Every lunch hour, and whenever I could wrangle trading coffee breaks for leaving early, I attended every open house, film show, tour, and lecture I could find. It didn't matter what the topic was. I just wanted to learn. Plus the architecture fascinated me.

Two incidents stopped me short, and changed everything.

The first involved leaving work early and leap-frogging across town to attend a lecture about the Unified Field Theory held at the Space Aurum, National Air and Space Museum. I barely made it before the doors shut. No kidding, not only did I understand every word spoken by the physicist, I could see what the man was talking about played out in the air above him. The next day one of my bosses asked me to file a paper for him. Nothing he said made sense to me. Not a lick of it. He repeated his request. I drew an absolute blank. As he began to speak a third time, I could see the muscles in his neck and arms tighten. Anger was rising. Alarmed, I did something I try never to do . . . I entered the sanctity of his brain/mind assembly without permission to search where pictures are stored. There I recognized what he wanted me to do . . . *extend an arm, take the paper from his hand, turn, walk from his office into mine, go to the file, pull out a drawer, lift up a given file folder, drop the paper into the folder, push the folder back down, shut the drawer.* I performed accordingly. That night I collapsed and leaned against a bedroom wall in stark terror. How could I possibly understand physics with no training, yet be completely baffled at work by a simple request? How could I support myself now that my brain had flipped?

The second incident occurred the following Saturday. Dressed like a field hand, I drove to the post office to mail a letter. The minute I turned around to leave, a man, almost as wide as he was tall and with a voice like a bull-horn, yelled: "You're an angel come to save us. Your aura, huge, mighty. I recognize you, and I'm here to help you save the world." All eyes turned to me and all I could do was wave everyone off. I tried to quiet the guy by denying everything, but he wouldn't stop. He trailed me for several days before I finally convinced him I had no such job and he should leave. Poof! That quickly, he disappeared.

Several had commented previously about my aura being plainly visible. How do you stop that? And how do you live with a mind that is busily soaring past anything you can handle? I started going to meetings: spiritual groups, psychics, churches, health-care centers. One Saturday I stopped at a Unity Church in Reston. I walked right in and yelled: "If anybody is here, tell me how to live in this place. I come from Idaho and I can't make sense of anything." I heard a man answer: "I come from Spokane and I can't make sense of anything around here either." A kindred soul. The guy turned out to be the church minister.

The answers I sought lay in one direction: give talks about my near-death experiences so others like me would come forward. I volunteered with every type of group I could find. That's all it took. I was inundated with offers, newspaper interviews, radio shows. People, many of them experiencers, showed up in droves—all willing to stay late so they could get personal. I recognized common traits right off, both in how the phenomenon tended to play out, who had what imagery pattern and who didn't, and how it affected not only them but their families, friends, jobs, and any sense of future. The more people I met the more dedicated to research I became, doing what I learned as a child back at the Twin Falls Police Station: focus on the individual's words and body movements. Check in with family members and friends. Verify.

A dear friend of mine, back in the days when I trained with a shaman, reminded me of a promise I made. If I ever found myself in Virginia, I was to call David McKnight, a psychology professor at a community college in the Shenandoah Valley. Talk about fate. David turned out to be my main supporter, finding me audiences, experiencers, medical people, opportunities to "knock on doors" everywhere imaginable . . . for decades. He never stopped making sure I had another door to open or another group or individual or family or school or class or hospital room to visit. He was truly "on assignment" with everything he did.

The highway I traveled between where I lived in northern Virginia and the Valley during the early days of my research crossed the fabled Shenandoah River—a breathtakingly beautiful place. Long past midnight on my first trip, as I neared the bridge, my Self instantly soared high into the air, looked around, then plunged straight down into the River, merging with every stone, every twig of moss and plant, every lifeform—fish, bug, or minion—every chemical and offal, every shell, glass, sand, and breath bubble. Spirit Keeper. Me. Here. The truth of this helped me realize how important Spirit Keepers are and how each of us, at some point in our history, may have taken on this task or are doing it still. As suddenly as I had soared away, I plopped back into my car seat. Me at the wheel, busily traversing the miles ahead, even though—absolutely so—I had been gone for a while. My childhood "lessons" on that log back at the home place finally made sense.

The double life I was living—administrative assistant on week days, researcher of near-death experiences on nights and weekends—pushed me flat against truisms I had no knowledge of. A biggie was diplomacy. To me, people around D.C. and in Virginia talked in circles. Their speech went round-and-round but they never actually said anything. Typical of my heritage, I spoke up when appropriate, said what needed to be said, then shut up. On a brief trip back to Idaho, a retired detective from the police force pulled me to one side and with his whole heart said: "You have to come home. You're learning that eastern diplomacy lingo and we can't understand you anymore."

No more than a few weeks later, a lawyer who worked at the Pentagon cornered me after a talk I had given. A tall man, he looked way down to my level and barked: "When I first heard you I thought you were a druggie and I tossed you off as some kind of kook. Now I know better. You are doing a tremendous job and you are doing it well." Needless to say we became friends.

Comments from these men hit me, and I had to ask myself: what is happening here? First there's this situation related to the Unified Field Theory, then at work I couldn't understand how to file a letter; then this character at the Post Office who thought I was an angel sent to save us; then discovering the truth about Spirit Keepers and that I was one of them; then the constant differences I kept finding in speech patterning versus meaning.

Why the jumble? Why the near-constant contradictions?

You know, sometimes overload can push you into exquisite simplicity. What I repeatedly saw with the hundreds I kept meeting was . . . *near-death experiencers seem to become more whole brained—logic and intuition merge—as if the life we lived as a human being is now concurrent with the reality of our soul.*

I saw myself in the eyes of every near-death-experiencer I spoke to. In my determination to block out my own experiences (put them "on a shelf in my mind" so I could be a blank slate on which others could write their own story), I discovered many things that helped me as much as it did them. A no-no. I lost "distance" doing this, a clarity necessary in any type of research. How could I be objective if I constantly blended in with whomever I was researching?

A dramatic confrontation quickly sealed the deal on what my real job was and how to do it. That experience occurred in, of all places, a police station in Arlington that had a large room with a stage for public events.

The room filled, some stood. When my talk was over, a woman quickly advanced, gazed at me with stars in her eyes, and crooned: "I wish something like that would happen to me so I could have the experiences you did."

Horror!

Words tumbled from my mouth about meditation, prayer work, spiritual disciplines. She didn't have to die like I did to open herself to greater realities.

Then I froze, yelling inside my head . . . *what had I said that would lead anyone to think they had to die to transform themselves? Had I misled this woman and all the others there into thinking experiences such as mine were something to pray for? Did I leave anything out? Had I betrayed what I now know to be true? Was I a failure doing the job I was led to do?*

That night was the last time for many decades that I spoke of my own story. Mention it, yes—describe the whole thing, no. Only recently have I felt comfortable divulging more (hence this book). What I was told to do in my third near-death experience covered not only the phenomenon and its aftereffects, but enlightenment itself. A rather broad venue, decidedly scary.

Several times I almost quit. The job ahead of me proved beyond difficult. I wasn't quite as strong as I'd thought.

Take this literally: my monthly menses went from a healthy red to a pale yellow/green. The Doc said I was starving to death. Turns out, a carrot from an Idaho farmer's patch isn't the same kind of carrot purchased from a D.C. grocery store. They may look alike but they don't "sing" (vibrate) the same. Soils are vastly different, as well as atmosphere. For the first time in my life I became vitamin-pill dependent, and had to wear progressively different weight-belts around my hips to shift the alignment of my bone structure to that of East Coast energy grids.

The changes I had to make, all of them, were radical.

Chapter 17

With the Coming of Spring

"Everything changes once we identify with being the witness to the story, instead of being the actor in it."
—Ram Dass

Good news. In the mail, I received a flier from Arleen Lorrance and Diane Pike, founders of The Love Project (spiritual principles that transform lives). I had sponsored them several years before to present a program at Boise State Student Union. Not many came because of mistakes I made in advertising the event. Strangely, the debacle wound up cementing a life-long friendship between us and opportunities for me to study in some of their programs.

Their next stop: Roanoke, Virginia. I immediately registered. On the long drive to Roanoke, I was surrounded by trees in full bloom and splashes of bird wings. Spring. The perfect time to move. There. I designed a poster featuring my picture and resume, pinned it to the bulletin board on the church wall where classes were held. A retired couple saw that poster and recognized me as "one of their own." They called. We made a deal: help out with groceries and I could consider their home my home. Don and Neddy Repp—angels in disguise. My son, stationed then on Governor's Island near New York City, had time and helped me move. I happily traded D.C. for barns and a bustling southern city that was once a main center for the railroad. Repp's had a large basement, so I flew back to Idaho, rented a U-Haul, said more goodbyes, and trucked the last of my things to my new home. A quick trip. No difficulties. Those strange energy balls I had seen the first time I drove this route were there again. Just floating along—for no reason I could discern.

I hurt myself at a temp job in Roanoke, necessitating that I see a doctor. For the first time since leaving my home state, I faced the type of danger most experiencers eventually must face . . . calling on a physician when in need. Within hours the medicine I had been given nearly killed me. A frantic call to Doc Reimer, now living in Nyssa, Oregon, pulled me out of the crises. Afterward, he put me on an even better regimen of vitamins and supplements than what I previously had (this new program I still have checked and maintain today). Later on, when researching near-death-experiencers, I found that most become so sensitive afterward that they can no longer handle the medications most people take for granted. Physiological changes after an NDE can be that extreme.

To ensure full recovery in my own situation, I immersed myself in every type of natural healing I could find: color breathing, solarized water, sun baths, walking barefoot on grass, chanting, affirmative prayer, and mineral soaks. It took several weeks, but the plan worked.

Money was next. I needed a real job. I found one working for an interconnect company before the divestiture of Ma Bell. Translation: computerized telephone switching systems for large businesses—something very new back then. My charge: train operators. Ha! Never heard of the stuff. Yet, instantly, *I just knew what to do and how.* When precedent failed, my bosses would give me extra time at various assignments to push systems and try out new ideas and procedures. The manuals we had to use were worthless, so I challenged my boss by writing a better one. He liked it so much, I wound up rewriting all of their manuals . . . a job formerly done only by their engineers.

Training people to use the new telephone systems (and manuals) required constant travel throughout states east of the Mississippi River. That meant living out of a suitcase, working in conditions that stretched the imagination—anywhere from military bases to new construction—from hotels and motels to office buildings and high-rise giants. You name it and I was there. And I loved it. So much so that I painted "Idaho Phyllis" in large black letters on my yellow suitcases. I didn't have to worry about theft. No one in their right mind would touch 'em.

Everywhere I went I encountered near-death experiencers. Lots of them. This research, what I was doing "on the side," rolled into over-drive. Truly, forces beyond my knowing or any sense of logic "arranged" to immerse me in extremes, 24 hours a day, seven days a week. Examples:

1. Driving to a job site near Minneapolis, I queried the cab driver about the local economy, any schools/colleges, the politics of the area. Frustrated by his inability to answer me the way he wanted to, he finally yelled: "Lady, I'm from Egypt. I got a scholarship for school here so I don't know anything about what you're asking. I died two years ago. Can I tell you about that and what I saw instead?"

2. Working in what would later become office space, the ceiling suddenly gave way around myself and the four ladies I was training. As we scrambled to safety, one

woman moaned that this accident was similar to one she had several years ago when she was almost crushed and saw "the other side." Two others piped in with similar stories.

3. I took a quick coffee break at a nearby truck stop south of Macon, Georgia. I had just sat down at a table to read a book when a giant of a man walked over. "Lady, anyone sitting in that chair opposite you?" "No." "Can I sit there?" It felt okay to do this, so I said yes. Hardly a second later, this burly guy put both elbows on the table, stared me in the face, then spit out: "I want you to know I still chase women. I still cuss and I still drink. But I also want you to know about the time I died and what happened to me."

4. I was walking down a street in a large city, when a woman gingerly touched my shoulder, looked me in the eye, and said, "I gotta talk to someone. You look like a nice person. May I tell you about the accident I was in? They said I died, but I didn't really. I was busy in heaven and I saw a lotta things."

5. The power died at the Air Base where I was teaching (hit by lightning). I was speaking, and right in the middle of a sentence when all of our equipment fried. Before I could juggle subjects, a man stood up and talked about his near-death experience after he was hit by lightning. Another followed with a similar story.

6. Construction at a large office building halted. Workers were cursing at each other big-time. I walked up and, in

a soft voice, invited each man to express what was on his mind. Everyone took a turn. Civility reigned. "Yup," said one, "doing this is like what I learned to do when I died. Help folks be their best."

7. A cabbie in D.C. had the blackest skin I had ever seen. I found myself staring. Embarrassed by my behavior I started to apologize, when he laughed: "I can see in your eyes, you died like I did. I can tell you everything and you won't laugh at me." Skin color? No such thing. We were the same.

8. I was standing quietly in an elevator with a few other people, when a fellow to my left murmured, "I'm one of those people who died and saw things. Can I tell you about it?"

9. At a nunnery, the sisters were more interested in talking about near-death experiences than they were in learning how to use the new telephone equipment. I did nothing to cause this. One of the sisters mentioned what happened to her when she nearly died. That got the others started.

10. In Kentucky, whole families sought me out. They were concerned about their kids. They'd heard about me from motel workers where I had previously been. Word quickly spread that I knew something about what their kids kept claiming.

Can you explain any of this? I can't. I finally decided I must be wearing one of those sandwich boards that only experiencers can see. And it reads: *Tell Me About Your Near-Death Experience*. Any explanation you can offer would be just as outlandish as whatever I can invent. I worked at this company for almost two years and encounters like this happened hundreds and hundreds of times, sometimes almost constantly.

Still, the assignment given to me to trouble-shoot an installation at a large hotel in New York City topped everything that ever happened to me at work. You see, for some reason beyond anything I recognized at the time, I had become hyper-sensitive to electricity and anything electrical, making me the perfect pawn in a conflict brewing between two large telephone companies.

Our company had teamed up with Japan's finest to install the best telephone service any hotel in the United States could offer. This very big deal involved dignitaries, newspaper reporters, cameras, flashing lights, and headlines. After two months, the world's finest failed, so we sent up our smartest to fix it. So did Japan. The problem was, neither crew spoke the other's language. Frustration broke into all-out rage when hotel management threatened, "Either you fix this mess or we'll throw it out."

Panic. And, in that panic, my boss sent me up for four days. "I don't care what you do, just give me a written report when you return." He scurried out the door and I flew to New York City.

The hotel was large, unique. I interviewed people on every floor, paying close attention to first floor check-in arrangements and the top floor where all the telephone cabinets were hooked up and the main operators worked. I tried to speak with installers, both ours and the Japanese. I could see in their minds what the deal was, but I proved useless as a translator. Thus, I spent most of my time with the main operators, pulling night shifts with them. Each night, when they weren't looking, I'd go back to the main cabinets, open all the doors so they couldn't see me, leave my body, enter/blend into flashing lights, and, one at a time, flow wherever that pulse led me, feel around while there, come back, pick another flashing light, enter/blend, inspect what was going on and where that led. I did this again and again, each night, until I experienced what I needed to know from every possible viewpoint. I wrote a report detailing what I found and gave it to my boss when I returned. Three days later, my boss called me into his office. Looking down at his desk pad he muttered: "I want you to know that because your report was so thorough we were able to fix the entire system in two days. Do not ever tell me how you did what you did." With that, he got up and left. Never once did he look me in the eye or say another word. Once alone I nearly cracked up, I laughed so hard.

Oh, at that Air Base in Florida's panhandle, something else happened. One day I was heading into work when I passed a movie theater marquee emblazoned with *The Empire Strikes Back,* the second film in the *Star Wars* series. Suddenly I envisioned myself there that evening with a physicist. I also saw myself easily finding the perfect parking space and walking in with him. I thought no more of this until late afternoon when I scurried out the door to catch the movie and bumped into a fellow walking in—the same man I had seen in my vision while rushing to work.

Without skipping a beat I queried, "You've been wanting to see the latest *Star Wars* movie, haven't you?" He was so shocked at what I said, he could hardly mutter: "Yes, how did you know?" I countered, "You're the physicist I saw myself watching the movie with tonight." "Uh . . . well, yes, I am a physicist. . . brought in for the new project." I grabbed his arm and turned him around, saying

I would explain later, and away we went. Cars were everywhere, yet the perfect spot opened up and we slid right in. The movie thrilled both of us. I later find out this man explored esoteric matters in his free time and was especially curious about near-death experiences. Imagine that! We came together at the very second we each could fulfill each other's needs and wishes.

My research into near-death states, now full-steam ahead, was about to take an abrupt turn, fulfilling a prophesy I had forgotten.

Chapter 18

The Topic is Zen

"Faith is taking the first step even when you don't see the whole staircase."
—Dr. Martin Luther King Jr.

Special doings happened Friday nights at church. For once I was home and the topic was Zen. Couldn't believe it. Zen in Roanoke, Virginia? You've got to be kidding. Must be a mistake in the bulletin. No mistake. The church where Don, Neddy and I attended did indeed advertise that a speaker would stop by and give a talk about Zen, a favorite topic of mine. The three of us went, arriving early. I sat on the floor in the yogic lotus position, front row. A fellow by the name of Terry Atwater sat on a chair in the back, eyes glued only on me. During the break, Neddy stationed herself at one door of the Fellowship Hall, and Don was at the other. Their goal? Grab each of us and bring us together so we could meet. Neither of us knew about their plan until years later—that they were playing match-maker because they were convinced we would make the perfect couple.

That Saturday Terry drove some distance to Repp's place, just to make certain he knew how to get there (they had invited him to a spaghetti dinner I knew nothing about). I had just left the house to take a walk and when I rounded a bend, there he was. I recognized him from the night before, so I asked if he wanted to take a walk with me. He thought about the invitation, then said yes and parked his car. We joined hands and walked together until the road ended. As we were about to turn around, clouds started to pour. Terry panicked. "No problem," I chortled. "Just look for a ditch with a good weed cover." We quickly found what we were looking for and burrowed in, laughing, dry as could be.

Don and Neddy, worried about me, took off in their big rover, hoping to save me from the deluge. You gotta know Neddy. Short and a little plump, she had the strongest, loudest voice anybody had ever heard. Apparently Terry's legs could be seen from the road. Neddy jumped from the rover and screamed, "Terry Atwater, what are you doing in the weeds?" Then she saw me. "What are you doing in the weeds with him?" After we crawled out, Terry turned pinkish red. He was so embarrassed. The rain stopped. We turned down a ride back, preferring to go on chirping like a couple of canaries as we walked along.

The prediction made by that psychic back in Idaho returned to memory. *On a day filled with the coming of rain, we took a walk. He, taller than I, younger, had black curly hair, bronze skin, a conservative fellow, refined, well-traveled and well-educated, unique in his devotion to the spiritual path. He recognized me immediately. It took me three days to recognize him. He was a twin himself; we felt that the two of us were "twin souls"—exact opposites of the same energy.*

Three times with three different astrologers, we had our charts drawn. We were indeed exact opposites: the position of Suns, Moons, Saturns, and Venuses opposed what appeared in the other's chart. All three astrologers advised against marriage with this type of "difficulty." Their verdict told me they did not understand the true power available in direct oppositions—a power that can blend all parts into an equal whole.

Our first date was high up a mountain at the reservoir. He parked in an assigned lot, then we took off into the woods, exploring as we went, until we spotted a large tree trunk laying on the ground near the water's edge. We sat on that log and sang the moon up, each taking a turn vocalizing our favorites: he, music like the Bee Gees. Me, tunes such as "Coming in on a Wing and a Prayer," a World War II lament. Differences in generations faded. Hearts together. Sheer magic!

Once darkness fell, he panicked. How do we find the car? Neither of us knew, but I had an idea: create a sound ball, toss it high in the air, then follow the sound it makes as it seeks out the target. Nutty, but . . . energizing my hands, I saw in my mind a ball formed entirely of sound—a sound that would lead us where we wanted to go. I tossed it and we followed what I heard. Terry, flatly mystified, kept up like a trooper. The moon's light barely covered the very large area of forest as we stumbled along. The ball landed exactly atop his car hood. I jumped with joy. He shook his head in disbelief. "Get used to this," I laughed, "cause my world has no boundaries." Love defined the night.

The dating scene in downtown Roanoke, however, proved to be more than what we experienced in the woods. Each time we'd enter a restaurant, people would put their silverware down and glare at us. Their muscles tensed. I always smiled and waved as we walked by as if nothing was amiss. In my mind, nothing was. Each time I did this people would smile back, pick up their utensils, and start eating again. One time, Terry pulled me aside as we left a particular restaurant: "Don't you know what they're doing in there?" With utter confidence I answered yes. "They are giving me the power of their attention, and I happen to feel that is a precious gift so I was simply saying thank you." We had many opportunities to test this truism: *Wherever you put your attention, is where you put your power*. The old Jim Crow laws still existed in some parts of the state: a black man with a white woman was still a concern to many. What always puzzled me, though, was the question of color. Terry is certainly not black, he's light brown. And I'm spotty, with moles and freckles all over the place. Hardly white.

One night, after we saw the movie *All That Jazz*, it rained so hard I could not get out of the car. The windshield morphed into revelation: the two of us were plainly visible as opposite carriers of the same energy factor. We were both stunned. When Terry proposed, "yes" was a given.

I tussled afterward with the notion of what name I should use. Then one night I had a most extraordinary vision. Across a background of soft shiny black appeared huge block lettering that spelled out "P. M. H. Atwater" in the brightest white I had ever seen. This was so unexpected, I jumped from my bed and wound up in the middle of the bedroom floor staring at a white wall with that name now reversed to a stunning black, hanging in mid-air. One of the letters nearly bumped my nose. I yelled, waking up Don and Neddy. The three of us huddled in the breakfast nook, with me complaining that this was the most egotistical, stupid, ridiculous name imaginable, almost cursing its awfulness. Surely this wasn't to be my new name. But . . . I decided to pray about it for nine days. After that I would know. To my great surprise, on the ninth day I felt as if I had been born with that name. According to the Court, a woman could choose how she would use her name at marriage, fill out forms, and it would become legal. My choice: PMH Atwater (with or without periods). Six weeks after we first met, we married.

Terry walked away from a television job as a "human interest" reporter (*man bites dog*) in a major market so he could return to Roanoke. He said it just felt right for him to do so. He then traded Roanoke radio for an announcer position in Harrisonburg. We moved . . . smack into the reality of . . . we didn't know each other.

Does love really conquer all? Well, kinda sorta. We agreed on two rules: 1) if we couldn't agree on something—coin toss, two out of three, winner rules; 2) if we got mad at each other, take it out with the person you see in the mirror first, find out where that person (you) is coming from, then go back and talk things out with your spouse.

We never imagined there might be a number three, which turned out to be the elephant in the room: Terry loved flashy clothes and I loved beige, beige, beige. I had spent decades working with the public. People by the thousands. No more. I much preferred to be "woodwork." Terry's biggest boast? A particular coat that was so gaudy I refused to be seen with him if he ever wore it. This became such an issue that I hid the thing in a far corner of a second closet. I loved the man but I couldn't stand that coat!

After flying home early from one of my jobs, I determined to have it out with the coat. I pulled it from the closet in such a way that it would face me, yet still remain on its hanger on the closet rod. When opened full-out, I discovered that it really was fancy and very expensive. It even had invisible "French-seams." The dark green velvet collar and sleeve cuffs were soft to the touch. It had huge, double-breasted rows of bright gold buttons down the front, like mirrors. You could see yourself in them. The fabric was silk brocade in yellow/pink/green swirls. The lining, quilted gold.

After appreciating its worth, I pulled it off the hanger and danced with it. Round and round across the floor. Satisfied, I rehung the coat and hurriedly fixed a great meal. As he began to eat, I carefully pulled his arm down, food and all, and asked: "If you accept Plain Jane me, I'll accept Nevada Flash you." He thought for a moment, then agreed. From that moment on we never again criticized each other's clothes.

Six months later we happened to notice the clothes hanging in our closet. He had easily and effortlessly replaced everything (including that coat) with fashionable conservative styles, and my clothes now matched the colors of the rainbow. Neither of us made a decision to do this. Our tastes simply changed, naturally, easily. This caught our attention. What we had learned while dating turned out to be equally true with anything that bothered us: *Take the attention away. Tension dissolves. Problem solved.*

These simple measures worked for us, but not Terry's mother. She made it very plain she did not want me in her family. She blew up halfway through our wedding and loudly stormed out of the church with her husband following right behind her. Throughout the days and years that followed, I always deferred to her. I did everything I could to let her know how beautiful she was—a lady of fashion. She certainly knew more about fashion than I did. I learned that she prayed her twin boys would marry women of "their" color—that is to say, a rich golden brown. What a joke that turned out to be. Terry's brother married a woman with very dark skin—a former model who had earned two doctorates. Of course you know what happened with Terry. He married whitey me. At first she disowned both wives.

I knew precious little about African-American customs or lifestyles (for what we now call Blacks). Racial issues in Idaho were wrapped around the Chinese, Native Americans, then later Mexicans and Japanese. We had a lot of Basque immigrants, especially in southern Idaho, and people from Owyhee. A direct route once existed between Owyhee, the West Coast, and southern Idaho. Many of them manned Old Fort Boise. Today we call people from Owyhee "Hawaiians" because Morman Missionaries changed the spelling of their name. The fabled Old West ran along different color lines and customs than those in the East.

I didn't recognize anyone's racial rules because they meant nothing to me. Not so with Mom Atwater. This misunderstanding, this "difference," came to define our relationship. To her, Terry was a failure and she never let him forget. His twin not only had a doctorate, but won appointment as a college professor and later became college president. Terry's many accomplishments meant nothing to her: a second-degree black belt in karate, years as a body-builder who ran for miles each morning across the shorelines near Hampton Roads, excelling in voice training at a special school in D.C., receiving his college diploma in jig time, well-studied in the esoteric arts as well as Christian mysticism, and on and on. He was a doer. His brother, a teacher. Both were innovators. I had hoped that someday she would feel differently about both of us. I don't know if that ever happened for her. We loved her dearly anyway. She really was quite a lady.

We went through a lot with "our" children too. All three fully accepted Terry as special—the girls most of all—especially the oldest one. She couldn't make it to our wedding, but called soon after to meet Terry over the phone. Right off the bat she told him she didn't care if he was purple with pink polka-dots. "Just get my mother pregnant because I want a baby brother." To say her request surprised Terry would be an understatement.

We tried. I miscarried again and again. I took a quick trip West to attend my son's wedding. Once there, I had to feign specialness because for me everyone was my son, my daughter, my father/mother, aunt/uncle, brother/sister. All special. All family. Other near-death experiencers felt the same way. We returned from "wherever it was we were" during our episode to discover that the unconditional love we were once bathed in is actually as challenging as it is glorious. The idea of "play acting," joining in with others to meet whatever situation or need presents itself—behaving as others do—solved the conundrum. Everyone benefits when this is done. A haunting question remained for me though. How could experiencers be displaying this same trait unless it was typical to the aftereffects of near-death states? And if that is so, what, really, is unconditional love?

Soon after I returned from the wedding, my menses turned black. A hysterectomy was required. I told everyone I was going to birth my uterus. As things turned out, the hospital was so crowded on the date of surgery, they had to put me in the birthing ward. Funny! An even funnier thing happened when I took a quick trip down the hall during first time walking after surgery. A large clock displayed the month, day, and time of my son's birth. Exact. The energy that it took to open my womb closed it. I shifted from blood to light, from personal to universal. As one cycle completed itself, another began.

Art Yensen came to visit. Two scrappy Westerners under the same roof. Terry winced.

Years before, Art had written a little book called *I Saw Heaven.* It chronicled what happened to him in 1932 when he barely survived a car roll-over that smashed him through a cloth roof . . . into a world he could only describe as heaven. A staunch materialist, the experience so changed him that it took him three years to even begin processing the event. After reading his story at one of our many visits, I sat at the kitchen table with he and his wife Alice, in awe of everything, especially their home . . . a unique creation he built himself out of pumice from a nearby quarry. All the how-to's he needed in construction came from asking detailed questions every time he meditated, then doing exactly what he was shown. Everyone in Parma thought the man a fool. Yet his beautiful one-of-a-kind home, warm every winter, cool every summer, proved the magic of pumice—and, the magic of Art Yensen —who often visited "other realms" for answers to questions.

Back then I had said to him: "I wish something like this would happen to me so I could write a book about it that would help people, like you did." Stop everything! Did I actually wish for an episode like his to happen to me? So I could be like Art? Really? The pause between us was a long one.

My youngest came knocking after Art left.

The previous year, the image of her face had suddenly covered the entire windshield of our car as we drove from Roanoke to Harrisonburg. No, this wasn't a dream. Without warning or explanation, the self I was hovered over her as she tried to kill herself in the bathroom of a Sheriff's office near Spokane. I saw her break a drinking glass, take a shard and begin to cut her wrist. Instantly, I projected the face of the man she thought she loved onto the mirror. Seeing that face, she collapsed into a wail of tears and screams. The view disappeared. I told Terry what had just happened. He thought I was daydreaming; me, a worried mother. Soon after we arrived home, she telephoned. "Mother, I have something to tell you." Before she could utter another word, I countered: "Let me tell you what I just saw and what I did about it." Every detail was given. Silence. For what seemed long minutes, she finally spoke. "Isn't there anything I can do in my life without you knowing about it and intervening?"

"Live any way you want," I advised. "But if you ever try to kill yourself again, I'll be right there and I'll stop you."

Childhood memories of her flooded my mind. "Am I going to die now?" — the first words she ever spoke. No little one talks like that. Was this a troubled soul, my daughter? Were there other reasons for her saying what she did? Past life reasons, maybe?

Living with her dad wasn't working. Desperate to leave, she found a trucker who would take her half-way across the country. She phoned Art for help. He telegraphed her enough money to bus the rest of the way. She wanted Terry to be her new dad.

Hardly recognizable when she got off the bus, we both knew that in order to clean up her mind, her body had to come first—a "flush out." This meant she could only eat vegetarian dishes. No sugar. No spices. No alcohol. No drugs. Complaints netted her more house cleaning and more job hunting tasks. Her foray into a "new and better life with Momma" introduced her to a humid climate, heavy vegetation, and people and customs foreign to her. We might as well have been living in Greece. Differences between southern Idaho and the Blue Ridge of Virginia were that huge.

She had a lot to learn. So did I.

Chapter 19

Tilt

"All tempest has, like a navel, a hole in its middle, through which a gull can fly in silence."
—Fourteenth Century Japanese Saying

Soon my travels morphed into opportunities for me to give talks on what I kept finding in my research, plus a broad range of spiritual topics and how-to workshops dealing with the aftereffects of transformative experiences. I resigned from the telephone company, then penned a little book called *I Died Three Times in 1977*. Sorta like Art's. Fifty copies were printed. How a copy got to a bookstore in Hartford, Connecticut, nobody knows. Kenneth Ring, Ph.D., the man who validated the research of Raymond Moody, M.D. (the man who coined the term "near-death experiences"), just happened to be in that bookstore and bought a copy. He tracked down my telephone number and asked if he could stay overnight with us on his way to a meeting with experts in the new field of near-death studies, arranged by Moody. We agreed. He and his lady friend came.

I knew absolutely nothing about this group, nor had I heard of Moody or his famous book *Life After Life*. All I knew was what Elisabeth Kübler Ross had told me and what I had discovered myself by asking a lot of questions and making observations of the countless experiencers I had met or heard about along the way. We visited 'til morning, with Ken overjoyed to learn about what I had accomplished. "What you have done is staggering. You know more about the phenomenon than anyone else. Now you must come up to Storrs, Connecticut and meet your colleagues." Colleagues? He was quite serious when he said this. "I teach there and the office of the International Association of Near-Death Studies is near mine. You can sleep on the front couch in my cabin, go over our research, see what you think."

I went, stayed nearly a week, and devised a questionnaire that could test both their cases and those I had addresses for. I spent a lot of time with Nancy Bush, the newly appointed Executive Secretary. She puzzled over the pattern of her own NDE, one that seemed to defy those already collected. She wanted to hear any ideas I might offer. In the meantime, the Board of IANDS approved my idea for a test questionnaire to be sent to both groups, theirs and mine. I went right to work reading everything they had, asking questions whenever I could. I sorted through cassette tapes and studied each file. Numerous times I made the journey back and forth from my home in Virginia to Connecticut, finally joining IANDS as one of their earliest members. When asked to write a column called "Coming Back" for their newsletter *Vital Signs*, I jumped at the chance, basing everything I wrote on my discoveries.

This newly opened door introduced me to egos both devoted and competitive, squabbles of every kind imaginable, scientific prerequisites, and a mad dash to satisfy the growing demand of a public titillated by any proof that there really might be life after death.

Results from the questionnaire came in. Every single experiencer, those from the IANDS archives and those I had personally interviewed all responded exactly the same way: *their near-death experience was the most incredible thing that had ever happened to them and the unconditional love they discovered in dying was the only answer to every problem.*

Really?

I had been in the homes of many in my group. Whenever possible I had also spoken with their health-care providers, neighbors, co-workers, and friends. Every single one faced contradictions that all-too-often morphed into all kinds of problems—some serious. Divorce rates were sky-high. Most found it impossible to verbalize what they really wanted to say, as words no longer fit.

What I had encountered in my work convinced me there is much more to the story of the near-death phenomenon than anyone else had discovered or admitted. Experiences are real, yet what is laid bare challenges every culture, every belief system, every personal preference. Yes, unconditional love is wondrous, truly beyond what anyone can say or know or even attempt to describe. Still, the phenomenon itself, every inch of it, has edges, schisms, and gaps both positive and negative between the power of the experience and how it unfolds in people's lives. It's not enough to focus on stories, miracles, or challenges. There are aftereffects: patterns of physical, mental, emotional, and spiritual changes that can alter "the known way"—mostly for the better, sometimes not.

My life suddenly turned somersaults. Terry volunteered to take on two jobs to pay the bills so I could begin to write my first book. Ken suggested talking to his agent. I did. "First send me your manuscript," she advised. Manuscript? Gulp! I felt like sweating blood before words flowed. At last the book came together and I sent her the result. "Come up here," she urged. "I need to talk to you." The drive to New York was a quickie. I sat in her office for what I thought would be a discussion. Didn't happen. Right in front of my face she threw the whole thing into the trash. All of it, except for the Table of Contents. With my heart in tatters and tears beginning to gush, I managed to somehow ask why she kept that one page. "I want to show publishers up here what's coming. Once you quit trying to write like Ken Ring and write like yourself, there's a book in you waiting to come out."

Her assessment blew a hole in my ego.

How to deal with this? And above all else, how would I continue with research while satisfying a growing demand for appearances and lectures? Receiving money for anything I did countered what sponsors expected. Finally I asked for donations. Pass the hat. Airline tickets are not free.

This conundrum actually enhanced and increased research opportunities—an unexpected "windfall" —like what happened because of Wally Johnston, a psychologist I met at Shanti Nilaya. He opened a number of doors for me where travel and giving talks were concerned. For years. At one particular gathering with a Grief Group that met in a Funeral Home in Winona, Minnesota, I faced a type of fear that cut deep. The room was large and chairs were arranged in an oval shape, with me on one end and an older fellow with a mustache directly opposite. As a door-opener, I began with some of what happened to me, hoping to use that as a springboard to a conversation about aftereffects. Not even half-way through, the man opposite me abruptly stood and angrily shouted, "You have not been washed in the blood of the lamb." With that said, he marched right out of the room, followed by over half of the audience. Turns out he was a popular Lutheran minister and the walk-outs were mostly people from his own congregation. No one knew what ticked him off, but I knew exactly why my heart so suddenly filled with such a deep pain that I could hardly continue. The man was an exact double for Daddy Sogn, the Norwegian who helped raise me. He and Momma Sogn were the only source of love I had ever received throughout my childhood.

Pain, the Lutheran minister's and my own, showed me the extreme spread that life's beginnings and endings can take. *There isn't any right or wrong to this.* For sure, what makes the phenomenon of near-death experiences so miraculous is that we in the modern world have, at last, a passionate yet reliable source of how to see past and beyond what we once thought were absolutes.

Later, while attending a program at a library in Falls Church, the speaker took me aside afterwards and predicted I would soon be flying up to New York and New Jersey to give presentations. Total surprise. I never saw the guy before, yet, sure enough, opportunities to do just that opened up as if on schedule. I mean it when I say "just opened up." It was that curious. The entire Northeast, in fact, became like my backyard. While out and about, I brought my runes with me. It wasn't long before research of near-death experiences also included research about the symbol-signs I had been introduced to at that full-moon meditation back in Boise before I left.

These so-called Runes of Njord were actually group or family runes in the sense that they could only be used as a single unit in free-form casting to obtain answers to questions. Whenever possible I "planted" myself in libraries to search out runic histories. Additionally, I spent extra time with elders who understood sacred objects and symbols wherever I could find them. What seemed to make sense when I first received my set was to associate them with Viking and northern Germanic rune forms. It took decades and several trips to Turkey before I could trace what very well may be their actual origination: areas around Caspian and Black Seas, Volga, and the Bosporus. Runes of Njord they certainly were not. Eventually

I named them Goddess Runes because their symbol-signs matched what researchers kept discovering about ancient Goddess cultures. Into a cedar box they went, as sacred objects never to be touched by anyone but me. Prayer came first whenever I used them. Actually, prayer first describes every morning of every day since I died, as God to me is now a living pulsebeat . . . That Which Breathes Me.

Meanderings around West Virginia, Pennsylvania, and Maryland enabled me to set up "Playshops" where anyone could come, bring pebbles and marking pens of their own to fashion their own set, learn runic how-tos, then practice, practice, practice. The average female learned "the way of a cast" in about an hour; the average male maybe two to three hours; the average kid, ten minutes. By 1986, I self-published *The Magical Language of Runes*, a collection of what I learned during those early attempts to pass along to others what had helped me.

For reasons unclear to anyone's way of thinking, my rune set was ever-ready during the decades I went on the road to conduct near-death research—both as a way to help people circumvent conversation in favor of deeper digs into their psyche (what they truly wanted to know about their own life), and as a way to help cover my travel expenses. What modality I used with the general public made little difference. The astrology and numerology technician I once was vanished. In its place was a me that rippled with color, rhythm, and a feeling/sense that often led me in directions as natural as the rising sun—flowing more with what wasn't said rather than what was. Many times I seemed able to "see" right through people, pinpointing the unspoken.

This change of mine matched that of other experiencers. Fact: if you weren't psychic/intuitive before your experience, you became that way afterward. If you were psychic/intuitive to begin with, you became even more so afterward. Appreciated or not, the near-death phenomenon opens anything closed or held in secret. I talked about this in my *Vital Signs* column. "Coming Back" quickly became a conversation starter about an increasingly large range of aftereffects—what is natural and normal versus what is ignored or denied. Experiencers moved towards wholeness afterwards, becoming freer somehow—more of themselves.

No researcher pursued the pattern of aftereffects to the extent I did. I was incredibly curious and had endless energy. It seemed as if I could not learn enough fast enough. Still, hanging over my head was that book I was supposed to write though. Others to follow. How could I ever find the courage to do such a job? Writing a book was a bigger issue to me than words on paper. It meant the possibility of losing again what I had already lost in death. Ken's agent said there was a book in me, a really good one. But where was it and how was I supposed to find it? It took a ghost to show me what my mind could no longer deliver. And that happened one day as I walked across the elevated gangway from where Terry and I lived in order to reach the apartment mailboxes located at street level.

A sense of importance overcame me. Reaching inside our box, a very hot letter wiggled. Well, at least to me it was hot. Strange though—it was from a woman I'd never heard of. Hurriedly I opened it and found a letter filled with grief from a woman who had lost her eighteen-year-old son the previous year in a motorcycle accident. Could I please contact him—somehow, some way? Did he suffer in the crash? Where was he now? Soon it would be his birthday and she was desperate. Could I help her contact her dead son?

Mediumship had been a part of my life in the sixties and again when the famous *Seth* books came out (which detailed what medium Jane Roberts learned from a disembodied entity). I found then that I could do the same thing as Jane. Meetings were held. People from all over came to hear what came through me. I cut this off after a few months though. I didn't like being in a position where desperate people hovered around me to hear the latest about their dead relatives. Not my thing.

The letter I now held brought those memories back. The heat in the letter—her son. He rode along hoping to reach me too. I saw his form and spoke with him. He loved his mother so much and wanted to get a message through to her. Would I help him? It took a lot of persuading, but I finally agreed. I would allow him to use my hands to write his mother a letter. While in the spare bedroom where my office was, busy with the task at hand, my daughter walked in the front door. She yelled for me, then stopped short, peered around the corner of the living room and asked "Who's that guy leaning over your shoulder?" "Oh, that's John," I answered. "He was killed last year in a motorcycle accident. He wants me to write a letter to his mother."

She cocked her head. I could hear her talking to herself, saying, "There's a guy leaning over my mother's shoulder. He died last year in a motorcycle accident yet he's right here talking to my mother. I see him. But he's dead." She promptly left, yelling "Mom, I can't handle this." That night, I asked Terry if he wanted to meet our new visitor. He agreed. Terry walked into my office, stood exactly where John was standing, then immediately jumped away, questioning: "Why is it so cold there, right by your files?" "Well, dear, that's where John is." I explained everything but Terry couldn't handle the situation either. He had never seen a disincarnate before, much less stood right in the middle of one.

John and I finished the letter. I mailed it to his mother. It was a crazy letter, filled with repetitions, like a child would do. I almost didn't send it, thinking I had somehow goofed. Surely this was not what an eighteen-year-old would say to his grieving mother. She promptly replied, utterly overjoyed. He really did speak like that. It's how she knew he was actually with me.

After that day, allowing another to speak through me, spending time with John, laughing as my daughter talked to herself, cheering Terry on to experience something he had never felt before, all of it, the whole experience of it, let loose a plug in me. I had been trying to resurrect the writer I once was. Not possible. My charge now was to make sense out of the senseless. I could allow my research to be in charge, write itself, as I had done with John. Articles quickly tumbled out once I did. *East West Journal* took the one I wrote about Perelandra—a place where one learned how to garden with angels and fairies.

Chapter 20

All that Glitters Isn't Gold

"To be fully alive, fully human and completely awake is to be continually thrown out of the nest."
—Pema Chödrön

Perelandra is located north of me, in Jeffersonton. The miracle maker is Machaelle Small Wright, aided by Clarence, her partner. She was drawn there to create a sanctuary, where humans, nature spirits, plants, soil, and weather could co-exist as an expression of their essential spiritual selves within the same physical environment. The result? Proof-positive gardening.

I was drawn to write this story because, back in the sixties, I fell in love with The Findhorn Gardens, a magical place in northern Scotland that was too cold, windy, and sand-packed to raise anything like flowers and food—a place totally transformed by three people: Peter and Eileen Caddy, and Dorothy Maclean. These three believed that if you talked with God and worked with angels and fairies, you could accomplish the impossible. The crops that resulted shocked the world. Today they "garden" *people*, helping them find and cultivate their own spiritual selves and live accordingly.

The impact The Findhorn Gardens had on me was deep and profound (later on from Perelandra too). As a child I had played with wee folk peeking through each patch of earth, especially 'round roots of trees and bushes. None looked like people. Rather, they spun like whirligigs of color and sound. I'd open up my hand near them and they'd whirl across my palms and fingers, tickling them as they did. Fun! I never saw them again after my birth mother took me away from the Sogns.

We moved to Williamsburg during this period. Terry tried selling time share projects while working as an "on-air" personality at the local radio station. Our daughter surprised us by moving in too, along with her new baby. This first grandchild was birthed at 10:31 pm on October 31st. Exact. A miniature spook. I created a bed of blankets across my legs for this tiny treasure to lay on as I spent hours typing away. He loved this nest. I mused that maybe someday he might grow up and become a writer because of such early exposure.

Article writing honed the skills I needed to craft my first major book, *Coming Back to Life: The After-Effects of the Near-Death Experience*. Terry found me an agent, and away my manuscript flew. It wound up on the desk of an editor at Dodd, Mead & Company—one week before Shirley MacLaine gave that funny demonstration of Chakras (the whirling energy flares that can come from each endocrine gland) on *Late Night with Johnny Carson*. It broke viewing records. Overnight, New York publishers clamored for anything "far out." My book—right there—sold. I even got to choose the author photo that went on the back flap (a pic of me holding my daughter's newborn after I picked them up at the hospital). The photographer I wanted did the cover. His name came to me in a dream.

My new editor turned out to be an exact duplicate of the one I had back at the Statehouse. She was just as stern and strict. Her goal was to polish what I had submitted, not fire me as my former editor tried repeatedly to do. The Boise version carried a loaded gun in her purse, was a chain smoker, and tried to drive out every writer who came onboard. The fact that I lasted two years drove her nuts. She told me so in a haze of cigarette smoke laced with epitaphs and air-borne books aimed my way. Soon enough, State politics flipped sides—which means heads rolled. I left when neither the new politics nor my previous husband's strange behavior seemed based on any kind of truth.

The ad campaign my publishers laid out for me was unbelievable! With perks. I was sent to every daytime television show that would have me, along with the best of nighttime radio. They were convinced my book could be a best seller, so they shoved books out the door with me and I did the best I could to sell them. My first foray was with radio; a tall building, late at night, black-curtained-cozy. Another woman ahead of me also spoke about her new book *Coming Back* (same title as mine but it tackled *Divorce* issues). Believe it or not, she too was a near-death-experiencer. She stayed on afterward to teach me how to dress for TV (including which colors to stay away from, and what to say and not say when interviewed). On top of that, she fleshed out my show by volunteering as a guest. The audience loved us.

It took six years for me to reach this moment. During that gap I gave countless talks and sought out more experiencers, while at the same time helping IANDS spread the word—to both experiencers and the general public—that the organization was there to help experiencers handle what they had gone through. IANDS was paramount in helping to inform the public about the phenomenon and its aftereffects (the full spread was unknown then, except for the pattern of psychological and physiological aftereffects I had found that still needed further scrutiny).

Truth with a capital "T" seemed to define what we all had discovered. For the first time in recorded history the entire world had an opportunity to investigate, in a logical and scientific manner, what lay at the crux of the greatest of all human dilemmas: is there life after death?

Yet, what seemed wondrous at first glance wasn't necessarily a blessing.

Experiencers were having real challenges adapting to family life again, holding down jobs, and facing physicians who failed to understand or even care why they no longer fit standard models of health care. On top of this, Psychiatrists' single solution to "variables" always seemed to be . . . commit 'em. IANDS and I wanted everyone to know what was typical and what was okay. We provided experiencers with guidance in order to help them deal with everything they might be going through. Near-death miracles could be tricky, as one woman who was quoted in the original best seller, groaned: "I'm not perfect. I'm not like the others in *Life After Life*. I'm ashamed to be in that book."

The original kerfluffle regarding what I said in my column suddenly mushroomed. This time, gripes reached such a crescendo that the then-editor of the newsletter put his foot down. Either I write like all the other researchers and forget about the patterns I kept finding, or I was out. The "bug in the package" turned out to be my insistence that the majority of experiencers became psychic (outward directed awareness) and intuitive (inward knowing sense) after their episodes. Some extremely so. This claim finally led to outright war. A phone call from the newsletter editor put things plainly: either I recant or I was fired and my column would be pulled. My answer? No way! Had I cooperated with him I would be going against what I had found true with well over a thousand people. (I only claimed around 700 at the time but the actual count was much higher.) I did soften what I was saying somewhat because I recognized the challenge this new organization faced within the scientific community. The editor, by the way, became embittered—not just because of me, but because his vision of unconditional love backfired (probably because of a love interest he fancied with an experiencer who ignored his advances). After writing the most incredible book about unconditional love I had ever read, he committed suicide, shocking everyone.

Overall research, mine and others, backed up what experiencers shared. Stories were that astounding! Pressure from the media became unavoidable though. What saved me was my name, P.M.H (or just PMH). People assumed I was male. I'm convinced that if I'd had a female name, few, if any, would have paid much attention to what I had discovered. The vision I had of three initials for a name given to me before I married turned out to be right on . . . neutral.

Chapters of the organization sprung up across the country (they're now called Friends of IANDS). We were all new back then, dipping our toes into unknown territory, totally devoted to the mission we all shared—helping to alleviate the fear of death. Unfortunately, disagreements betwixt and between almost destroyed the organization. I didn't realize how serious this was until an offer came for me to appear on *Sally Jessy Raphael* (a very popular daytime television show at the time). Everyone I met en route was either an experiencer or knew one. This charm hardly dampened my fear though. Me on national television? What if I goofed or made a mistake or walked on stage looking like a fool?

When ushered into the Green Room, the first thing I noticed—it wasn't green. I asked about this but no one knew or cared. One by one, each person took their turn. I could see them via the in-room set. Once on stage, people acted half-crazy vying for attention—shouting in order to shine. More than a half-hour passed. Still, no one came for me. Finally a sour-faced man opened the door, sat down, and began to treat me as if I were a criminal. He accused me of all kinds of things, finally stating that according to IANDS I was mentally ill. Their office had heard I was to appear, so a woman claiming to be the head of the organization called ahead to warn the television staff not to let me on. Since the official administrator of IANDS had resigned and left her post months before, I had no idea who made that call. Why the ruse? I defended myself, finally convincing the man I should be allowed on stage. In the last five minutes I managed to boldly proclaim we all had a lot to learn from people who survived death. That's it. Show's over. Out the door I was ushered, without the slightest clue as to what had happened or why. Whoever made that infamous call remains unknown.

Refusing gloom, I labeled the whole affair a learning lesson and went on participate with Raymond Moody on the *Geraldo* Show. I was also a guest on *Regis & Kathie Lee*, *Larry King Live*, and *Entertainment Tonight*. But I lost a major magazine interview, then another and another, before television scouts and reporters finally located me a year later. All told the same story: they had tried calling me about my near-death work using the central number they'd been given, but got another woman in my place who simply took over. I have no idea if this was intentional. I only know that requests for interviews were consistently re-routed. How many interviews I lost remains unknown.

These mix-ups turned out to be harbingers of things to come. I had extra time while in Connecticut, so I made an appointment with a woman I deeply admired. She was so good as a speaker, she left me in awe. I had hoped to get some advice from her. What seemed like a really great meeting between us ended with her advising me to stay away from all near-death chapters. My voice, she claimed, wasn't needed there. I left the office unsure of what had just occurred, so I called her right back. Did I hear her correctly? Might I have misunderstood what she said? She erupted in rage on the phone, not only affirming what she had previously said, but adding that if I ever visited a near-death group again she would call a lawyer. Stunned, I scurried back to Virginia. I couldn't believe this, nor could anyone else I checked with.

The first national near-death conference was held at a college in Rosemont, Pennsylvania in 1989. It seems like a scheduling conflict "suddenly manifested" when I got there. There was no room available for me, so they tucked me into a music room that didn't even have a stage. There wasn't even a sign marking my talk. A handful stopped by. Make no mistake, that conference excited everyone and I met many wonderful people. Still, the feeling of being unwelcome grew . . . so much so that I called a cab and left early.

I returned to find out that the agent we hired had left town with most of my book advance money. He couldn't be traced. A corporate raider had tricked the management of Dodd, Mead & Company and bankrupted them—the first of many such takeovers to come in the publishing industry. My book, scheduled at the time for a third printing, vanished. Once booksellers across the country learned about what happened, they pulled anything Dodd/Mead off their shelves and shipped it back to New York, hoping to get their money back. I had just completed a series of successful shows when this occurred and was inundated by calls from people wanting to buy my book. But no books could be had. Poof! Gone. I inquired at the warehouse. A woman there said she had plenty, but they would all be remaindered (destroyed). I objected loudly. To quiet me, the corporate raider's sidekick claimed I had been lied to by warehouse personnel—my book was little more than a flop. Eventually I was offered some payoff money to shut me up. A lawyer advised: Take it. It was the best I'd get under the circumstances. I did, and used the money to buy myself a do-it-yourself-desk-kit.

For days afterward, I spent every hour I could spare and more immersed in every forgiveness technique I knew. Eventually life felt okay again. Then a miracle occurred. Dodd/Mead, without my knowledge, negotiated a handsome contract with Ballantine Books to release a paperback version of *Coming Back to Life.* It was scheduled for publication the following year. Unfortunately, my agent took all the money from this deal before he skipped town—but at least *Coming Back to Life* would be doing just that.

What was saved? All firsts:

- An extensive discussion of the seven major aftereffects I had discovered.
- Hellish cases as well as heavenly.
- Comparisons from the work of Dr. Richard Maurice Bucke (and his search for Cosmic Consciousness) to patterns I found in many near-death experiences.
- Differing points of view expressed in speech patterns of the deeply religious versus those who were not.
- Important discoveries between Eastern and Western views_of enlightenment as a corollary to the phenomenon of near-death.

Plus this surprise: how closely human transformation mimics lightning. Example:

> *Lightning is an explosion in our external environment that, by releasing built-up pressure through a sudden visible charge, equalizes energy differences while stimulating physical plant growth. A near-death episode is an implosion within our internal environment that, by releasing built-up pressure through a sudden burst of light, equalizes energy differences while stimulating the expansion of consciousness for human growth.*

New findings throughout the field were revealed, like:

- "Deathflash" (where anything that dies releases a flash of light)
- "Lightflash" (where anything that is born also releases a flash of light)

Facts about the lure of psychism and how one can be betrayed by what seems true, but isn't.

Tackled as well were reincarnation, walk-ins (souls trading bodies), and the mammoth puzzle of consciousness versus brain. Also featured: the true story of a young woman who was committed to a psychiatric institution *just because she exhibited the typical aftereffects of an average near-death experience.*

The Ballantine Books version would save this research. What I had at first believed would be a best-seller would now at least survive. Words do not exist to describe how deeply this affected me.

Then my mother, after reading the book, cut to the chase with one swath of brutal honesty: "You made the near-death experience look like a disease."

Chapter 21

A Walk on the Dark Side

"Any fool can know. The point is to understand."
—Albert Einstein

As a result of this debacle, we came within a "hare's breath" of bankruptcy. Fortunately, paperback sales translated into a string of events, not only about the many aspects of the phenomenon itself, but how similar the aftereffects are to those following intense transformations of consciousness—no matter how caused. I breathed a sigh of relief. All was not lost. We could at least pay our bills and my work could continue.

The idea that Eastern and Western versions mimicked lightning in the natural world surprised everyone. And that bothered me. Don't researchers also check in with nature to see if there are clues that may be helpful in their work? I have always done this. That double-blind study I did at age five with a control group enabled me to discover why mudpies had different colors and consistencies. It depended in part on where they were found—but mostly on how much light exposure they received. Playing? No way. Serious stuff.

Nature's hues, sounds, pressures, and rhythms alter in response to more than just earthquakes and planets. Clues are always present as to why shifts occur and where aftereffects might lead. This means human relationships and lifestyles can be involved as some form of intervening consciousness—positive or negative—at every level, including the in-between.

One particular talk changed how I regarded people's stories and the consciousness behind them. It was held in a large hall, standing room only. After I presented my material I asked if anyone in the audience who had yet to speak of their episode might want to come up and share what had happened to them. One man and one woman volunteered. The man looked to be in his late twenties, the woman a little older, maybe in her early or mid-thirties. The man spoke first. He mesmerized the crowd with his story of angels and beautiful landscapes and music beyond that of Earth. There was hardly a dry eye in the crowd. Everyone was deeply touched. Then he shocked the crowd by saying it was the worst thing that had ever happened to him. He was sorry it had occurred. He felt cursed by it, and wished it would all go away. The woman jumped up and told of darkness, high winds, and an unearthly wail as she felt suction pulling her downward into a growing whirlpool. She had to fight hard to reach the shore and crawl to where she would be safe. The entire audience gasped at her next words: she declared this horrible encounter to be the best thing that had ever happened to her. She learned that no matter what life hits her with, she could turn it around, find a way out—win.

The despair of the man who cursed heaven's beauty—offset by the woman trapped in a swirling hell who learned how to save herself and find joy in life—presented everyone with a strong message: it's never the experience. It's how we feel about it, what we learn. Be careful of language and how people describe things (because it's almost always a reflection of culture, religious and/or societal pressures). We can be deceived by stories and how they're told. The important thing is to look for *the experiencer's view; how they interpret their story*.

Unexpected news. A publisher wanted to buy my self-published book, *The Magical Language of Runes*. They kept the same title, hired a great artist for the illustrations, and created a truly gorgeous cover. Soon the first printing was out the door and calls started coming in. But . . . drawings of rune casts did not match the interpretations. The artist either drew them upside down or backwards. None of us had checked before launch. Costs of correcting the book at that point exceeded any possible gains. The project was dumped.

Thanks to these two book disasters, my name, now a known commodity, impressed an "idea-man." He was convinced that a nationally syndicated phone line of great psychics, me included, could serve anyone's need for advice—any kind of advice. Just dial the magic phone number appearing on the television ad. He featured me in his first two shows. I think he named this venture "Psychic Counselors Network," but I can't validate that. I worked the line for more than a year, then resigned. The money I made paid for research costs. Three months later he went bankrupt, and the line resurfaced as "Dianne Warwick's Psychic Friends Network." My grandson knew all the times he could see Grandma on television, sitting on a stage tossing rocks. According to his babysitter, he watched every single ad every single day and knew in advance everything I would say or do . . . for months on end. In his mind, I was a superstar. I've tried to find copies of those early TV ads, but haven't been successful. Probably just as well, considering the calls I got (like people wanting to commit suicide, rich folks who were after cheap advice, fetishists who preferred sex with animals over people, the drunk and the lonely, and children play-acting like adults).

I have no regrets about this venture. But I do regret what came next. Senseless rumors about my sanity and the manner in which I conducted my research (as well as the findings I made) spread to the point that I lost it. I mean I got really angry, which is unusual for me. I wrote a letter to the one who had forever banned me from visiting near-death groups, then sent copies of that same letter to everyone else who appeared as parrots of the same threat. A few weeks later there was a knock on our door. When I opened it, a lawyer from Connecticut stood there, demanding that I show him a copy of that infamous letter. Fortunately I saved one, invited him in, gave it to him to read, then exited the room. Soon, my husband and I heard the man laughing. His conclusion: "You were just pissed. There is nothing in this letter to prove or even indicate mental illness." With that, he got up and walked out the door. I breathed a sigh of relief.

Before I jumped back into full-time research, I re-examined everything. I was doing my work because of that Voice. No college, medical, or scientific assignment here. No knowledge of how researchers like myself were expected to behave. The idea of writing "abstracts" and "papers" about my findings and then submitting them for approval from professional committees who would then decide whether or not my work would be published in a peer-reviewed journal . . . all of this wasn't just foreign to me, it was pure Greek. Yet I knew deep within that until I learned *that Greek,* I could never expect to achieve recognition or respectability in my field of work. Translation: helping people, sometimes, is not enough.

My next step had to be school, getting a degree. I had taken classes back in Boise to re-learn how to think and speak again. Anyone who goes through a near-death experience, especially an intense one, returns different—often unable to understand standard speech and language phrasing. Words just aren't there. You've been "elsewhere" and the language necessary to share that doesn't exist. 'Tis a puzzle.

Initially I attended classes at the Science of Mind Church in Boise (today these churches are called Centers of Spiritual Living). I learned how to do what they called "Spiritual Mind Treatments"—which is just another term for affirmative prayer. The catch here is to learn how measured and proven techniques can retrain the very depths of one's being when tackling a given goal. Drills included writing everything out, turning in your paper to be checked by your teacher (who invariably used red ink to emphasize better ways to phrase what you wrote), learning the difference between just dreaming or playing with language in a way that gets to the heart of an issue, and pin-pointing where you're kidding yourself versus when you're clearly centered within the spiritual truth at the core of your being.

A specific assignment changed everything. Goal: to create a spiritual mind treatment that would enable me to manifest something I truly needed. But there was a catch. This treatment could in no way interfere with the rights of others to also manifest good for themselves. In my case: a pair of shoes. My need for a new pair had become critical—oxford style, lace up, beige, $15.00. Not a penny higher. I handed in my paper. That week I had several errands to run for the bank department where I worked, and those errands took me right past the most expensive shoe store in town. I'd never been in the place. As I walked by, two hands grabbed me by the shoulders and pushed me inside. But no one was there. Yet the pressure from those invisible "hands" was totally real, very physical. Inside, at the top of a display in front me, was the exact pair of shoes that I wanted. I tried them on. Perfect fit. When I put them back and began to head out the door, a clerk yelled: "They're on sale today, $15.00." As I paid for them, I asked that the shoes be put in a brown box wrapped in brown paper. I took that package to the next class, put it in the middle of the large table, and announced for all to hear: "Prayer treatments work. Here's proof."

Such power! To learn how much we have . . . what a gift.

That experience gave me the courage and confidence to listen to Dr. John Rossner, Ph.D. (an Anglican priest and Professor at the Department of Religion at Concordia University in Montreal, Quebec), and his wife Dr. Marilyn Rossner, (special educator, behavior and yoga therapist, medium, psychic, and clairvoyant). The two of them described the degreed programs available through their school—The International Institute of Integral Human Sciences in Montreal. They could give credits for what I had already accomplished back in Idaho, which made the price they offered for a doctorate in Letters of the Humanities (L.H.D.) seem like a gift from heaven—even though it was still more than we could afford. I called Terry. We discussed the pros and cons since I would also need to establish Canadian residency each year until I could complete my goal (as well as pay for food, lodging, and education costs). Our vote: yes. Thus began my first taste of collegiate learning coupled with multiple opportunities to teach.

I hunkered down big time. My specialty was "Spiritual and Psychic Studies." My dissertation focused not only on my near-death research but more specifically on a particular phenomenon I named "future memory". . . exactly what had happened to me on that fateful Monday morning at the bank where, without warning, I had pre-lived the next six months of my life in only ten minutes. Everything I pre-lived came to pass except for a few timing flips that occurred when several people changed their minds at the last possible moment. But those people ended up reversing their decisions within an hour, which automatically moved them back to their original commitment.

Forget clairvoyance (the ability to see without the use of eyes); or clairaudience (the ability to hear without the presence of sound); or clairsentience (the ability to perceive emotional energy that's imperceptible to the five standard senses); or precognition (seeing or becoming aware of events in the future); or any of the other psychic "clairs" one might think of.

No to any and all of them.

Future memory is distinctly different. Here's what I found: One can feel a physical sensation at the onset (like a lift or sweep of energy, perhaps a ringing sound). Present time/space relationships freeze in place (this stoppage can be accompanied by sparkles in the air. Everything becomes brighter than before and sense faculties heighten). Expansion (as you expand, so does space). A future memory episode then temporarily overlays the present (a given scenario manifests in specific detail and is sensorily experienced as if it was a real event). Present time/space relationships resume normal activity (sparkles disappear, rightful proportions return, regular living restarts). Aftereffects: sensations of being startled, "chilled," or puzzled. The event remains in mind as long as awareness is vivid, but, eventually, it's either forgotten or set aside until the pre-lived event actually occurs.

People who experienced the phenomenon of future memory felt as if it was a type of preparation, an opportunity to rehearse in advance what would soon occur. When re-examining cases, I became convinced that future memory can be, and often is, essential for some, especially near-death experiencers such as myself. It can help someone move past the shell-shock that often occurs when "reality consciousness" makes little sense. It's as if we revert back to the same behaviors a child has in dealing with the past, present, and future—and for the same reason: to adjust and stabilize behavior.

Living in Montreal enabled me to "think outside any kind of box." Other anomalies needed a rethink: not breathing for periods of time (as a function of the vagus nerve—the physical component to the silver cord), electrical sensitivity, psychokinesis (the ability to move things using only the power of your mind), and why some people experience the fullness of near-death states (along with all the aftereffects too) *who were never near death.*

The year before graduation, I presented my dissertation before a large gathering at the Institute. Dr. Douglas Dean, a breakthrough researcher of extrasensory experiences, ran the overhead projector for my transparencies. It was a large room, with many people present. My fear of being there, doing what I was about to do, quickly morphed into the joy of showing everyone how important the future memory phenomenon is. I became so excited that my energy melted the insides of the projector (how electrical sensitivity often works). That meant someone had to run out and buy new parts, as well as a new bulb. The delay cost me 45 minutes of a one-hour talk. I did my best to "entertain the troops" while we all waited, showing them the different ways some aftereffects can change people. Finally, the overhead was fixed.

I rushed the transparencies. I wanted so much to show what future memory is and why understanding it is so important to the why's and how's of consciousness transformations . . . that I didn't notice nearly two-thirds of the crowd had walked out. In my final five minutes, I revealed the "big wow" to the loyal few. At that exact moment, a seven-foot-tall kangaroo marched into the room. I kid you not . . . *a seven-foot tall kangaroo!!!* I came to find out later that the hotel was having a special promotion for trips to Australia and they had hired someone to dress up as a kangaroo and visit every room where people were gathered. All I could say to that kangaroo at the time was . . . "Please, not now." With a mighty swish of his huge tail, the giant left.

As I stepped from the stage, a man approached me and cautioned: "You know you will be hated, don't you?" This caught me by surprise, so I asked what he meant. His answer: "You're ahead of everyone else. The world always punishes people like you. They'll hang you." When I walked out to mill around with the crowd and get people's opinions, it was like I was invisible. No one saw me. No one spoke to me. No one even acknowledged my presence. I heard nothing but derision throughout the crowd: people calling me mentally ill, crazy, someone to stay away from, a fraud. That guy, he was right. A cloud of darkness descended like nothing else I had ever experienced.

I had thought baseless accusations would now be over and the value of my work would finally be on the upswing. Wrong again. I received my doctorate on May 19, 1992, the very day Montreal celebrated its 350th anniversary as a city. Because of trouble brewing between Quebec and the Canadian government, my graduation affair had to be low-key—no frills, no cap, and no gown. When it was over, I marched out into the street and joined the crowd carrying Montreal's flag, shouting "Viva La France." We marched to the waterfront, transfixed by a massive fireworks display that emblazoned the dark sky.

The transparency challenge I had while delivering my dissertation presaged what greeted me when I flew home. Horror of horrors, all of the boxes of my personal transparencies (colored slides of a lifetime with my former husband and our children, the family we had then, trips we took, birthdays, happy moments, rodeos and parades, ghost town adventures, daily miracles) were now in box after box of goo. How did this happen? What could I have done to better protect those pictures? Those miracles?

How can anyone lose forevers? Can't they be preserved? Memories flooded of my son having to sell his blood for enough money to eat. A daughter with continuous surgeries who was always suffering through more and more pain. Another daughter making a flurry of mistakes with money, men, and her children. Had I stayed in Boise, would that have made any difference with them, or would the challenges they faced have somehow happened anyway?

The commitment I made to The Voice Like None Other grew thin. Obstacles just never stopped stacking up, and they were getting tougher to handle.

I gripped and squeezed the diploma I earned, drew a breath, and kept on walking forward . . . one foot in front of the other.

Chapter 22

Time to Fry

"The sun, with all those planets revolving around it and depending on it, can still ripen a bunch of grapes as if it had nothing else in the universe to do."
—Galileo Galilei

This I know: all life begins in darkness. Everything that exists came from darkness. A good reminder.

As if on schedule, another opportunity opened up. IANDS wanted me to be on their Board. With new leadership, new goals, and a dynamic new energy, what they offered rang true. Still, my yes had a catch: I would have to sign legal documents prepared by their lawyer stating that I would never give readings, pass out my brochures, or in any way mention "esoteric or psychic skills" while engaged in IANDS business. Members apologized for this, but I understood. Signed. I'm the only one in the history of the organization who ever had to do this.

Being on the Board turned out to be the perfect next step. I met new people, took trips to attend meetings, and had plenty of heated arguments. There were sacrifices galore, including having to pay the bills of IANDS out of our own pockets if contributions and conference fees did not cover costs. And that happened several times! Later I moved up to Second Vice-President. This opportunity both fulfilled my personal vow to always be there for IANDS in whatever way possible, while insuring that I learned more about what still puzzled me: the so-called "scientific model," a method of research that, to me, missed the boat. Using that model relied heavily on questions written down and asked in advance. My training strictly forbade any such behavior. To me, asking questions in advance of the experiencer describing things (including what they saw or went through), was wrong. A good cop asks if an individual saw or heard anything and only says something after the individual's information has been given. Always the experiencer first. You're guilty of leading results otherwise.

Tales of anomalies, especially the electrical kind, quickly took center stage in my work after an episode I had while recording two audio cassette tapes. A friend hooked me up with a media company that had dollar signs in mind. They planned to professionally create, sell, and nationally distribute any tapes I recorded. They'd pay all expenses and I'd get 50% of proceeds. A local studio with a surprisingly expensive setup (like the kind you'd find in New York City), offered to do the job. They were located in, of all places, a building on a little side street in Charlottesville that few even knew existed. My job was to write and voice the scripts for two of my books: *Coming Back To Life* and *As You Die: Know That You Live Forever.* The latter evolved from a phone conversation I once had with a young man dying of AIDS in New York City. He told me he'd attended all the conferences by all the greats who help people make peace with death, but none of them could tell him what death actually felt like. Could I? For an hour I described everything I had learned from countless near-death experiencers, including myself. A year later, word came that my session with the young man gave him the courage to die in peace, without pain, without fear. (By the way, the *As You Die* material is still available as a video. I receive no commissions from sales. All proceeds aid an outreach group. Nothing has become of the *Coming Back To Life* tape. It still sits on a corner of my desk like a child nobody wants.)

The day I voiced those tapes—pumped up—no ego allowed, I kept saying to myself: *only by God's Grace and in accordance with God's Holy Will.* To ensure this would happen, I did what I called "letting God out" (while in prayer I felt my energy rise to such a level that it seemed as if I would surely explode with joy). I signaled the studio engineer once I was ready. No sooner had I begun the actual recording when . . . a loud "pop" occurred. Electricity surged. Fuses blew. Everything fried. The engineer was beside himself, screaming "What happened?" He ran out the door and into the street to see if anyone else had experienced the same power surge. Businesses and residents within a three-block area were hit, including a print shop across the street that had just purchased brand new equipment, but hadn't insured it yet. *Exactly five minutes before the pop, the owner of the print shop heard a voice in his right ear say "Unplug all your equipment."* That voice saved his equipment and his pocketbook. He called this a "come to Jesus" moment.

Losses were high throughout the area—things like burned-out coffee makers, ruined computers, and so on. The incident garnered a small article in the newspaper because the electrical company traced the power surge to the building where I was—*and it occurred at the same moment when the recording began.* No accusations were made. Still, I was overcome with guilt. I discussed this with a fellow researcher, asking him if I should go to the electrical company and tell them what happened. He asked me: "Are you ready to pay for everyone's losses?" "No." He then advised: "Forget about it. No one will believe what happened anyway." Years later I took the studio copy of those recordings and had them checked by a sound specialist. Result: marked "drop outs" throughout. Translation: *My voice often didn't register as being present—even though I could be heard.* Figure that one out. Or figure out what happened in an attempt of mine to obtain some papers for my husband from a maker of robotic equipment. The only door I could find to enter the building had two banks of light beams that you had to pass through. Once in, I walked by a number of offices. Each had large signs saying "Wear Your Badge At All Times." A female engineer saw me, but before I could say anything, she started yelling: "What are you doing here? How did you get in? Where's your badge? Who are you?" I calmed her down enough to explain my mission. The two of us walked all over that plant. I never found the papers I needed though. Not once did I set off an alarm anywhere in the place. Finally, the engineer just stared at me. "No one can be in this plant without a badge. Otherwise loud alarms go off. You haven't set off a single alarm." Then she added: "Maybe it's because you're a mother and mothers can do anything." Funny, yes. Serious still.

Anomalous behaviors and strange phenomena occur so often with so many experiencers, that I wrote *Beyond the Light: The Mysteries and Revelations of Near-Death Experiences* . . . as a way to explore more of the story and from a much larger research base.

I held nothing back this time. I made it plain that the idea of a single overall pattern to near-death experiences doesn't match what actually exists. I found four major types:

> *Initial Experience*: one to three elements, like a loving nothingness, the living dark, a friendly voice, a brief out-of-body experience.

Unpleasant or Hellish Experience: an encounter with states like a threatening void, stark limbo, hellish purgatory, scenes of a startling indifference.

Pleasant or Heavenly Experience: features reassurance and self-validation, loving family reunions with the dead, affirmative and inspiring dialogue, and how every effort has a purpose in the overall scheme of things.

Transcendent Experience: more universal, has expansive revelations, alternate realities, seldom personal in content, a "mind stretching" challenge to whatever one deems as truth.

I had many case studies . . . like what happened to George Rodonaia, a vocal Soviet dissident who, with his family, tried to flee Russia. They managed to escape, but the KGB (Russian police) knocked him down with a cab and then ran over his body numerous times—a political assassination. His body, stored in a freezer vault for three days, miraculously began breathing during autopsy—shocking doctors (one his own uncle). Every story he told about what he did during those three days, what he saw and heard, held up. I spent some time interviewing his wife Nona. She validated everything. Then there's Mellen-Thomas Benedict who died of inoperable brain cancer. He recognized a near-death experience as it began to form and said: "Stop a minute. This is my death and I want to think about this." He is the only experiencer I've ever heard of or met that changed his near-death scenario *as it occurred*, leading him to an idea-rich matrix of new inventions and the marketing plans for each, including the use of specific light arrangements to heal problems in the human body. I laid on one of his light beds and can attest to its effectiveness. Unfortunately, he ran afowl of various laws in the State of California and lost everything—a common problem experiencers can have when trying to materialize what they were shown during their episodes.

I tackled the *Near-Death-Like Scenario*, where someone who's not in crisis can have a complete near-death experience as well as the same aftereffects. Some name this a "fear death," but what I discovered was far deeper and more puzzling than that. Case in point: a young man in Canada got up from his apartment sofa, walked across the room to look out his window, turned, and, while walking back, *he had a full-blown near-death experience that resulted in the same pattern of aftereffects.* During the experience he was shown which Biblical translations were wrong and which ones were correct, so he spent the following years of his life "knocking on the doors" of numerous Ministerial Colleges and telling them the difference between correct and incorrect Bible teachings. My final conversation with him occurred by phone as he lay dying in a Canadian hospital. I assured him of the importance of his path. He died minutes later. I'm told he died with a smile on his face.

By then, just about everyone knew about the psychological changes that occurred after an NDE (loss of the fear of death; becoming more compassionate, caring, loving, psychic, and intuitive; having a desire to change careers to that of a teacher, healer, or minister). But the physiological changes often seemed a stretch too far (changes in brain structure and function, challenges to nervous and digestive systems, increased skin sensitivity, plus a full range of electrical sensitivities).

The Body Electric: Electromagnetism and the Foundations of Life helped me understand the importance of electrical changes in the human body. This incredible work by Robert O. Becker, M.D. directly challenges the medical community's almost universally accepted chemical-based model of life, saying instead that the electrical model is, and always has been, primary. We see this challenge appear in near-death cases across continents.

To further explore the scope of this, I sent out a questionnaire to forty-one experiencers entitled "A Survey of Electrical Sensitivity Reported_by Near-Death Survivors." The results surprised everyone, including me: 85% claimed to have had an experience where at least half of their scenario was filled with bright, all-consuming etheric light; 52% said they merged into and joined with that light or being of light; and of these totals, 80% became unusually sensitive to physical light afterwards. *It was never about what kind of near-death experience the person had, or how long/ how complex it was. The single indicator of electrical sensitivity afterwards was the* intensity *of exposure to etheric light during the episode.* This finding, by the way, has held up throughout the decades of my work with thousands of experiencers.

I finally took the chance in this book to explore what it feels like to die, what death is, what existence is, the realness of God, the big picture, priorities and values—even "the small stuff."

Sensing a large market, my new publisher, Carol Publishing Group, brought out the first edition as a hardcover (normally a good sign), but the cover wound up looking like a black slab (solid black with a white title in the middle of it). No other writing. No other color. When I asked my publisher why they did this, the answer was: "We wanted to depict death."

Their publicity agent sent me to speak at a nighttime radio show in New York City that specialized in hellish stories. Reason? I had mentioned that my life review during my second experience overwhelmed me. That notion, to them, labeled me as a hellish experiencer . . . a good promotional gimmick. No explanation I gave made the slightest difference. I swallowed hard. Same story. The book bombed. A year later, the paperback version saved my research.

Heard that story before? Hold on. There's more.

My rune book and *The Book of Runes* by Ralph Blum made it to the desk of an editor at St. Martin's Press around the same time. The House picked up Blum's book instead of mine because rune casting seemed too abstract (even though they loved the idea). I renamed the book *Goddess Runes* and sent it over to Avon Books. They picked it up and promised to include a kit (rune set and bag) as a package deal. The book came out sans kit and hardly sold. My editor at Avon suddenly quit. Rumor had it there would soon be a buyout of the company, with the new publisher cancelling extra expenses involved with any book. The copyright was returned to me. No charge.

And more.

Other researchers and those involved in studying the near-death phenomenon began to think of me as careless. Who was I to counter or expand the work of physicians and psychiatrists and scientists? *Beyond the Light* didn't even have an appendix. The truth is that I paid for one, but Carol Publishing Group dropped the ball and never printed it. No apology given.

The "rumor mill" had a field day. Some openly declared me a disgrace to the field.

Four books. Four flops.

My work survived . . . sort of . . . but my soul hurt.

Chapter 23

God's Left Side

"In nature we never see anything isolated, but everything in connection with something else which is before it, beside it, under it, and over it."
—Johann Wolfgang von Goethe

The runes somehow took care of themselves. Maybe the world wasn't ready yet for "abstracts." My near-death research? My goal of being dedicated to examining and digging deep slapped me in the face. I'd finally had enough. I quit. That's it, quit. With files in hand, photos, caseloads, everything, I headed for the door and the garbage dump. Just as I was about to leave, the phone rang. I put everything down and answered.

It was the head of IANDS, Dr. Elizabeth "Pat" Fenske. She asked me how I was doing. Did I ever unload. One solid hour. Named names. Revealed every single thing. Left nothing out. No interruption. She just listened. At the end of that hour she offered: "I had no idea any of this was happening. Don't quit. Let me talk to some people." Pat Fenske is the *only* reason I kept going. Whatever she did, whatever she changed, I never saw any results. Yet somehow I felt better. Encouraged.

The next day I returned early from shopping and noticed that the rubber mat in front of my apartment door was gone. Arcing across the door itself in sparkling letters appeared a message: "It is now time for you to move." Instantly, in my mind's eye, I saw the boys who took the mat. I walked over to the main office, reported what had happened, described the boys, and asked for my mat back. They recognized the boys from my description (they'd had problems with them before). The mat was returned the next day.

Terry worried about the message. We both wanted to move, but with no money, how? I decided to try anyway. Whenever I had seen sparkling messages like that before—appearing out of nowhere—good things always resulted. Especially in stores. Since I'm not a shopper, the phenomenon cuts time while insuring value. My sister would soon witness this. She had swung by on a trip East and agreed to go house hunting with me and a real estate agent. We saw a lot of houses, most with prices too high for any down payment I could afford. Soon enough though—while driving down a cul-de-sac to view a particular home—another one caught my eye. It was painfully plain, without much of a front yard or driveway—still, it somehow called to me. We stopped. As soon as I touched the doorknob of that house, I saw sparkling writing materialize across the door: "This is it." The minute I walked in, waves of love washed over me. An elderly couple lived there. They had spent many years raising miniature dogs in their daylight basement, but, as it turns out, age and health problems were forcing them to leave. They had a great deal of love for the house, so their concern, first and foremost, was who might buy it. Without hesitation, I made an offer—a little less than what they were asking. My sister thought I was crazy. Actually, so did the realtor. While leaving, we passed a young couple headed for the front door. I knew they would beat our price. With Terry out of town, I signed the earnest money agreement alone.

The elderly couple accepted our offer. They acknowledged that the younger couple that came in after me offered more, but the elderly couple felt so much love from me that they knew my husband and I were the right ones to live in the house. When my sister and I sat down with the broker and went over how this could happen, my sister shook her head. Not possible. Papers were drawn up anyway. Terry got home in time to sign; the loan was submitted. In jig time, word came back. The loan went through. We had a home.

My sister couldn't figure out how the loan went through so quickly. A month later, our broker explained: *That Monday morning the woman who approved loans faced a large pile on her desk. Ours was on top. Her doors were open so everyone in that section heard her yell: "PMH Atwater. She's famous. Approved."* I came to find out that she had just read *Coming Back to Life* and loved the book. She never read our file. Not one word. Our home doesn't look today as it did then. We had to refinance twice to remodel. A miracle still.

After the move and a massive cleaning (my office is located where they once raised their miniature dogs), I started to scream—for fifteen minutes non-stop. I would have screamed more if I'd had a voice left. The rape that led to my deaths—I never screamed at the time, even though I wanted to. Twenty years had passed. Suddenly it all came back—that moment in time—and now at last I could grieve. I spent the rest of that day allowing pain and emotional grief to ease away.

A steep drop-off at the end of our driveway led to another lawn below. In the back of that lawn lay a fair-sized forest with vines hanging down like a green curtain. The vines were covered in wild berries and flowers like the ones I used to see on a small cliff overlooking a river snaking past hay fields. In an effort to create an "Idaho forest," I asked the life there if it would cooperate.

I heard multiple choruses of "yes" as I pulled out bushes, vines, and weeds—all by hand—blessing each as I did. One day a man who sprayed throughout the subdivision asked what happened to all that wild growth. "I removed it," I replied. "Did you spray first?" "Nope, did it all bare handed." He had a shocked look on his face and said: "Lady, that's poison oak." Not an itch ever, even when I brushed my cheeks with the plant leaves. The forest and I were friends. Simple as that.

Research resumed thanks to Fenske. Since 1978 I'd been on a track, even considering some "stopovers" that nearly derailed me. The way I wrote my books altered after the first two though. That alteration continues today. Here's how it goes: Each book-to-be arrives first in a cloud-like dance of sparkles, about face level, in the air over the left extension of my desk. When those sparkles fall flat, they spell out the name of the next book I'm going to do. After that occurs, I go into prayer and ask if this new project is best for my highest good and the highest good of all concerned. If I get a no, I forget about it and move on to the next project. If I get a yes, I grab a large pad of paper and begin the process of planning the book: chapters, material, cases, style: how I will use what I have. Always . . . prayer first, decisions second.

Don't think for one moment that this manner of doing my work fits in with the schedule of others or in any way protects me from a clash of minds. I have been threatened several times by near-death-experiencers who accused me of profiting from their story or trying to steal from them (I always get permission first in writing, then again after the final copy). Nothing I do offers a slick way to guarantee ratings, sales, interviews, or offers. The only thing this does is keep me in line with The God of My Being—for better or worse.

Often leaders in the field, not liking or approving of what I did, unknowingly criticized me in front of the very people who knew better. Soon after, my phone would ring or I'd get a letter. Charges of my work being "worthless" or "phony" never meshed with facts. The 1995 conference in Hartford put me face-to-face with Kenneth Ring—a surprising critic. We quickly found a room where we could be alone and hash everything out. Yes, he apologized, but I couldn't fully accept his apology until I understood why so much negativity was constantly directed at me. I discovered: scientists and doctors avoided and criticized my work because I wasn't one of them. I didn't use scientific protocols like all good researchers do. How could they trust me, even when I was right? They use formulas, math, careful screening, peer review. Me? I'd never heard of that stuff. I just knew how to "read" people, listen deeply, study every single little thing, and test answers, especially with significant others.

Ken and I healed our relationship and he became like a brother soul. At one of our many visits, he shared stories of his childhood and some photos—one in particular of him at around age nine. I knew that photo, that boy. Suddenly I began thinking about my return to Twin Falls a few years earlier. I was sitting on the upper balcony of the Methodist Church I'd attended when I was a child, when, in my mind's eye, I witnessed once again that fateful day I'd had when I was seventeen. While seated in the choir loft, invisible "hands" suddenly lifted me from my chair, walked me across the aisle, down the stairs, and to the spot just in front of the main altar where our minister stood asking: "If anyone wants to join the church and devote the rest of their life to God, step forward now." Without intent, yet feeling a certain rightness, I said yes.

That instant a bright shaft of light broke through the domed skylight and lit up where I was standing. I left my body and floated up the shaft to a light-filled world where a ring of children were dancing. There were ten of them—boy/girl couples, all about age nine; each couple dancing with exuberant joy about the task they would soon begin on Earth and the help they would give each other. While seated in the balcony, I remembered how I had cast aside the whole scene once I discovered that the sky outside was as stormy and dark as ever. Even if there had been sun, light can't travel in an oblique angle like that. I convinced myself that the whole thing must have been my imagination. Yet others saw the miraculous beam and said so. It took me twelve years to reassess what had happened then.

Ken's photo at nine years old matched the boy I saw in that beam of light. True enough, it was Ken who first learned of me and almost "burned up" telephone lines trying to reach me. He didn't want to leave during his first visit with me because he was so interested in the things I'd done. It was Ken who went out of his way to invite me to stay on in Storrs, sleep on his couch until I could read all of the IANDS archives, compare theirs with mine, and create a questionnaire for both groups to see how the results matched or didn't. It was always Ken at my side trying to steer me in the right direction. Still, I think the scientific pressure everyone faced to impress and prove the reality of the near-death experience made a difference. He did not have the same nine-year-old memory I did, yet the scenario I shared felt right to him. It explained our relationship. Certainly, there's no way any of this could ever be proven, or perhaps even believed. But for us, it was enough.

My phone once again kept ringing, this time to be a guest on one radio show after another. There were so many, I lost track. Around the same time, a plague of condemnation spread loud and strong from various Fundamentalist Christian and Catholic churches—aimed at everyone in the field, not just me. I never saw this coming until it hit. These people, as a group, claimed near-death experiences denied the presence and power of Jesus and all the holy fathers of Christianity—even God and the Bible. Supposedly, both experiencers and researchers were possessed by the devil. Ministers preaching from the pulpit who based the strength of their sermons on "the good news" revealed from the accounts of those who literally "rose from the dead". . . were fired! None of us could believe the sudden hysteria.

As an overall statement gleaned from experiencers, I could note: *after discovering death isn't, came the discovery that God is.* I could also say that most of them fall head over heels in love with God. Experiencers claim to have been bathed in God's Presence, immersed in God, filled to overflowing with God, returning to life convinced that God was real. They *know* God! Belief was no longer needed. This discovery brings an exhilarating freedom for each to walk and talk with God without reservation or restriction. Reference terms often change from traditional Father, He, Him or Mother, She, Her, to the more open, unlimited and unfathomable realization of the immensity of That Which Cannot Be Denied.

In tracing where comments came from, I discovered that about two-thirds of the experiencers I had interviewed either left the church they were attending, were not churchgoers to begin with, or started up a new church more in line with what they had discovered during their episode. The one-third who stayed became more involved, energized, and desirous of making changes. A few went on to become evangelists.

At a conference in San Antonio, Texas, a mother and son drove many miles to see me. Recovering from brain surgery, the youngster surprised everyone with how quickly he healed, talking almost non-stop about God and what he had experienced on the Other Side. Every week though, the mother and son had been visited by church members condemning them to hell for what they believed was trash-talk about God. To them, he was possessed by the devil. Church elders did this. The son handled the visits better than the mom. He just considered the church members ill-informed.

The Catholic churches that came to my attention mailed out letters to their parishioners telling them outright that children who had near-death experiences were possessed by the devil. (Pardon me while I scream.) I contacted each church where I traced such newsletters and did what I could to acquaint them with research that validated the reality of such experiences. I reminded them that most of the people who later became Saints in the Catholic Church had near-death experiences when they were children. I never heard back from a single one.

Muslim cases, and yes I had some, were the strangest of all. Mothers and fathers of child experiencers did everything they could to kill their child because they didn't want their family name besmirched by such a disgrace—an experience they felt insulted Allah. The viciousness of the mothers challenged me like nothing ever had before. Most adult experiencers either fled their country of origin or "kept things secret." It was the children who concerned me the most. I spent some time working with one who managed to hide in Germany.

The clash of Fundamentalist Christian ire continues today, though it's not as mean-spirited as before. Perhaps that's because several very famous cases made them reconsider their positions about NDEs. The story of Colton Burpo's episode, who almost died during emergency surgery when not quite four, challenged not only his parents but the entire congregation of Rev. Todd Burpo's church.

Audiences packed in to see the movie version of the book, *Heaven is For Real.* The same thing happened to Annabel Beam who barely survived being trapped inside a hollowed-out tree. She spoke of seeing Jesus in her ordeal and returning to life miraculously healed of a chronic intestinal condition. The book and movie about her is called *Miracles from Heaven.* Another one, *The Boy Who Came Back from Heaven* (about six-year-old Alex Malarkey who was paralyzed and in a coma for two months following a horrific car accident), made the book scene big time—but not as a movie. There were continual arguments, religious backlashes, claims and counterclaims, with demands later on that the book's publication cease. His parents divorced. Alex stayed with his mother. Once he reached the age of consent, Alex denied his story during a nationwide interview, saying he lied and made the whole thing up for the attention he would receive. Last I heard, there was an ongoing lawsuit in the Malarkey family as to where all that money from the book sales went. Apparently nothing went to Alex.

How did this religious rebellion affect me? Long before the two movies, and for years on end, attacks against me and others in the field happened almost constantly. What kind of attacks? Letter campaigns, phone calls, magazine articles, public interviews, physicians and scientists—all claiming near-death experiences could be explained away as hallucinations or wish-fulfillment. The most difficult to handle though were the twisted, hateful prayers (almost like Black Magic), sent by so-called devoted Christians . . . for my ill-health, injury, accidents, heart trouble, mental illness, and more. Some did this openly, others in secret. This plague of so-called "believers" got so bad that I had to hire a healer to work with me on a monthly basis to help clean out all the dark energy directed towards me. It cost a mint, but was worth every penny. Surprisingly, the Catholic Church eventually did a 180: through research of their own, and by validating the work of others, they came to regard the near-death phenomenon as credible and worthy.

My work continued, but I'm not sure I did. I had surgery for a "fatty tumor" on one side of my upper leg. There was no reason for it to be there, and it was larger than the doctors suspected. The procedure went well, but the surgeons made no effort to "sew me back together" properly in order to prevent scarring. I was left with a sizable "dip" midway in my leg. When I complained, they just told me to hire a plastic surgeon. That was that. I never wore a swimsuit or shorts again.

Chapter 24

Three in One

"Sometimes good things fall apart so better things can fall together."
—Marilyn Monroe

I walked into a wall. For no particular reason that I can remember. I hurt my nose and almost broke my glasses. I walked into it because I couldn't see it. All that surrounded me—walls, furniture, rooms—registered in my brain as nothing. Not there. The me of me existed. I took up space but sans identity. Chores, cooking and cleaning, walking in and out of rooms, the house, my husband, our two cars—nothing had identity. All was there, yet nothing was there. I remained in this state throughout the winter. I turned down drugs and doctors. Eventually one word made sense . . . depression. Leave me be, I begged. I need this. I need to be nothing. The lower I sank, the more I alarmed others. Colors were gone. Feelings were gone. I felt it would be okay to stay like this for the winter. So I did.

Looking back, several things could have precipitated this. I had made a choice early-on to let go of any trappings of what most people call a normal life. Normal to me now meant flowing in and out of dimensions, spaces, worlds, life forms. I loved this, the new ways I had of living and the ease in which I could flow amidst vibratory "strings." And above all else, I had the honor and privilege of seeing past creation's myth. What enabled me to be so comfortable was exactly what took me away from what I had promised The Voice Like None Other I would do: I could not remain "the new me" and still do that kind of work.

I went through a lot with "our" children, too. All three fully accepted Terry as special and wonderful, the girls most of all. There were divorces, painful ups and downs with all of them. Both girls adopted Terry as their dad; our remaining grandchildren loved him dearly and still do. That first grandchild who spent a month of his new life with us went through nightmares with his own dad (and so did his younger sister). Their dad had a temper and was physically abusive. We intervened whenever we could, taking both kids on weekend visits and doing loving and fun things with them. But taking them home after each foray turned out to be an encounter with their "warden." If we were even a few minutes late, he'd bar us from seeing them again for months. Our daughter fled, mistakenly thinking she would not gain custody in a divorce. This led to the boy getting beaten so often that we urged him to complain at school. Maybe his teachers could help. They did. What seemed like the perfect solution led to a court case with the mother of my daughter's husband hiring a specialty lawyer who made everything sound like my daughter caused all the problems. Alcoholism eventually killed her husband though. His daughter found his body in a pool of blood. Passing years enabled a better life to form.

You could also say that one book after another, one opportunity after another, all crashing, would be enough to drive anyone nuts. Both of my first major books sold well and garnered a lot of attention—which pretty much passed me by. I never saw a penny from either. My other projects answered a need within me to share—to pass along what had made a positive difference for me, and I never understood why anyone would attack these extras.

I emerged from my gray, nothing world in the Spring. No words said. No reason given. No understandings. The past simply ended, so I went straight to work. What mattered, all that mattered, lay ahead. Quite suddenly, and without effort on my part, I had all the power and energy I needed to forge forward. Literally. My energy levels quadrupled—maybe more. I became superwoman. My work schedule zoomed to around 12 hours a day, at least six days a week, every week, every year. I traveled more, did more, wrote more. In a way, so did Terry. One day I purchased the full set of *A Course in Miracles* books for him (because I saw his name in sparkly writing on the cover). He sorta thanked me. He was uninterested at the time though. He tossed them into a closet and thought no more about them until we attended a very large conference where one of the speakers taught the Course. He attended, and instantly knew this would be his life path. He has since become a teacher himself, a man transformed by an ancient wisdom made new.

One day a child-experiencer I came to call Carroll Gray (not her real name) suggested I get a designer to create a website for me. She had just the right person in mind to do the job, so I took her advice and began setting one up. Understanding the world of computers and gigabits and this thing called the worldwide web, combined with my electrical sensitivity, created some very odd and unusual challenges for me.

Problem number one: how can you be a part of this new world if you have electrical sensitivity? I learned that getting acquainted comes first. Turn the computer on, go into a meditative state, then enter the computer with your mind. Yes, computers have a soul. It's like an intelligent energy flow you can communicate with. Just like with your car. When my computer and I met, it really listened. I explained what I had in mind, what I needed it for. We conversed. It agreed to cooperate with me; I promised to treat it with respect.

Problem number two: how specifically can this be done without injury to me and in keeping with my promise to my computer? Amber. If you've never discovered the power of amber, listen up. It can transmutate energies/radiation so your working area feels okay and you don't have to periodically "clean" it out with sunlight. Amber perpetually self-cleans. You'll need hunks of it, even unpolished will do—or old necklaces—bits and pieces. I put some amber in a narrow, open necklace box and set it between my keyboard and desk monitor. The rest I spread around my work area. What seemed like arthritis in my fingers vanished.

Problem number three: is there more to do? Go with yes. For instance, have some carnelian nearby. It lifts and heals body energy. Always keep a glass of water handy. I place mine to the right about two or three feet away. Add some lemon or lime to the water if you feel okay about doing that. Such a mixture works like natural lithium in the way it balances your body and lifts your mind. I also have lepidolite hunks around (the lithium stone). All of this keeps me balanced and able to work long hours without difficulty. Plants are good too, especially those with long leafy vines like ferns. And sunshine is very important (hopefully via a window). Never use a laptop computer without an insulated pad underneath. Modems should sit on a pad too—cork.

Heaven help our population once 5G towers are spread out near our homes and schools. Anything over 10 megabits viewscreen strength can redden your skin and/or make it feel as if you're burning. All too often this happens to any sensitive person who is not careful about proper protection.

Carroll's suggested website designer turned out to be a genius, even though she's considered "legally blind" in one eye. Don't believe it. She could actually see pretty well and would invent what she needed to compensate. Steff is her name and she has become my right arm in all things e-mail, website, design, manuscripts, newsletters, checking the law, running down book pirates, and managing my Facebook page (a particular portal energy I cannot handle). She sends me posts. I answer them. She then sends them back. The perfect go-between. She shaped my website, blog, and newsletter. What pays her salary? My Social Security check.

Since I mentioned Carroll Gray, here's a little more about her. She had five near-death episodes in childhood and five more as an adult—all because her father tried again and again to kill her . . . almost succeeding until, when older, she hired a bodyguard for protection. Her father finally died. Her case is in two of my books, presaging other cases similar to hers. Before birth, she remembers observing, as if a bystander, her father (in a drunken rage) throwing her mother into the edge of a large wooden table. Hitting the table caused her mother's amniotic sac to rupture. She was rushed to the hospital where a "dead" baby girl was delivered via an emergency cesarean section. But to everyone's astonishment, the child began to breathe. Among the many medical facts about this case: at the age of two-and-a-half, in front of both parents and visiting relatives, Carroll Gray repeated back to her father *every word he had said when he'd thrown his pregnant wife into the table's edge. She also described the situation and furniture placement.* The doctor never reported the father's drunkenness to the police because his history of being her father's drinking buddy might be discovered.

Three bursts of sparkles over the left-side of my desk, accompanied by a massive influx of energy, led to the three books that

I wrote and had published in 1999. My husband called me "the monk in the monastery," a name that still sticks (even though my work schedule has shortened to around five to seven hours per day and five, sometimes six, days per week.)

My first, about child experiencers, was called *Children of the New Millennium: Children's Near-Death Experiences and the Evolution of Humankind*. A serious challenge occurred on publication. The title and published content did not match the manuscript I submitted to Three Rivers Press. What I submitted was the first major study of children's near-death experiences, along with their aftereffects. I had many cases backed up with facts and drawings, plus a large resource section in the back for parents, educators, and children. Guess what my publisher did? Without my permission or knowledge, they cut out *two-thirds of the book*, changed the title, and waved it around as a fun piece they could use to "welcome in the new century."

No one knew or cared about what my publisher had done or why. Thus, researchers everywhere (or so it seemed) ganged up to condemn me for doing such a poor job. Major papers were written about my sloppy research. Some were even published in a peer-reviewed journal. I became the laughing stock of the field (again). Professionals used this as proof that I didn't know what I was doing and never did. Attacks went on for years. Ugly. Did you ever try explaining anything to Ph.D.'s and M.D.'s? My publisher ignored the whole debacle. Not even a "sorry." I put some of these comments on my website so others could know the truth about the screw-up.

With *The Complete Idiot's Guide to Near-Death Experiences*, I shared authorship with David H. Morgan, a former literary agent of mine whom I had met in Portland, Oregon. If you know anything about the "Idiot's" books (there's a whole series of them on about every subject you can imagine), then you know it's like tech-writing. You follow a script that tells you exactly how many paragraphs, words, sentences, photos, and sidebars go into the book. It's strictly formatted and strictly controlled. By then, David had moved to Richmond, Virginia. We had no way to actually "work" together, so we improvised. I had most of the material, but David managed to handle several chapters by himself. There was a time-crunch throughout because of publisher scheduling mix-ups. Our reward for handling their mess? They allowed in material about "spiritual transformations." We cheered. So did the near-death community. Then, klunk! Hardly anyone bought the book. During my various travels around the country, I made it a point to stop in at bookstores and talk to managers. Why weren't people buying the book? Their answer: no one would buy it because of the title "Idiot." Customers considered that word an insult, unspiritual. Six months later the publisher gave me the copyright to the book so I could rewrite it any way I wanted—except I could not use any of their Idiot monikers. I took the deal. I asked David if I could just redesign it myself. He agreed. We parted company. It's now called *The Big Book of Near-Death Experiences* and it's much larger. I gave the copyright to IANDS, so they'd always have money coming in while they helped experiencers and educated the world about NDEs.

Future Memory was really a "non-book" that I had used as my college dissertation. More importantly, it was the second book I was told to write by The Voice Like None Other during my third near-death experience. But I couldn't do it. Tried. Couldn't. Seven years I persisted. I produced a different version every year and each one was peer-reviewed. Everyone liked the material, but, unfortunately, they didn't understand it. *Seven years, seven different versions of the book, still no solution*. I gave up and decided to throw the manuscript away. I was kidding myself to think I could do anything with the material. Maybe that kangaroo butting in on my dissertation in Montreal knew something I didn't.

On a Saturday morning bright with sun, I started to step out of the shower when, quite suddenly, matter contracted while space enlarged. Everything froze, me included. Air filled with sparkles, everywhere sparkles. A voice spoke: "Turn it into a labyrinth. I will show you how." Just as quickly, everything reverted back to normal dimensions. I called to Terry nearby. No, he did not see or hear anything. Hurriedly I toweled dry, rushed downstairs, and began the final version.

The next day my effort blew out the monitor screen, as cyclones from my third near-death experience formed, then grew larger and larger until bursting through the screen, spraying visible particles all over the place. I could hardly move. Energy extremes were everywhere. Once coherent, I grabbed the monitor, unplugged it, got in the car, and drove to a computer repair shop. The fella there laughed, saying there was no way could such a thing happened—then he examined the screen. That hourglass shape had burned through it and was plainly visible. Shaken by what he saw, he quickly tossed the monitor into the trash as if it were poison and gave me a new one.

After that, the book was done in two weeks. The trick to making it a labyrinth turned out to be simple: use a rhythmic stomp-beat-heart-beat like the Aborigines of Australia do when making their paintings—which are really maps. By stomp-beating curves and waves in a synchronized rhythm and pacing them within your very heart and soul, you can follow any path and locate anything—accurately. It's pure math, performed/arranged differently than what we're used to doing, but still math: map-math. Every sentence, every paragraph, every page of *Future Memory* is part of that labyrinth, and it's purpose is to raise the reader's consciousness to the next highest level possible at that time. The book is literally a brain-changer. You cannot skip-read. To get the labyrinth effect, you have to stay on the path and read it straight through as is. No cheating, no jumping around, or you'll wonder why I ever wrote such a dumb book. Hampton Roads Publishing bought it and they've kept it in print ever since.

Some people report nothing when reading the book. Others say they feel a decided lift, as if their consciousness craves more, does more, and understands life more. I've heard from some who say they read the book each year to get another lift. That seems strange to me, but maybe it isn't really so strange when you think about it. The book is truly meant to be a brain changer.

A woman called me from London, England. She thanked me for putting my talks and interviews on YouTube. She said each morning she watches what she can because it gives her the energy and courage to get through the day.

What a surprise!

Chapter 25

Lightning in a Bottle

"There is something in every one of you that awaits and listens for the sound of the genuine in yourself. It is the only true guide you will ever have. And if you cannot hear it, you will, all of your life, spend your days on the ends of strings that somebody else pulls."

—Howard Thurman

Heavenly or hellish, lengthy or brief, a near-death experience is like lightning in a bottle. The container of your life, how you lived and who you think yourself to be, cannot and does not fit the strength of its needle point. It either blows you apart or pricks whatever is "norm." Understanding can take a lifetime.

This happened to me—three times—so I know what I'm talking about. Let me share a few of my cases so you'll know too.

A woman in the state of Arkansas (a minister's wife with two kids), had a long and involved near-death experience during surgery. Afterward, she could no longer be at her husband's side on Sundays. She always made up a story to stay home with her children. I asked her why. Her answer: "He's lying to the people. God's not like that. He's lying." She still loved her husband, loved her kids and the life they shared. She didn't want a divorce, yet looked away when I asked about how long she thought she could be absent on

Sundays without having to face her husband and tell him the truth. No answer.

Margaret barely made it to the hospital. She had severe phlebitis. As doctors fought to restart her heart, she found herself in a greensward with beautiful trees and bushes near a small stream separating her from a voice that boomed: "You will go back and be a healer, even in darkest Africa." Margaret was a single mother and school teacher who raised and showed horses, had a large garden, and was active with 4-H projects for kids. Be a healer? Nonsense. Yet once she was in the recovery room after surgery, she left her body and passed her new "healing hands" over a young man screaming in pain. He instantly slept. After that, she somehow flowed right through the wall of a black-curtained isolation room to find what she described as "a white boy turned black" from severe burns. She sat next to him on the bed, introduced herself, then proceeded to counsel him about what it's like to die. She comforted him and let him know that it's okay for him to leave his parents. The boy could see and hear her perfectly, and even felt the weight of her body sitting next to him.

Months later, now in a wheelchair, Margaret attended a horse show where her daughter competed. Her daughter won. The announcer barked out the daughter and mother's names. A rustling sound could be heard as two people hurried through the crowd to be at Margaret's side. They were the parents of that severely burned boy from the hospital. Yes, he died—but peacefully, with a smile on his face. He'd told his parents everything Margaret had said to him, including her name. No one could explain how she knew about the boy or even got into his room *while her body lay on a surgical hospital gurney some distance away.* Margaret fought the idea of becoming a healer, but finally relented. She moved to South Africa after her marriage ended, and ended up teaching sangomas (traditional healers) her healing techniques, becoming like "one" of them.

A trip to Las Vegas, Nevada, turned the tables on me. My publisher set me up at a bookstore in the older section of the city. Management put me outside under a canopy of flowering vines, and my table was boxed in by large signs. Many stopped to talk, tell their stories, especially a thin, wiry desert miner who spoke loud and strong: "Them experiencers on television telling all those stories about heaven and love. They don't know what they're talking about. They're lying. They're lying to all the people watching those shows. All lies. It's hell on the other side of life. Real hell. I know. I've been there. You talk about all kinds of experiences, that's why I trust you. You listen to real people like me. Not just them who act, who lie." The man paced the sidewalk, sometimes waving his arms in the air. Others joined in. Not a single person in the crowd spoke of heaven. Strange but true. Soon enough I was whisked away to the local television station for a live interview. That proved to be problematic, as my electrical sensitivity brought down both cameras, throwing the program off-air. When I tried to explain what happened (and suggested how they might counteract and set me up differently), they tossed my idea and gave up in disgust. Must be the cameras or the hookup, they claimed—not me.

Outside Portland, Oregon, during the dark of an October moon, the temperature dropped suddenly. A man driving his car on the outskirts of town didn't notice. Driving much too fast for "black ice" conditions, he lost control of his car on a curve and crashed into a large tree. As he put it, he floated to the top of the tree, and, looking down, he saw his mangled car and blood flowing from his now-missing right arm. He chose to save his body. He looked around, but there were no homes except for one on a far away ridge with the light on in an upper corner room. He went to that room. How, he did not know. But he did. He spied a man inside and started jumping up and down yelling "Call the police, there's been an accident." The man in the room later told police he saw fog doing crazy things outside his window. "Fog doesn't dance around like that," he said. So he made the call, went downstairs, found a flashlight, and was there to flag down the emergency vehicles when they arrived. The man in the car lost not only his right arm, but his sight as well. Three months later (still in the hospital after his many surgeries), his sight returned. The once professional right-handed artist asked for pen and paper. With his left hand he drew a detailed picture of the accident scene. The man in the house and the attending police officers agreed to see the drawing. They all said it was so detailed and accurate that it could have been a photo of the accident scene. When I met him, he was passing around copies of that drawing to everyone. His new job: proving that all of our abilities extend past what we think is true. Limitation is a joke we play on ourselves.

A woman in her late twenties, driving along farm roads, was hit broad-side by a huge truck. Though she was declared dead, surgeons tried to revive her anyway and managed to restart her heart. Despite sedation, her eyes popped open and she excitedly spoke of seeing her dad. Her dad had told her that he'd just died, but even though his time on Earth had ended, hers had not. She had to go back. Her joy at seeing her father caused so many problems during surgery, a doctor left the surgical room in search of her family. In the waiting room, everyone assured the doctor that the dad was fine. One had even called him that very morning and spoken with him at length. When the doctor returned and told her what her family said, she became even more animated. Desperate, the doctor went back, demanding that someone phone her father so he could take the phone to her and she could hear for herself that her dad was okay. Suffice it to say, after many attempts to locate her dad, the family learned that he had indeed just died— *five minutes before the daughter and in exactly the same manner the daughter had described.* I verified all of these stories except this last one.

I once met a father and daughter at an outdoor exhibit. I had a booth. The father trained dogs and had a large one with him on a leash. He came over to tell me that a few years back he had died on an operating table. At the moment of death, he "saw" his son hurled into the air because a truck had slammed into his motorcycle. The father, "instantly there," caught his son in midair and lowered him gently to the ground—all while doctors in the operating room worked frantically to save the father's life. Still shaken up, the father wanted me to hear his story. The daughter confirmed everything. No one would give me the son's contact info so I could speak with him though. When I asked why, the father, daughter, (and dog), turned their backs on me and walked away.

Do you think this story outlandish? Told to fool me? I'd come across episodes far more improbable than this one that evidence had proven to be true. I've also had situations where the evidence seemed proof positive, but was later discredited. You can usually tell the truth by a person's eyes and body language (especially if others are present. Watch the shoulders and knees).

With my cases—although many were brief time-wise—the majority averaged between five to twenty minutes without any sign of pulse, breath, or human response. One in particular, a woman, was revived in the morgue, shocking everyone. Less than a third of experiencers saw a tunnel of any kind, contrary to popular notions. Common greeters were deceased loved ones (always appearing as their youthful selves), angels, pets, and animals of various types—especially birds. Lots of birds. And the living. Yes, I said *living*. I found this to be true mostly with child experiencers, but also with a few adults. Consistently, *living greeters stayed only as long as it took for the experiencer to feel unafraid and comfortable. Then they disappeared, replaced by beings typically found in such episodes.*

In different parts of the world, with differing languages and belief systems, near-death symbols and expressions can alter as well . . . without changing the impact or aftereffects. Example: the differences we consistently found with experiencers in East versus West Berlin. I was only in Munich a short time, yet long enough to recognize that East Berliners tended to have "colorless" episodes (in the sense of being low-key, less involved, and less emotional). Those in the Western sector, however, were just the opposite—with loving greeters who radiated forgiveness and joy. I encountered this same disparity multiple times in the United States with people whose families lived for generations in low-income housing with little hope of change. I cannot claim "across-the-board" discoveries here, but I can say that such inconsistencies exist and we must acknowledge them.

I did a lot of traveling, asked a lot of questions, and invariably wound up doing strange things in strange places—like in Seoul, South Korea, where, if you want to engage with anyone, you need to walk the streets between 10pm and midnight. Most people there begin their workday late morning and leave work late in the evening. I also found that symbols in Eastern cultures tended to be more earth-based rather than having the religious themes often found in the West. Invariably, people with non-linear beliefs hardly ever experienced anything like a life review. Life to them was less of a linear progression and more like a mobius strip that wraps around.

You find this same pattern in the West with child experiencers of near-death states—mostly those who had their episodes between birth and age five. There are any number of countries where people think in terms of "we" rather than "I," which affects not only their episode but how they describe it. "Love" does not translate worldwide either, but empathy does, so I learned to fashion my words accordingly.

Cultural differences like these are the reason why I often asked experiencers to draw what they encountered, rather than just tell me. This is helpful because most experiencers have the same problem: how do you describe what cannot be described? They try to use the language of the culture they're in, but it often doesn't work. It can't communicate what they want to say. But when they use drawings instead of words, differences dissolve. Example: a horse trainer in Wyoming drew some pictures matching drawings that Todd Murphy, a fellow researcher, had shown me years before. Murphy's drawings, from Thailand, were of Yamatoots, servants of the Lord Yama, Ruler of the Underworld, who appeared in near-death episodes there. Both the horse trainer's pictures and the Yamatoots drawings were basically the same, with similar responses made by the ones who'd had the experience. There's a similar link between Christian "true-believers" and New Age/Spiritual folk. Meanings behind the words they use are basically the same.

There are "near-death-like" experiences, similar to what happened to an African-Canadian man who crossed through his living room to open a window, then walked back towards his sofa and *into a full-blown near-death experience followed by all the aftereffects.* He had no health problems, yet he remained forever changed by the event. Another: a middle-aged Southern woman walked out onto her porch, bent over to pick up the Sunday newspaper, stood back up, then *walked right into the rising Sun and was so changed by doing this that she experienced lifelong near-death aftereffects.*

There are "fear-deaths," where individuals suddenly become so frightened, (like when a car heads right for them yet veers off at the last possible second), that *they have a near-death experience as complete as any other and deal with the same pattern of aftereffects.*

There are "empathic or shared near-death experiences" where another person can agree to, or accidently follow, the one who is dying. In doing so, they experience what that individual does and in a similar manner. There seems to be a "line of demarcation" with these, whereby the one who is "extra" cannot continue on past a certain point. This type of experience can actually be caused or planned beforehand by the parties involved, using meditative or silent prayer as an aid.

Multiple personality types can also go through near-death events and face aftereffects that either heal their many splits, reduce the number of them, or cause integrative factors that are beneficial and long-lasting. A number of such cases appear in my various books (especially those covering child experiencers). I have yet to encounter any such event that was negative or harmful.

Get this: with near-death experiences—all of them—*there's a pattern of befores.*

What consistently caught my eye is the episodes that occurred *during major life junctures*: when a decision needed to be made and/or during times of deep dissatisfaction, disappointment, and frustration; when someone is feeling hurried all the time or excessively strained; while "running a tight ship" and insisting on too much personal control; when lifestyle maintenance overwhelms one's ability to keep it going; *when pushing limits*—at work, at play, in everything; when demanding/strict rules limit one's beliefs and activities; when one is without meaningful goals, or in strong denial; *when "happy" times turn out to be a façade;* and when one is overly complacent.

By far the most consistent "before" state I saw was over-the-top-stress—the kind that pushes one beyond his or her limits, beyond what is "safe." Known as "high stress," this is what has been regarded throughout the ages as necessary to cause "the death of the ego."

Is that what is happening with near-death experiencers?

Have you ever talked with one? Are you one? In a genuine near-death experience there is no ego. Gone. You're suddenly elsewhere. The world you've known and lived in since birth is either overturned or takes on different dimensions or disappears. Brief or long lasting, complicated or simple, it's like a lightning bolt crossing the windshield of your mind.

Tradition has it that one must die unto the self and leave behind previous desires and wants in order to take on the trusted role of healer-guide. This tradition is present in all forms of shamanism, and all religious and spiritual conversion rituals. To get a handle on this, consider the mythological traditions of the "hero's journey" (or heroine's). High stress is always the deciding factor—the big push—that forces one over the edge (the stress threshold) and into the otherworlds of spirit, where everything converges/suspends/expands into the collective whole—and is forever imprinted by the aftereffects of the journey.

Strip away all the fancy words and theories here, and just look at what's being said along with what that implies.

You died, or nearly died.

Lighting hit.

Your bottle broke.

You begin again . . . different.

Chapter 26

Little Bottles

"If you want to upset the law that all crows are black, you mustn't seek to show that no crows are; it is enough if you prove one single crow to be white."
—William James

In the early 2000's, I went into overdrive and started producing a book every year: *The New Children and Near-Death Experiences* (my attempt to reconcile the fiasco created by publishers when my first major book on child experiencers was cut to pieces); *We Live Forever: The Real Truth About Death* (about our granddaughter's death and what we all can learn about the soul); *Beyond the Indigo Children* (my first foray into what I believe to be the evolution of the human race now occurring); my final completion of *The Big Book of Near-Death Experiences* (a global encyclopedia of the near-death phenomenon). Plus, I finally obtained the rights to reissue *Coming Back To Life.* To cut costs, Steff put it online for me via Amazon.

So many have asked: how did I do it? How did I see so many people, hear so much, investigate on such a broad scale? Fair question. My answer: I work at my job night and day, every week. Even on vacation, I'm not on vacation. My job has been as much a part of my life as the air I breathe. Ask my husband, he'll tell you. I've even put ads in magazines and newspapers looking for experiencers, sent out notices from time to time on the Internet and through my website. On the home front, Terry helps me separate "researcher-from-experiencer-from-wife." He's a very involved partner—same, yet totally opposite—and at times not at all interested. He loves a good meal. I'm a pretty good cook . . . because . . . I first ask the food what it wants to do, then we both have fun. Surprises, always.

Do this for forty-four years and see how it works for you.

When the subject is kids, I refuse to accept standard ideas. That first book I wrote about child experiencers opened up so many new doors in near-death studies that the public mostly zoned out, preferring instead the cliché "out-of-the-mouth-of-babes" stories, rather than anything that challenged what they'd heard. Certainly, we all want to hear about angels and grandparents "ever there" to catch us should we fall—guarantors of life's meaning and purpose. If someone like me deviates too far from acceptable storylines, however, boundaries get crossed. I did that with my child experiencers study, which is probably why so many refused to support what my findings implied.

I know this isn't a research book. It is a memoir-autobiography. At least that's what it's supposed to be. But what if your life is research? Day and night, every week, every year? I promise I won't bore you. So hold on.

That first study of 277 childhood experiencers showed, quite clearly, that for kids dying isn't as big a deal as it is for adults. Returning is the biggie. I focused on experiences that occurred between birth and age fifteen. Most who responded had their experience when they were seven or younger. Teens and tweens just weren't interested. If still a child, I found that parents, adults of any stripe, would interfere . . . even when they didn't mean to. The youngest I worked with was four. Hear this: if you're doing one-on-one with kids, your eyes can *never* be above that of the child. You can pat them on the hand or arm once or twice but that's it. What you want is to build is a trust that says: "you're okay, I'm okay, you can tell me anything. " Children pick up on body language instantly. They "read" you faster than you can read them.

The vast majority of youngsters have Initial Experiences, and these can involve powerful feelings, knowings, and often a sense of presence which greatly affects the child. Adults talk a lot about "the light" they encountered on the other side of death. But kids are more specific about *what kind of light* they saw. Most described:

> *Primary Light*: usually seen as a pulsating luminosity—a radiance that is almost frightening in how awesome, piercing, powerful and all encompassing it is—as though it were "the origin of all origins."
>
> *Dark or Black Light*: sometimes described as black with purple tinges, or just dark; a shimmering, peaceful, healing place some kids call *The Darkness That Knows;* a source of strength and knowing; a sanctuary-like "womb of creation."
>
> *Bright or White Light*: can have a full range of yellow-gold-white hues; brilliant with an almost blinding glow that emanates unconditional love; an inviting intelligence you can converse with, like "the activity of truth."

Kids also claim that the white or bright light is Father Light. The dark or black light is Mother Light. And that powerful radiance is God's Light. And they are adamant while wiggling their finger in front of your nose and saying: Father Light and Mother Light come from God's Light. I cringe sometimes when adults insist that a near-death experience is always a white-light experience. Not so.

Kids often see prayer as beams of light moving out of a person's heart area, zooming over to wherever that prayer is intended to go: to help, to uplift, to heal, to bless. These are not rainbow-shaped bridges; rather, they are long, narrow beams of brilliant lights, with white tips front and back. I asked a youngster what it was like to be hit by one of these prayer beams. "Oh," he giggled. "It feels warm and tickly all over."

Most of my cases came from drownings, surgery, child abuse, and fevers—and they still do. Quite a few came from tonsillectomies, which puzzled me. I talked a number of times with pediatrician and near-death researcher Melvin Morse, M.D. about this. He noted that during the early to mid-1900s doctors regularly used too much ether for tonsillectomies. That's why so many near-death cases show up during that period (some still reported). Apparently, excessive amounts of ether can trigger full-blown near-death states with some children, above and beyond any simple hallucination. In my research, not only did I catch the same "error of judgment" many physicians made, verifying Morse's work . . . but I also discovered something else: *Medical mistakes of any type readily surface in near-death scenarios* (adult or child). Nurses and physicians should be alerted to this.

Most children continue to have out-of-body experiences afterward and see the dead as very much alive—at least to them. The youngest virtually never use the term "angel." Instead, they'll say things like "the people" or "bright ones." One young patient saw the deceased walking around the hospital so often that she drove the nurses crazy talking to them. If the parents were killed in the event that injured the child, those parents would often hover around the ceiling of the child's hospital room to help in any way possible. Ditto with pets. Deceased animals can and do snuggle up with children in hospital beds. In one such case, both doctors and nurses were so upset by the child's antics with her "dog," that she was released early and sent home.

Child experiencers are not like adult experiencers, especially if they had their episode between birth and age five. The majority of them don't fit back into their families afterward, even though they usually try to. Often there are mismatches when trying to compare them with other siblings. Usually smarter than parents and school teachers, almost half of the child experiencers in my research scored between 150 to 160 (the range for genius) on standard IQ tests when old enough to take them—without genetic markers to account for this. Sensing the future is commonplace for them, as well as some form of synesthesia (sensing in multiples), and having psychic/intuitive knowing on a regular basis. Shocking though—and I mean truly shocking—were the number of kids who somehow stole/found liquor from any source they could in order to drink their way back into crowd acceptance and not be "different" anymore. Being labeled "different" too often makes someone a target for bullying or being ignored.

Puzzles with children became more noticeable the younger they were. Because I was unable to interest other researchers in exploring this, I tackled the project solo again years later—only this time I went after those in their mature years who could remember and validate a near-death experience between birth and age five. By doing this, I could compare the young who were looking forward in life with the more mature who were looking backward in life. I asked them this question: did having such an experience when you were very young make any difference in your life? If it did, what was it?

In essence, I was asking for essays. What I received overwhelmed me. Some essays were fifty pages long, replete with family photographs, and others were so tear-stained I could barely read them. One woman complained that no researcher ever asked people in poverty what happened to them. I did—along with Native Americans and every other type of individual I could find.

Prepare yourself. What follows may be over the top for you. The information you're about to read directly affects the abortion question worldwide and shows that humanhood begins at conception.

Combining both of my studies with the present ones gave me 397 people total. Memory held, even with a woman in her eighties who was validated by a "slightly" younger sister. Those whose experience happened when they were babies or toddlers called themselves *birthers*. I did not make up that term. The people in that age group did it themselves, by themselves. They were literally "born aware and awake." Get this: about a third remembered being in their mother's womb. According to one: "The most profound memory was my mother smoking. I remember getting excited in utero when she would feel anxious—because I knew that the bad taste was coming and soon I would feel high." Well over half remembered their birth—in detail. Two remembered their conception. Those two were "there" to watch everything their parents did. One, when older, drew a picture of what she saw and showed it to her parents. To say they were shocked and utterly embarrassed would be an understatement!

The abortion question versus my research is one we had to face in our own family. A daughter of mine became pregnant far too early for motherhood. My research shows that abortion is really not the mother's choice and never was. It's the soul's choice. With this in mind I recommended that my daughter go into a deep meditative state and connect with the baby's soul. She did, asking if it would be alright if the child left and went on to seek out another mother. "Yes" was the answer, so she had the abortion without guilt. Abortion is a soul-level question, not just the mother's.

Look at this too: instead of continuing with concrete learning styles with kids of their age group (details), they move to abstract learning (concepts). Most child experiencers are forced by their teachers to go back to "what-everyone-else-is-doing," even when they are no longer able to. The majority displayed some form of synesthesia afterwards (blended or multiple sensing). Ninety percent lost the ability to bond with parents (many loved their parents but never took them seriously).

But get this: the percentage of those who became very successful in life (some millionaires) was 74%. The percentage of those with lifelong suicide ideation throughout their life was 74%. Same overall percentage. Why?

We do not understand what happens to a child's mind after a near-death experience. Many come to display full memory . . . of a world we dip in and out of as we pass from life to life. Some speak of reincarnation but the majority do not. *Their vision is spherical*—a wide-awake brilliance. The youngest of the young often go on to display a form of PTSD (Post Traumatic Stress Disorder). Yet if the truth be known, what they are is . . . homesick for heaven.

Children have an amazing way of picking up on anything hidden in their parent's psyche. Then, in some unfathomable way, they act it out. They will dig and test even when it's not clear why they're doing it. Near-death kids and their parents inspire each other, while at the same time testing each other's limits. Kids will pull every switch in their parent's psychological armor. Parents will welcome these tests because it helps them prepare for and better handle family life and all of its challenges.

Epigenetics shows us *how our environment influences our genes.* In my work with child experiencers (especially once they were older looking back), there is clear evidence of epigenetics. What parents learned from their near-death experience is often passed on to their children and grandchildren. Near-death experiences are that powerful!

After I finished *The Forever Angels*, I wrote a series of six children's books called *Animal Lights*. I wrote these books so adults could have fun with their children while exploring memories, including those their children might have about their birth or pre-birth. This is untouched territory we all would be wise to explore.

The average adult takes seven to ten years to integrate their experience, but it takes the average child twenty to forty years. An adult can make comparisons, seek out assistance, question. A child experiencer never really integrates . . . they compensate. Their challenge as a child is to grow up, mind their parents, make it through school, and find their place in a world that most of them do not understand. Example: a New York City police officer called me just a few months ago. He was in his late forties and crying. Finally he managed to say: "I just read *The Forever Angels*. I'm one of those kids. I've tried my entire life to understand why I'm so different. Now I know."

Imagine you're a child experiencer with abilities and thoughts outside the norm. What do you do? Where do you turn if you have no idea about the why of who you are?

Lighting in a bottle.

Even little bottles.

Honor their differences, then watch them fly.

Chapter 27

Time for Overwhelm

"The person who says it cannot be done should not interrupt the person doing it."
—Chinese proverb

Raymond Reynolds popped into my life just when I needed someone with credentials like his to speak up on my behalf. Retired from a career in Law Enforcement and Criminal Justice Training, he attended a workshop I taught about near-death experiencers and how their significant others tend to respond to them. "You've had law enforcement training, haven't you?" he queried. Surprised by his question, I countered: "I'm a cop's kid, raised in a police station. Does that count?" He rolled with laughter. We became good friends. Years later he wrote a piece supporting the way I do research. It appears near the back of *Near-Death Experiences: The Rest of the Story*.

People like Raymond have been few and far between for me. I do my work because it is mine to do. Aside from cuddling with Terry whenever moments allow, visiting with kids, grandkids, friends, and seeing a movie or two, you'll mostly find me knee-deep in researching where my findings lead me.

One day some percentages I'd previously found caught my eye like I'd seen them for the first time. With experiencers: 21% claimed no discernible changes afterward. 60% reported significant, noticeable changes. And 19% said changes were so radical, they felt as if they had become another person. This means *a whopping 79% were unable to return to "life as always."*

Oops. Time to rethink.

What we call psychic/intuitive abilities—all the many kinds of them—are simply extensions of faculties normal to us. Nothing more. They get bigger/better when we undergo some type of episode that causes what is known as high stress. And high stress is the key, not only for understanding near-death experiences, but for any type of spiritual episode that leaves us "changed."

Throughout time, sacred initiations of the greatest order demanded a "death"—seldom physical. That death was the death of the ego. One had to "die unto the self"—leaving behind previous desires and wants—in order to take on the role of a healer-guide who dedicated the rest or his or her life in service of others. Sometimes called a vision quest, the goal was to mimic or come as close as possible to actual physical death. If you study mythology, you'll find the same thing. The hero/heroine's journey is always preparation for that overwhelming/over the top fear that pushes one's panic button . . . how one handles that stress (the watcher at the gate), overcomes fear (passes through), enters the worlds of spirit (where everything converges/suspends/expands into the collective whole), and is imprinted from the aftereffects (bears the mark of ascension).

Get what I'm saying?

Just in case you don't, let me try once more. Intense or high stress narrows one's focus. Everything accelerates beyond any type of fear-panic. Usually there is a greeter (perhaps a loved one) waiting for you inside a space difficult to describe. Suddenly you are infused with knowing. Returning to consciousness leaves you "marked" by a pattern of aftereffects.

What's really happening here?

A colloidal condition has occurred and you have become a colloid.

One more time.

The colloidal state is a peculiar in-between condition that happens when forces suddenly collapse, then converge. This in-between state creates anti-force, which is antigravity. Particles caught in this unique state between implosion and explosion transmute and remain forever changed by that transmutation. On a molecular level, these particles show evidence of enlargement and of having taken on different and enhanced characteristics.

I'll make this simple by using water as an example of what a colloidal condition is. Rotate a vat of water. Spin the water. Round and round. Faster and faster. Now, stop the direction of the spin. Stop it dead in the water and reverse the direction. When you stopped the spin, the water collapsed into itself creating an implosion. But just before you initiated a reverse spin, where the water could explode back out, conditions mysteriously changed and both the water and everything contained within the water were briefly held in suspension. That suspension is what's called a colloidal condition and particles caught therein are referred to as colloids.

There's more. Right after the vortex of spin collapsed, surface tension increased dramatically and antigravity ensued. Antigravity continues to exist quite apart and disconnected from the water's movement until the reverse direction of rotation can be generated (or until the condition dissipates because of no further movement).

Hear this: gravity does not behave as a force. It behaves as if it were *the entrainment of the spin of a smaller object by a larger one* (literally the attraction matter has for itself). When such a spin is suddenly reversed, the entrainment momentarily collapses until the reverse spin can begin. During the collapse, that which was held together by mutual attraction is freed. *The same thing can happen to the human brain if suddenly hit, jarred, or severely jiggled, especially during an automobile accident or as the result of a fall.* Typically, a colloidal-like suspension of consciousness will follow such trauma, where space appears to expand outward as time slows to a standstill. The individual feels somehow caught *in-between realities* when this occurs, as if he or she had slipped through a crack in time and space and had suddenly become a resident in a world "neither here nor there."

What I discovered is . . . a colloidal condition best describes what happens during and after a near-death/spiritually intense transformative state. This colloidal condition reflects the core mechanism for the shift that energy makes—a shift that suspends, expands, and transmutes whatever is caught within it, either instantly or seemingly so. Step-by-step:

- A colloidal condition occurs where forces suddenly collapse, then converge.
- A momentary state of suspension results.
- Everything caught in that suspension expands and enlarges as antigravity is created.
- Inherent or unlimited potential is released.
- Whatever is present is imprinted (becomes permanently altered by what happened).

- Whatever is present then transmutes (takes on different characteristics).
- As reversal of motion is completed, forces are restored, suspension ends, but the imprinting (transmutation) remains.

Remember, a colloid is any particle caught in a colloidal condition. Once suspended in this manner, the particle will automatically enlarge, expand and remain permanently and forever altered by the experience.

This means you!

The process that creates colloids describes almost exactly what happens to most of those who undergo intense spiritual transformations and near-death episodes. The majority who go through such a process experience an enlargement/expansion of consciousness, exhibit the sudden surfacing of latent abilities, and face a confusing array of psychological and physiological aftereffects. They are never quite the same again.

It is my belief that this process of convergence and transmutation (transfiguration) is universal because everyone of us, now and throughout the ages, is and always has been imprinted by the same creative impulse that originated us. The mark of our creation is what we display whenever our consciousness is freed to rediscover itself and the source of its being. Rebirth.

Unfortunately we can't just tell our stories, no matter how wondrous. There is always some kid in the crowd that hollers, "Wait a minute. Something else is going on here and we need to take another look."

Right, so let's have fun with this.

The limbic system in the brain is the main "governing" area since everything that comes in goes through the limbic first. It is the limbic that decides what goes where for further processing. There is a direct link between the limbic and the heart and the nose. That's why so many of our memories are triggered by smell or odor. What I found shows us that the limbic (as the "gateway" to higher states of consciousness) is activated in near-death and other impactful transformational states. It is the key doorway to the collective, to mass mind, to higher realms. Not the right brain. Not the subconscious. *The key is the limbic* (in myth it is the "watcher at the gate").

Love, ecstasy, integrity of memory, upliftment, otherworldly realities, empathy, awareness that life continues, knowing, mysticism . . . all of these link up in and through the limbic. The limbic, as the oldest part of the brain, is that first arrangement of mind/thought that enabled us to survive. It is ancient. Primal. It is the base-point. You see this in education—how classes must be arranged and taught if children are really going to learn. There must be movement and rhythm to understand text.

Consider the limbic as the gateway to the colloidal condition. Walk through this with me.

> *External Colloidal Condition*: that state of temporary suspension which results from collapse/compression of time and space and "relationships-in-motion-moving-together." This releases unlimited potential through the sudden expansion and enlargement of energy/matter.

> *Internal Colloidal Condition*: that state of convergence which enables subjective and objective states of consciousness to momentarily overlap and expand, thus making it possible

for consciousness to be anywhere and everywhere simultaneously (usually coupled with a marked acceleration of awareness and knowing).

Colloid: a particle or potentiality caught in a colloidal state that is enlarged, enhanced, and expanded by the experience of being there, then permanently imprinted (altered or transmuted) as a result.

Don't believe me? Check out Matthew 13:33 in the Bible.

Jesus is quoted as saying, "The kingdom of heaven is like unto leaven." Leaven is that which causes dough to rise, grow, expand, and enlarge—like yeast. "Heaven" is a Greek word which conveys the idea of expansion similar to leaven . . . except leaven refers to that which expands, while heaven symbolizes *that which has already expanded*. Even the two Bible verses in advance of the 33rd convey the same message (where Jesus speaks of heaven as being like a mustard seed): rise, grow, expand, enlarge, because this is what heaven is (the realm of the expanded) and this how you get there (expand as leaven does).

When your consciousness changes, the first noticeable difference is how expansive your thinking, feeling, sensitivity, and awareness becomes. Afterward, you are more than you were before. And you are transfigured and transformed to the extent that you were affected. You expand into what seems to be "heaven"—a state or realm of the already expanded (the colloidal condition).

During my third near-death experience, I witnessed energy/matter/light being converted from one vibrational level of existence to another, recycled and renewed as if in a giant washing machine or flush tube. When I drew a picture of what I saw, those spinning cyclones looked exactly like a giant torus.

Okay, let's play with this.

The torus is the only self-organizing wave form in creation. Contained within it is all the basic motions we humans recognize as movement: up/down, in/out, across. It is a living gyroscope, and the tilt of its doughnut curve, as viewed from differing angles, reflects every essential color and image design we humans have come to recognize and use—plus every letter shape ancient alphabets ever came to have. This type of "information" emerges from the phases of shift that the sine wave makes as it forms the torus membrane—by rotating itself on its own axis.

The torus has been revealed, in whole or in part, through visions and dreams since time immemorial. It is the progenitor of sacred symbology and the guardian of sacred mythologies because of the way the human subconscious automatically models death and resurrection motifs—either through its shape, function, or qualities. Not only are the two cyclones I witnessed (and shapes similar to them) suggestive of a torus (or part of one), so, too, are the designs of the original zodiac, as well as the angelic and alien sky beings that were witnessed and recorded by the first peoples.

Fact: as a seed begins to grow and an egg is fertilized, they are enveloped by an energy field in the shape of a torus. Cut into the heart of a fruit or flower and you'll find a torus. Speak your word and the air blows out of your mouth like a torus. "In the beginning was the Word" and in all beginnings, once movement responds to its own need to move, you find a torus. Its shape allows light to stabilize and self-organize as matter.

So, what's at the centerpoint of creation? I believe the centerpoint is a continuous state of colloidal convergence (suspension, expansion, alteration, imprinting). We remember this state, all of us do, and we return there over and over again because we bear the "mark" of its "heaven."

My life, my deaths, and my research have convinced me that threshold experiences are a biological imperative . . . to ensure that we continuously evolve in form, capacity, and intellect towards an even higher order. Traits—what we learn and gain—can be passed on to the next generation (called Lamarckism).

During the early years of my work, I put together models based on my discoveries. They were big and thick with charts and explanations in great detail. The overall title was: "Brain Shift/Spirit Shift: A Theoretical Model Using Research On Near-Death States To Explore The Transformation of Consciousness." Phase One was published in September of 1996; Phase Two the following year; and Phase Three around the turn of the Millennium. All were dedicated to Bruce Greyson, M.D. because he couldn't figure out what I meant by "brain shift."

Few ever bought a copy, but at least I had something in hand to show questioners. On a trip to Canada, I took 50 copies of the completed version with me. I even had transparencies of each chart to present during my talk. Fifty people attended. They each bought a copy of *"Brain Shift/Spirit Shift"* once my talk was finished. They were excited at what I had done and felt it was cutting edge. I was asked many questions. They were Chinese. Every one of them. Not a single person from the U.S. or Canada or Europe or anywhere else was even remotely interested.

Of those fifty Chinese people . . . all were scientists. Why would they be interested in my work when no one else was?

Chapter 28

The Worm Turns

"It may be that some little root of the sacred tree still lives. Nourish it then, that it may leaf and bloom and fill with singing birds."
—Black Elk

In December, 2001, the *Lancet Medical Journal* published a paper on near-death research that was conducted in the Netherlands by cardiologist Pim van Lommel and his team. This study was the largest and most detailed examination of the phenomenon ever done. Among its many discoveries, there was mention of what I found: that it takes a minimum of seven years to integrate a near-death experience. I am also cited in Dr. Pim van Lommel's book *Consciousness Beyond Life: The Science of the Near-Death Experience.* Notification about this came in mid-December and I told everyone I won an "Oscar" for Christmas. This study, by the way, is the world's best thus far. I feel honored to be a part of it.

A little surprise. Months before all of this, I was visiting Pim and his wife at their home in the Netherlands. One night Pim was talking about the paper he'd written and he told me that it was still in his briefcase, unmailed. It languished there because he harbored a "what if" kind of worry about mailing it to the *Lancet Medical Journal.* I thought long and hard about that paper, then decided that even though I was just a guest, I was going to nag him until he finally mailed it. I didn't even know that some of my work was in the study. Later the next day as I descended the stairs, he walked in the front door with a huge grin on his face. "You mailed it, didn't you?" I yelled. His "yes" was triumphant!

Once the paper was published, I could at long last say that someone besides those fifty Chinese scientists thought my life's work was worthwhile.

It didn't take long before I was swamped with offers and paid speaking engagements. Several Publishers wanted my next book, and larger cross-sections of people were saying "yes" when I called for participants in future research. I set up workshop after workshop, some in other countries, where I could share my findings, search for more experiencers, and explore what all of this might mean. Some of the workshops and classes I developed were:

- "Evolutionary Factors in Near-Death and Other Transformative States"
- "Sacred Encounter—Visionary Episodes"
- "Our Minds, Our Attitudes—The Power of Belief"
- "The Life Continuum"
- "Children's NDEs"
- "Children of the New Millennium"
- "Visualization for Better Living"
- "Awake or Asleep, the Power of The Dream"

- "Impromptu Drawings—Reaching Deep Within" (based on some of the classes I attended with Elisabeth Kübler Ross)
- "The New Race"
- "Synchronicity—One Mind"
- "Meditation and Prayer."

You should see all of the lesson plans and folders I made. Massive. I used props like tuning forks, measurement wheels (so people could see how large their auric field was), and strings hanging from the ceiling with paper circles and squares knotted at the end of each. Students would have to pass through this "jungle" of strings without touching any of them. They could only use the energy of their own hands to move aside whatever was in the way. It always tickled me to watch people discover the power they have in just their hands.

In the midst of all this activity, my granddaughter Myriam died. I mentioned before that we'd lost her. Bacterial meningitis. My son called, sobbing. He told me she was seizing one day and died the next. That fast. My youngest daughter and I flew out to California the next day.

A crush of aunts, uncles, grandparents, and friends gathered to do what they could to help. Myriam's older brother was awestruck by all the touching, sharing, crying, and hugging, as photos of happier times passed from hand to hand. Memories found voices. Grief. Sobs. Laughter. Pain. We formed a circle, and everyone shared their stories. By doing this as a family, we discovered something quite surprising: every single one of us had a premonition that this would happen. For some it was a few weeks, some a month, and one even six months before. In dreams. Sometimes even "voices" warning of what was to come. No exceptions. Everyone received a warning of some kind. Even Myriam's mother perceived it . . . *as she was giving birth to her!* She'd had a vision of Myriam at around two-years of age, climbing up escalator-type-stairs until she disappeared into an immense light. And that's exactly what happened. Once Myriam passed the age of two, her brain seemed to "burn up" and she disappeared into a flash of light. *All* of us *knew* —even those who could not bear the thought.

After her death, Myriam stayed with her older brother every night for two weeks so he could get used to having her gone and be okay with it. Yes, he could see and hear her. The two visited regularly. Funny thing, though. One morning, while my youngest daughter was taking a shower and I was reading a newspaper in the kitchen, Myriam manifested and hopped down the hall towards the bathroom. Then she bent over slightly so she could see past the bathroom door and yelled "Pawwe, Pawwe." She was so happy she could finally see her Aunt Paulie. Myriam actually ran up and down the hall several times, and "appeared" at other moments when no one expected it. She enjoyed doing this, surprising people. It was like she had no realization that she no longer "wore" a body —that to us, she was dead.

Her body was cremated. On a night when the Moon was bigger than big, her parents and brother flung her ashes into a heaving ocean ready to receive her. I later wrote a book about our family's story called *We Live Forever: The Real Truth About Death.* I wanted to share the discoveries we made about dealing with the trauma of losing a loved one, and give everyone a voice who wanted to speak. The book helped us, too.

Afterward, talks and workshops popped up like magic to once again fill my life, and I kept interviewing more and more experiencers for future projects. Even during all of this, part of me always remained with my son as he struggled with Myriam's death. She was his angel. Part of him never let go.

One day I found myself run-walking the many corridors of Pittsburgh Airport, not thinking as clearly as I should have been. When I arrived at my terminal, the entry doors were already closing. As I rushed to get there in time (screaming about how I had to be on that flight), I tripped. I had bag handles wrapped around both wrists in such way that I couldn't protect myself, so I fell face first. Smack! My upper and lower jaw was push/pulled. My left arm and wrist were crazy-shaped and instantly worthless. The medics were slow to arrive—I mean really slow, leaving me begging for help. When I was finally scooped up, they took me first to the front desk to arrange a flight out the next morning. Overnight accommodations were provided. That's it. No doctor. No X-rays. No pain killers. No way to even call my husband. I should have been taken to a hospital, not some low-cost motel. Much later, I somehow managed to call Terry and let him know what happened. No sleep. Going to the bathroom was virtually impossible, yet I somehow managed. The next morning a taxi took me back to the airport so I could fly home. Authorities made it very clear that the fall was my fault, not theirs. My injuries? Too bad.

I was still in shock when I arrived home, and there was much more to come. Yes, Terry found a surgeon—one of the best for the type of surgery I would need. There was one problem though: all the surgical facilities were overbooked for at least ten days—and if I waited that long, my bones would have to be re-broken in order to reset them properly (and even with that, there would be no guarantees). I feared losing the use of my left arm, wrist, and hand forever. Terry and I just looked at each other. My left arm was in a cast and sling. Drugs were offered. I said no.

With Terry at work and me at home cradling my twisted parts, I became more aware of my mouth and jaw damage. What could be done with that? No one knew. Wait it out, I thought. Maybe it might get better on its own over time.

No solutions. No cure or help. So I gave up. I gave up on ever writing again, ever doing research, ever traveling, ever doing anything. I just let go. Totally.

I entered peace, and nothing existed in that space but peace. It didn't matter if I ever resumed my life as it once existed. All that mattered was the peace I found in being nothing at all. Simple joy. Every day, a miracle. Every day, gratitude. 'Twas enough.

On that crucial tenth day, surgery began. It was a complicated break that required steel hardware shaped like a twisted spiral. It took hours and hours, plus hours more just to bring me out of the anesthesia. Both the doctor and Terry were worried. I told them afterwards that I "bought a ticket to the other side" and was thinking about using it.

Three weeks later I went in for my first X-ray to see how well I was healing after the surgery. The verdict? No break had ever happened. There was nothing there but a healthy, perfect arm/wrist/hand. It was a complete and total miracle. The doctor was so stunned, he rushed into my room and hugged me. A doctor had never done anything like that to me before. A miracle? Yes, but maybe the real miracle was something else. Maybe it came about because I had completely given up on everything . . . content to be nothing special, with no spiritual contract, no job to do, no pressure of any kind. I had found peace just being whatever I could with whatever was left of me. My bones simply fit back into place perfectly and that was all there was to it. This can happen to children, I'm told, but not to adults of "my age."

I soon resumed my schedules and appointments as if nothing had ever happened. I was given a letter from my doctor to use at airports if questions arose about all the metal hardware in my left arm/hand/wrist. But there were never any issues at airport checkpoints. About two years later, I had another surgery to remove all the hardware. Afterward, it felt like no surgeries had ever taken place. There was almost no scarring. The doctor never could figure out the why or how of any of it.

A few years later, I fell again.

But this time I didn't just fall, I sailed.

I was outside trimming the Crepe Myrtle tree on our lower lawn. I love ladders, so I was in my own kind of heaven near the top as I strained to reach the crest of the tree with the long trimmers. Suddenly my intuition warned me: *get off the ladder.* Before I could heed the warning though, I fell. My left foot searched for a lower rung on my way down. Couldn't find one. Seconds later I sailed away like a bird in flight, enjoying every moment. Landing posed a problem though. Not because the lawn might be too hard—I had just watered it. The problem was that hard blocks of wood lay to the right and metal tools and a wheelbarrow crowded the left. A narrow wedge between them was the only place I could land without breaking my neck.

I managed to land in the narrow wedge. My left arm kept me partially upright, but hyperventilation suddenly took over, with no sense of air or breathing. My body was rigid. I could feel blood rushing to cushion my heart as oxygen pushed into my brain. Clearly, something else ran the show—and that something else continued its charge irrespective of any choices or thoughts I had.

I finally recognized the power of that something else. It's identical to what enabled me to exist, do things, and continue living after all of my near-death experiences. It had helped me many times, including one time (a few years prior) when I was driving and suddenly stopped breathing. Out of nowhere, it (whatever "it" is), "drove" my car through downtown traffic in Boise, past first and second benches, through Vista Boulevard, around the Capitol, then out on State Street heading towards Floating Feather Airport. Not a whiff of air. Five minutes passed. Then seven, eight. I became alarmed. Not because I needed to breathe, but because *I knew that lungs need air and mine weren't getting any.* I pulled over, parked my car, and went into a meditative prayer. I visually restarted my lungs and kept doing so until air, real air, whooshed in. This freaky occurrence happened every once in a while . . . for a whole year after my deaths.

During my decades-long quest since then to find other experiencers and talk to them, I ran across multiple reports of this same anomaly: periods of time when experiencers didn't breathe and didn't miss the lack of oxygen. Breath returned on its own. For some this happened a few minutes later, others longer. No one knew the why of their breath coming and going as it did.

Fortunately, I didn't suffer any serious physical injuries from falling off that ladder—but my body's immediate, powerful response brought to mind everything I had ever heard about the vagus nerve.

Medical research reveals that the vagus nerve, one of the largest and longest in our bodies, runs from the base of the head to the abdomen, connecting all of our vital organs. It's programmed to keep us alive—no matter what. It tracks body responses, while also making certain that one part of the body "talks" to another in order to keep everything functioning properly. It is known to be involved in wakefulness and attention. A friend of mine, Karen Herrick (a transpersonal psychologist and author of several books), had some ideas about why some near-death experiencers don't breathe for long periods of time. She thinks they might be switching to the vagus system. To her, that means they've actually connected to "the silver cord". . . that which connects us to spirit. "Do experiencers see such a cord when they die?" she asked. In truth, a few experiencers have indeed spoken about it—but only a few. Any kind of cord that connects the soul with the body is rarely mentioned in near-death stories—until you do a double-think.

The vagus nerve could well be the missing link we've all been looking for since it ensures that, even if we're stone-cold dead, we can return and breathe again. I say that because it is a major carrier of nerve and emotional responses throughout vital organs. It makes certain that the main parts of our body hear each other, respond to each other, and help each other—sort of like the ultimate in "body talk." Experienced yogis who remain stuffed in a cell or box for days go through periods when they switch from breathing through their nostrils to an inner breathing technique that utilizes the vagus nerve. Their descriptions match experiencer stories. It is long past time, in my opinion, for other researchers to come forward and take up the baton on this one. I'd like to see them investigate why some experiencers go through periods of time after their NDE without breath . . . even the need for breath . . . and face what could very well be a fact: that the vagus nerve is the physical component of the silver cord—that which connects us to the spirit of our being.

There are more clues to the miracle of life, and my research is helping me try and unravel them. Good or bad doesn't matter. Terry shares my way of thinking. We are two peas in the same pod. And we laugh a lot. He explores *A Course In Miracles* with the students he teaches. Me? I explore the miracles of the near-death experience—the raw and open puzzle of death itself.

Chapter 29

God's Right Side

"Ever since happiness heard your name, it has been running through the streets trying to find you. And several times in the last week, God Himself has even come to my door, asking me for your address!"

—Hafiz

Light fills me now. Morning or night. When I truly let go, it's like the viewscreen of my mind wraps the planet. I see lights appear as new life comes in and disappear as older ones go out. Lights. Us. Birthing. Deathing. The lights of us are biophysically real. Even our bones emit light. I'm thrilled when I see the scientific community confirm this. It was recently discovered that a light flash occurs at the very moment sperm meets egg, and that a light flash also happens the second life fades away and disappears. Back and forth. Motion and rest. Cycles unending. Always light in some form. Flash!

In all my experiments as a child, I found life to be electric. This should be no surprise to anyone, really. Well over half of experiencers develop electrical sensitivity after their NDEs. Once an episode of near-death is over, the whole world seems suddenly larger and more real, especially if someone experienced The Void. The more spiritual and loving you become, the more biophysical light expands into radiant light and spiritual light. All of us, lights.

Vocalized or not, experiencers come to know God as the one presence, the one power, the one force, the one source of All. God is without competitors because no reality exists outside of God. God! Omnipotent (all powerful), omniscient (all knowing), and omnipresent (existing everywhere). Quite simply, there is no place where God is not. In our worst nightmares and terrible truths, you may want to argue this and say it couldn't possibly be true. But it is.

More truths. God is neither man nor woman nor thing. God is no one's father or mother or benefactor. We use human terms of parentage to help us understand our relationship to God. Such personal (even neutral) pronouns either serve as a matter of convenience or fill the need we have for comfort and security. We say we're Children of God because we don't know what else to call ourselves, and it seems as good a term to use as any. We are made in the image of God, not in the sense of physical appearance, but with respect to the power in our souls and the potential in our minds. Truth: God is Creator; we are co-creators. It would be more appropriate, even more in line with the truth we've come to know, if we simply called ourselves "Thoughts in the Mind Of God. "

God is more than name, protocol, hierarchy, concept, or grandiosity. Amazingly, God is truly as near as our next breath and as close as our next thought. We are part of God and existent *within* God. A belief in separation—that we could possibly exist and have a life apart from God—is the most erroneous idea that exists. Such a belief in separation is of our own making. God has not decreed any such thing. We did this ourselves by pretending that somehow, some way, we could transcend That Which Cannot Be Transcended. We are programmed as a species to evolve. We possess the exact apparatus we need, which, when triggered, will advance that growth.

Because of this truth, this hugeness, staying in a particular church or house of worship, clinging to holy books and bibles, seems either a waste of time or insufficient. With experiencers in my study, those who left their church (which was the majority of them), returned to a church setting about a decade or so later— but they were now drawn to a metaphysical or New Thought church (Transcendental). The Transcendental/New Thought Movement actually began with Plato (yes, that far back in history). Modern revivals began in the 1800's with those determined to practice self-healing and talk to God directly (similar to near-deathers). Ernest Holmes, who wrote *The Science of Mind*, was one of many revivalists. He defined love as "the self-givingness of spirit." Sound familiar? Maybe you also voice the same exquisite grasp of what is truly real. The class I took at the local Science of Mind center in Boise the year after my three deaths made a huge difference in my life. It gave me the clues I needed to re-evaluate my thinking processes and more fully grasp the God in me—with me, as me . . . me, a co-creator with the Creator . . . Universal Creative Intelligence (I AM THAT I AM).

The Bible we know has been altered throughout the ages. The most accurate one is, hands-down, the Ethiopian Bible, which was written shortly after Jesus left us. This huge Bible includes "The Book of Enoch" (which reads like a UFO trip. That's probably why it was nixed from modern translations). Early Gospels never mentioned a virgin birth, Christ's suffering, or the crucifixion. The resurrection did not appear in the Gospels until the 12th century—coinciding with the upsurge in Christian militarism and the beginning of the Dark Ages. Did you know that?

Many experiencers discover different types of modern translations. Seldom does anyone refer to the Revised Standard Edition of the King James Bible anymore. They light up instead when discussing The Holy Bible from the Peshitta (The Authorized Bible of the Church of the East), translated by George M. Lamsa. Of interest here is that Lamsa spoke Peshitta as a child (the language of Jesus's youth). In a vision, he was told to do a translation directly from Peshitta into English. The task took most of his life. Today his student, Rocco A. Errico, Th.D., Ph.D., helps people understand the original metaphors and language, which makes a huge difference in figuring out what Jesus may have actually said. I've had the opportunity, in a classroom setting, to compare King James passages with identical ones translated from Peshitta. Sometimes there's not much difference, but other times the differences are shocking. For example, the King James Bible refers to and lists the *sons* of this and the *sons* of that. The Lamsa translation says "the children of" instead, emphasizing, in a powerful way, the value of females. As you might think, there are experiencers who, in coming back, are convinced it's their job to create reliable versions of an even newer, greater gospel. One of these is Carol Parrish. After her near-death experience, she was "told" to find a special place to erect a biblical/spiritual seminary devoted to training ministers in the new gospel of spiritual truth. Sancta Sophia Seminary is the result, located in Tahlequah, Oklahoma. I've spoken there before, and to say I was impressed by the seminary would be an understatement.

Ohmygosh, prayer! Forget about types of religion, holy books, churches, and belief systems. Experiencers, sooner or later, fill their lives with prayer—especially group prayers and worldwide prayer events. That's because *prayer is the soul, talking*. We each have a soul; that invisible powerhouse that keeps us going, keeps us breathing, gives us a mind and the thoughts inside our mind. Just ask any experiencer . . . our soul is the real us! To speak of essence, your being's actual core, you refer to your soul. Some can see the soul.

Most can't. 'Cause when you're talking soul, you're talking about that invisible spiritual essence—that power deep within that moves us and keeps us moving.

Healing ability is linked to soul ability and to powers beyond the soul: God, Allness, The One. I learned long ago that before action is taken where healing prayer is concerned, a simple "check" can solve questions of "rightness." Dowsers, for instance, first ask: "Can I, Should I, May I," then check answers with their pendulum. My version: first I focus on the situation at hand, then silently ask those questions. If it feels right to proceed, my body will lean forward. Should this happen, I offer prayer with the steadfast strength of knowing that the needed healing occurs. But if I find myself backing up or I feel my chest folding inward, I step aside, knowing that any energy I could offer is not what's needed. Sometimes getting out of God's Way proves the wiser choice.

An astounding fact: more than 90% of near-death experiencers come back knowing God—not believing—knowing. And prayer becomes a dynamic driver between the heart and the desire to serve. Same in my life. How about yours?

Chapter 30

Unconditional Love—A Surprise

"We see the universe as solid fact; God sees it as liquid law."
—Emerson

God's love, freely given without barriers or conditions, is truly wondrous. Yet "love" and "feelings" of love do not translate globally. Some countries don't even have a word for love. Believe that. Yet everyone, everywhere, relates to empathy (altruism). With experiencer divorce rates sky-high, we need to admit something: *None of us knows what unconditional love is.*

We think we know and act accordingly; some of us try to be saints. Still, there's more to unconditional love than most of us care to admit.

My oldest daughter confronted me in the kitchen several months after my three near-death experiences occurred. With her hands on her hips, she looked me straight in the eye, declaring: "You're easier to talk to now than you used to be. You're easier to be around." Then, giving me the pointer finger, she yelled, "But you're not mom and I want mom back." You know, we both spent years looking for that woman. Never did find her. That "mom" utterly vanished. It took decades before she could accept that.

"My whole life is an aftereffect," shouted John (one of my case studies). With the natal cord wrapped around his neck, he died in the birth canal—seeing everything—all the why's and what's of life. A quick-thinking physician saved him. He grew to adulthood exhibiting typical aftereffects—accepted by no one, considered a freak. He later married, fathered several children, and was openly helpful and loving to all. Yet his wife constantly accused him of flirting, of betraying her. She misunderstood his friendliness. When he began to have health problems, his family turned away from him—so he left and went to live with a relative. Because he felt a need to defend himself, he called me and several other near-death experiencers for advice. He died lost and angry because those he loved most never "saw" him or "heard" what he had to say. Today, whenever IANDS holds a national conference, special sessions are available to help families understand their loved ones and the aftereffects they "grow" through.

Individuals who have a near-death episode (NDE), or a profound spiritual transformation (STE), are never quite the same afterwards. Some play-act and hide their feelings. Always, though, there's that "hole," that unexpressed truth that either screws up their concept of self or denies them their newness. And don't think for one minute that unconditional love is truly unconditional. There's a whole cadre of experiencers, usually those more fundamental in their beliefs, who, even after a near-death experience, refuse to attend talks given by Hindu or Buddhist experiencers because they're not Christian. Shocking but true. Popular films about child experiencers do not mention the phenomenon by name . . . lest the purity of their story become somehow "tainted."

Unconditional love. We instinctively know what that is and instinctively open ourselves up to it. Unconditional love is agape—God's Love, love of each and all without reason or condition or desire or want. It is a love that's big beyond bigness, beyond language, beyond preferences, beyond words—the stair steps of love spread across a healthy life. But what if you jump a few stages on the learning curve and suddenly find yourself feeling a sense of completeness?

Unconditional love means every woman is your daughter, mother, aunt, sister, and wife. Every man is your son, father, uncle, brother, and husband. Can you handle that? Can your family? Can anyone?

Near-death experiencers give this situation their best shot. Most succeed. But not everyone. And not all the time. Jealousy is a common reaction in families where members misunderstand experiencers, think they're flirting when they're just being helpful. Tempers can flair. I've gotta admit this: some near-death experiencers, in a desire to raise large sums of money for various projects—do indeed become shysters or hacks. Supporters have lost money. Some, a lot. Unique to the power of unconditional love (the real stuff), is a deep sense of forgiveness that covers most of the pain from mistakes that were made. Notice I said "most." Not everyone bounces back.

Trying to define "unconditional love" is a bit murky. Trying to live it can be almost impossible. Yet, as an experiencer, there it is. In your face real. Here's how this manifested in my life.

True story: I hated my mother. She was the most negative human being I'd ever met, and I hated her. Others loved her. I couldn't. Conditions in my childhood made a difference: her various husbands, constant upheavals, the war years. My sister and brother, born a decade later, were loved—but not me. One day she accused me of being something so horrible, I had to look up the words in a dictionary (and those words definitely weren't me). I turned her off after that.

When I married and had children of my own, I thought there must be some way I could forgive her, forgive myself, forgive both of us. After much prayer, I got to the point where I could feel love inside of me for her. Early in this book, I spoke of the first place I went when leaving Idaho: my parent's house. She looked golden, pure to me. Love itself. So I kissed her fully and told her that I loved her and I meant it with all my heart and with all my being. Immediately she backed off, stiffened, turned white, and said nothing. Dad smiled. Years later she took ill. I called her almost every week for two years. It was always the same routine: she'd answer the phone by cussing out everyone and everything she despised. I never said a word until she finished. Then I'd say with all my heart that I loved her. I missed those calls after she died. Why, I wondered. Then it hit me. Unconditional love means you love without question or reason. You love because love is all there is. My mother's negativity was her gift to me—enabling me, through stages of love and pain, to experience the truth of unconditional love and the power of forgiveness. Her abusive behavior taught me that I was never a victim, nor was she.

My determination to forgive my mother, myself, the two of us together, helped me dig deep into the depths of my very soul. Writing this book enabled me to fit together the various puzzle pieces that my life came to have.

> *First Truth*: Of course my mother felt the way she did about my having polio as a youngster. Information about polio back then was sparse; nobody knew it had levels of paralysis and one could get a milder form (still polio), but not as bad. As an adult, most therapists and some doctors asked me if I ever had polio when I was younger

because I displayed a particular type of difficulty with my right leg. It was weaker, and I'd fallen several times because of it. Sometimes my leg was just "not there." This made them suspicious. I also had problems swallowing thick foods such as mashed potatoes. Both are recognized symptoms of childhood polio, even when it's a mild case.

Second Truth: Buoyed on by the polio affair, what happened to me in the first grade was the last straw for my mother. What would any mother think if she had a child who smelled color, saw music, and heard numbers? No one at that time had even heard of synesthesia. What else could she think? Looking back, there was never anything wrong with my mother, or with me. She had a nightmare of a life as an immigrant's child. She grew up in extreme poverty, and, even though she was gifted in music, she had no way to develop her talent or support herself. She was also a victim of World War II and its aftermath. We were both wonderful, gifted people, who, through no fault of our own, lived in worlds totally foreign to each other.

Third Truth: For me, a constant drone throughout my forty-four years of researching near-death states was the way I approached it. Folks said, "She must have made everything up because no one could have possibly done what she did. Obviously, she's a liar." One of the best scientific researchers in the field of near-death studies put it this way when I asked: *Will my work in the field of near-death studies ever be accepted?* His answer: "No!" Even being mentioned in *Lancet Medical Journal* for some of my findings? Still, no!

Fourth Truth: Why did that Voice tell me to do the research during my third near-death experience? I dutifully started the following year. Of all the people on this planet, why me? And why did I never argue or bargain or question? Look at my childhood history—filled with fairies nature spirits, and otherworldy adventures. I never knew "different," nor did the Sogns ever admonish me.

Fifth Truth: During his younger years, my husband Terry was paddling around a motel swimming pool when he suddenly sank to the bottom. A nearby woman jumped in, pulled him out just in time, then disappeared. Terry told me about this experience, saying that he observed the whole scenario from high above, while out-of-body. Nothing else. Throughout his life, he has been quite different from his twin, his family, and others. Yes, the two brothers are "mirror twins"—exact opposites (as if looking in a mirror). Yet Terry's pattern throughout life matches not only the aftereffects of a child near-death experiencer, but also that of a quiet innovator who can move mountains, sell anything, and see past life itself. We get along so well, it's like we're opposite versions of the same soul. Yes, our skin tones differ and he has the curliest hair I've ever seen. Still, the joy we share is limitless.

Once, when playing around with the idea of consciousness, I wondered if I could actually feel consciousness itself. I came up with an experiment where I walked down the stairs of my townhouse, extended my right hand, and asked the wall if it could feel me as I felt it. How can I describe what happened next? Unexpectedly, the wall and I switched places. The feeling of this in the gut of my stomach was so eerie, so different from anything I'd ever felt before, that I nearly lost my balance on the stairs. Clearly, I was the wall. Clearly, the wall's consciousness was my consciousness and vice versa. My heart leapt, giddy in the wonder of what had just been achieved. Consciousness, by flipping presence betwixt and between, allows us to experience each other's essence in and through primal reality. The "we" that we are can switch places, letting us explore the very essence of body, mind, and awareness.

I discovered that everything has memory. Every idea, every thought is forever part of the universe as living information. I've seen this to be true. Some call this state the Akashic Record, a skein of time readily available to any and all who can match vibrations with those who desire entry—a match similar to what I did with the wall along my staircase.

Consciousness is not bound by the brain or by what we believe. That's why it survives what we call death. During my many decades of "knocking on the doors of the mind," I discovered that unconditional love (what it really is), actually forms and maintains the patterns we've used throughout time in order to test who we are and what we're capable of. Reincarnation, then, is the staircase love travels. Some examples from my own life follow:

Seoul, South Korea

When I spent some time in Seoul, I was home. I knew the place, the palace grounds, the air, the land, the people. They didn't appear Chinese. Most people I saw had Mongolian features, maybe

Tibetan. I was amazed when a room full of professors agreed that Koreans —real Koreans—aren't really Chinese. They're more like Mongolians. They were surprised I noticed this. I smiled.

I walked everywhere I could on my own. Once, when taken to a street filled with touristy stuff, I asked for time alone and then made my way through "this way/that way" alleys. Almost like I was being led, I wound up in a walled enclosure that hugged a Buddhist temple. I walked up a huge set of wide steps and into a sanctuary filled with people. They were all sitting cross-legged on the floor and listening to chosen words from a man with a sing-songy voice. It was a spectacular place—clean, colorful, heaven-like. When it felt right, I walked to an outside platform. I felt drawn to the right corner, where I stood watching a line of monks climb a set of stairs leading to a high open-air building. The building housed a giant gong and a bigger-than-big hunk of tree used to strike the drum (which was as large as a car I once owned). The power-punched tones they created reverberated throughout every bone and muscle I had, shaking me as if I were mallet. Gong, tree trunk, drum. The power of Korea was why I was there: in this place I could echo the "shimmer of me" throughout time and space —feeling myself—a soul in a body at one with Itself.

Moscow, Russia

My trip to Moscow in 2010 was strange from the start. My sponsor never said anything that made sense (speaking off and on about schedules until finally I agreed to pay for tickets). It takes months to get passport clearance from the Russian Embassy. My son-in-law, who was accompanying me, had previous military service—some nuclear—which raised concerns. My stamped approval still sits atop my desk as proof of miracles.

Once we were there, everything we'd hope for flipped: small bookstore audiences, empty workshops. I found out why much too late. People there didn't want to hear about research. They wanted to learn brain mapping, meditation, and body-beautiful exercises. To make up for crowds that never came, our host offered to provide a cultural tour of the city and pay for our hotel and meals. You bet we said yes.

In the United States, we once had service stations almost everywhere. In Russia, it's churches. Our guide told us that most were torn down by Stalin, but many still remained—gold-onion-domed wonders. We toured as many as we could. It's as if these were *my* churches and I wanted to pray at each one. The Kremlin and Red Square were very different than how they were portrayed in the United States. The Red Square is a lot like the Mall in Washington, D.C.—only much smaller. The Kremlin itself is really no more than a walled fortress surrounding a few government buildings, a large concert hall, and more churches. These historical wonders took my breath away. Take the Church of the Assumption, for example. The minute you enter, you find yourself in another world, another dimension. You're not you. You're something else. Immediately I left my body and floated upwards to the dome.

That mystical spiritual high from just walking in the door, sitting on a bench, and "drinking" in the splendor of the place not only overwhelmed me, but directly flooded my being with awe-inspiring art. The breath of the place, the power of God filling me, overwhelming me, holding, protecting and loving me, was endless and forever.

As I continued upwards, I suddenly ceased to float. I ceased to be. The me I was smiled back at the me present in every speck of wall, ceiling, and tower. I was part of its energy—energy created by the sacrifice of workmen's hearts and hands in ages past. No matter where I went in Moscow, there was always that sense deep inside of me that I was already there—long ago there. When we left, we headed for one of Stalin's architectural masterpieces on a high bluff overlooking the river and city. It's hard to understand why this marvel was ever built—or for that matter, any of his marvels. None served design purposes or the needs of his people. As I stood there, grateful that Stalin was gone, a clear strong voice from the right of where I stood, spoke. "Stalin is back. Putin is his name." I looked around. No one was there. I said nothing at the time. Today that warning makes sense. It's about freedom—not only in Ukraine but throughout all of Europe, Scandinavia, Turkey and all democratic countries—including us. Stalin really is back.

Frankfurt and Munich, Germany

I flew out of Frankfurt, Germany exactly one year after 9/11. To board the plane home, all passengers had to line up and parade past uniformed German soldiers with guns drawn. Instantly, I was back in Twin Falls during the war years, with wardens checking each home to make certain there were no lights during air-raids. Now 9/11. Soldiers. Guns. German soil. German plane taking me home. The power of that moment was almost too much to handle.

In Munich, I faced another moment of true horror. 'Twas late. A fellow researcher ferried me to where I would spend the night. As we drove past a strikingly plain, forever-burning-light memorial to victims of the Holocaust, I saw "tumbleweeds" of grief from everywhere imaginable, rolling towards that light. I suddenly felt my heart grabbed by a fear that ate at my soul. This strange pain didn't dissolve until I returned to the United States and found a doctor who knew how to help me handle it. Lesson: even if you know what you're doing, a little help once in a while can make a big difference. None of us knows as much as we think, nor is life always what it seems.

Istanbul, Turkey

Three times I flew to Istanbul. How do I describe the impact that city had on me? Homesickness. Instant grief. Joy. Horror. People always tour you around during your stay.

On my first day in Istanbul, a local school teacher met me at my hotel. She wanted to thank me for a small book I wrote and self-published called *The Challenge of September 11: A Memorial.* Her class (what we would call 6th and 7th graders), was horrified that Muslims had flown into the New York City Twin Towers—destroying themselves, killing so many people, and doing so much damage. Her students were deeply ashamed. The teacher had found the book on my website and made copies of it for each of her students. That little book brought peace to everyone, as it focused on the higher aspects of the meaning behind what happened. I could hardly believe that this little book I wrote and put on my website would find its way to a classroom of students in Istanbul and help them heal. (That book, by the way, is still available on my website.)

My favorite place was Hagia Sofia Church/Museum, and I'd often stay there as long as people would let me. Talk about a "blast from the past"—this place held me as if I'd been born there and died there. Years passed between my trips, enabling me to do some deep digging. There was a pillar on the right side of the sanctuary (third one from the front), and I'd often hug that pillar and cry. Again and again. Trip after trip. I could see/feel myself in the past as the man who led the group in charge of altering the Christian Bible. It was my responsibility to remove anything that even suggested reincarnation was real—and that we might have to pay for our sins. Cover it up. Lie. Change the text. Control labels of "Christian" truth. After the translations were complete, I hung myself. I couldn't go on living with the weight of my guilty conscience. The last time I went there, I hugged my pillar and forgave myself for what I'd done. I let go. In so doing, the horrors of that memory dissolved. What needed forgiving was forgiven. The publicity photo I use today—wearing a blue dress and caught up in realms of pure joy—was taken after that final episode at Hagia Sophia in Istanbul.

Norway

Norway was another three-timer (along with various cities throughout). I always felt as if my first trip there was for the Sogns. I visited the Sognefjord and stayed on its shores as the Sogns had before they immigrated to the United States. Large family. Very close. I thought of myself as part of them, but I really wasn't. They just cared for me as a babe and young child. Still, I grew up absorbing Norwegian values as my values, learning how to cook Norwegian style. The people I stayed with in Oslo appreciated knowing about the old Norwegian recipes because so much of their history had been destroyed by Hitler's Nazis when they took over the country during World War II. When my host family drove me to Sognefjord, we passed where "perfect babies" were housed to fulfill Hitler's dream of the "pure Aryan race." When the war ended, people abandoned the clinic/hospital. Children, even babies, were left behind. Many died before those willing to forgive the past came forward to help the helpless.

We made it to the Fjord, near Vik and Balestrand. Through a waterfall of non-stop tears, I discovered that I wasn't there for the Sogns. I was there for me. I had a vision of my life there as a Viking, steering long ships and silently sliding from shore to shore where we fought and plundered. Later, as I was walking the slopes behind the hotel, I was again "me the Viking." I suddenly had that vision again. In a massive burst of heavenly brilliance, I could see Father Olaf welcome me and call me Son. That moment—every bit a spiritual transformation—led me far away to join forces with Olaf and help him bring Christianity to Norway. We declared our independence as a sovereign nation. I died with him at Stiklestad (the Norwegian version of Gettysburg in the United States). On my last visit, friends took me to the actual Memorial. Memories packed my brain. My death there was a victorious one. I felt a sword split open my chest. Such joy! Such power! A good day to die! Father Olaf died too, on a nearby ridge. While there, I found the actual spot where I had died and took a picture of it. A farmer's tractor is parked there today.

Brexit, England

My sponsor in Brexit was an herbalist from Ethiopia who had his own shop and a reputation as a healer that any M.D. would admire. Of all the things I did there, I'll always remember the night of my talk as a pure miracle. The large room was filled with people and children of all ages, including babes in buggies. Only one person was white like me. Everyone else was black, brown, and every shade in-between. No babies or children cried or made a fuss during my talk: total quiet, total respect, total interest. Afterwards, the whole room burst into activity—children were blowing up balloons and knocking them everywhere. Women gathered in the kitchen to stir up a feast. Everyone was visiting/eating/laughing/talking to me/asking questions. Never in my life have I received such respect and such interest. People everywhere, especially in the United States, could learn a lot from the folks in that room. Skin color makes no difference whatsoever! Greeting one another, sharing a meal, and learning together is unconditional love in action.

During all of my travels I discovered that I'd been to each place before, lifetimes ago. People were familiar (some more than others), and a few even felt like "family." With some I held back, uncertain about the wisdom of making contact. It didn't matter who I'd been. What mattered was the feeling of each place and the memories that surfaced. Many of these memories needed another look, because there's always an opportunity to heal what's unfinished—good or bad, real or not.

I knew when I was young that my mother (in this current life) had, in a past life, been my daughter. In that previous life, I lived in France and was a prostitute who wore green sleeves like Lady Greensleeves of English and Irish lore. One night a man of means impregnated me and then later insisted I give birth to his child, even though I didn't want any kids. He even funded the birth. But because I was forced into having a daughter I didn't want, I had no love for her. Eventually, my daughter ran away in a rage, vowing to get even with me some day because of how uncaring I was.

In my current life, my mother showed me no love and often forced me to wear green, sometimes with green sleeves. I couldn't stand the color. It took me years to realize that my mother in this current life was "karma" for how I treated *her* in a past life when she was my daughter. Remembering this made no difference until, as an adult, I began to research past lives as part of a class I took in the Edgar Cayce group. That class helped me to understand the true power of forgiveness.

Is reincarnation always what it seems to be? No. It's not the switch and roll of incarnations that's really in effect or even important. It's really about the growth of the soul (which explains why so many people remember being the same famous individual learning the same/similar lessons under similar conditions).

Although unconditional love is a wondrous component to (and aftereffect of) the near-death phenomenon, it is the trickiest to understand. Not until "I" disappears into "We" and "We" disappears into "Mystery" can any form of resurrection—dying and being reborn anew—begin. You suddenly slip into a state of consciousness that is clearly beyond consciousness. This is where love takes us if it is truly unconditional.

Chapter 31

In-Betweens

"Don't adventures ever have an end? I suppose not. Someone else always has to carry on the story."
—J. R. R. Tolkien

I stood there, fixated on his grave. J. R. R. Tolkien. My hero. Paying homage. He and his wife were together in his stories of Middle Earth, and they were also together in death. I know Middle Earth is real—physically real. I had a chance to see it. In 1978, some friends and I were climbing the flat-tops in Owyhee County around midnight. Coyotes were baying at the full moon. As we ascended, the four of us found ourselves only a few feet away from a group of shadowy figures riding horses. Dust exploded from hooves, pushing time. We all thought about taking that next step and joining them. But we knew that would mean leaving our reality zone—perhaps never to return. So we all backed away. We had work to do here. The riders swept past us and Middle Earth disappeared.

I put a penny on his gravestone—a little teary-eyed, but happy. Their graves are on the upper left in an old-fashioned cemetery off the Oxford Parkway in England. Becoming every character in the *Lord of the Rings* books (both heroes and monsters), enabled me to begin the integration process after I died—to see how good and evil can emerge from the same glory. Great therapy.

Middle Earth is a parallel universe—as real as the ones I explored every summer for years in the Sawtooth Mountains where my parents vacationed. On a police officer's salary, what other kind of vacation could we afford? While my parents fished, I'd lose myself in worlds of trees, bushes, slopes, mountain sides, abandoned mines, massive rocks, pop-up streams, and rolling river bends. Doorways into "other" worlds were everywhere. Always doorways. I was lucky as a kid. I could disappear with no one the wiser. Imaginary worlds, parallel worlds, different levels of life-living: a universe of us, rejoicing in itself.

Interrelationships with the inert and non-living stretch old-fashioned ideas about what being psychic is. Here are three mini-stories, deeply meaningful to me. I hope each will inspire you to rethink what you think you know.

Given a block of stone as a gift, Michelangelo sat for hours contemplating it until he finally asked the stone, "What would you like to become?" One evening, as Michelangelo was meditating, the stone revealed to him the form of the *Pieta* within it. "The act of creation was simple," Michelangelo stated, "for all I did was remove what no longer belonged."

Architect Louis Kahn talks to bricks. To quote him: "You say to the brick: 'What do you want?' And brick says to you, 'I like an arch.' And you say to brick: 'Look, I want one too, but arches are expensive and I can use a concrete lintel . . . What do you think of that, brick?' Brick says, 'I like an arch.'" By asking buildings what they want to be, Kahn created structures of striking beauty and functional excellence.

Cleve Backster (a pioneer in the development and application of the polygraph technique for researching cellular communication), established that an unfertilized egg will register the heartbeat of a three-day-old embryo as a way of preparing a protective energy shield should fertilization occur. He also found that every cell responds to consciousness, and that all cells are "notified" in advance of what's about to happen through *nontiming* (a term Backster coined to explain the instantaneousness of cellular signals).

Let me repeat what Backster found: all cells are notified in advance of what is about to happen. All cells. That means all of us, or at least most of us, could be aware of what nontiming signals are so we can recognize them as they occur. This goes beyond hunches and intuitive knowing. Dying showed me that even the cells in our body, not just our senses, respond to futurist signals—especially in the heart muscle. Even as a kid in the police station, whenever I peered through the keyhole into the interrogation room, I'd hear victims say: "I just knew something like this was going to happen" or "I had a dream not to take that trip." Again and again I witnessed body movements indicating that the abstract and the physical communicated with each other via nontiming signals. As I matured, I came to realize that our world (and everything around and within us) is constantly, daily, reflecting back to us whatever is going on.

Everything talks to everything else. Everything is aware of everything else. Everything is conscious on some level and in some manner.

Forty-four years of research have shown me that both near-death experiences and spiritually transformative experiences tend to strip away the veneer of "society" and fling us into domains outside space and time—like entanglements (what some call "missing domains").

And that happened "in spades" with me. All that I knew before I died—and had previously proven to myself and others—exploded.

This type of explosion occurred when I was working on *A Manual for Developing Humans*, the final book I was told to write during my third near-death experience. Surprisingly, it turned out to be the first book I wrote. When I sent it out for review, every reader said the same thing: "The world is not yet ready for this book. Put it in a box." So I did—a very big box. It remained there for decades. At the funeral of a dear friend, his photo (which was on his coffin), "told" me "The time is now." I knew what that meant. I practically flew home after the service and opened the box. Horrors! Have you ever opened something that's been sealed for decades? The smell is overpowering. After I aired out my office, I went through the material. All there. All good. Still, how can I take this stuff and create the kind of book I know it must be? Blank brain. Honestly, I had no idea. Then something impossible happened. The air in my office folded over.

I'll try my best to describe this for you. I was standing up, mid-room, staring out the windows of my two large patio doors, when suddenly the very air in the room—space itself—folded over from ceiling top to mid-way down towards the floor. It hung there, folded, while continuing to fold more. Space billowed as if switching dimensions, yet there were no dimensions to switch. I felt the need to walk over to my computer, sit down, and write the Manual—even though I had no idea where it would take me. I just felt a need to put *something* on a blank page. That "something" flowed through my eyes and hands with an unmistakable feeling-sense of its own. No sense of mediumship. No sense of dictation or being shown a single thing. There was only strength and the fullness of that strength flowing into every press of every key on my computer's keyboard.

This fold of space guided me through a "felt-sense" of movement. Honestly, that's it. The resulting Manual has six sections, covering a wide-range of topics. It contains the basics on every level of life: how to use your mind, develop and use intuition, understand color, sex, relationships, children, and death. It also provides instructions on how to take out-of-body trips, interact with spirit beings, meditate, bend time, and re-think money. Thought-form drawings abound—simple drawings of phrases that suddenly took shape mid-air. All I did was draw what I saw. No plans. No choices. I just drew the invisible and made it real. *A Manual for Developing Humans* is based on the fact that, ages ago, people considered "Hu" to be the sound of God. "Hu-Man" to them meant "God-Man, God-Woman." What school on this planet teaches kids how to be who they really are—children of God, Co-Creators with the Creator? This miracle of a book does that, and it wrote itself through a felt-sense of movement and purpose on my part. The Manual is a *known-text* in the sense that the material in it comes from a lifetime of living, searching, testing, and re-testing. It was sorted through and clarified in ways beyond any form of thought I was capable of. The "who" in this project scared me, as, quite literally, "no one in any form" was in charge. Prayer kept me going.

Parallel worlds do exist and interact with our world. *A Manual for Developing Humans* is proof of this.

One day I received an email containing a quote from Howard Wiseman, a physicist at Griffith University in Brisbane, Australia. He said: "The idea of parallel universes in quantum mechanics has been around since 1957." Wiseman is one of the physicists who came up with the "many-worlds" theory. He added: "In the well-known 'Many-Worlds Interpretation,' each universe branches into a bunch of new universes every time a quantum measurement is made. All possibilities are therefore realized . . . in some universes the dinosaur-killing asteroid missed Earth. In others, Australia was colonized by the Portuguese."

Crazy, but real-world true.

Admit it—time and space are just concepts relative to how they're perceived. Near-death experiences prove this. Then there are the stories we've all heard: stories of dimensions and worlds, angels in charge of each "flip of the vibrational switch," and secrets revealed by the High Order of Light and the Masters of Time. Each is empowered by name, vibration, color, and sound. And each experiencer has his or her own measure of time and space. Beyond what I found to be true, beyond the experiences and knowings of others, are realities without number. Yet the illusion of time, space, and stable matter—life as we think it is—serves an important purpose.

To understand why this is so, consider electrons. The *actual electron* is stable, like true north on a compass. But the *virtual electron* can fluctuate, like magnetic north on a compass. The former presents a model considered "true" because it is long-term and consistently dependable. The latter offers an "approximation" based on its short-term capacity for maneuvering. The short-term version could not grow or change or alter without the long-term's stability, yet the long-term needs the short term in order to experience itself.

Stop right here—I did. What I just said explains how creation works. It's so simple that most of us miss it.

Now think of God (or Greater Intelligence) as the actual electron. Think of creation and all created things, including us, as the virtual electron. "Central intelligence/God" (the actual electron) is steady. But everything created by God (the virtual electron) can change, grow, alter, and have endless variations. The virtual electron only *seems* real. But it isn't!

The truth is that, as long as the world around us appears to be what we think it is, we have all the "elbow room" we need from time, space, and matter to learn, grow and evolve (like with the virtual electron). We would be lost in a meaningless jumble if we could see everything that exists *as it really exists* (the actual electron) . . . before we're ready to. Both fixed and flexible futures are real and exist *at the same time* . . . because that which has already happened, *is still happening*!

Take a breath.

I discovered that what we call fate can waver. But, what we call destiny, our job in life, seems fixed in our cycles. We are each here to accomplish a given task, meet certain people at certain times—unless, by altering how we feel about the task at hand (and our response to it), we change our direction in life so much that our job and the reason why we're here changes too. Think thunderboomers (near-death experiences and intense spiritual transformations). Think about those of us who underwent such experiences. Now think . . . edge space (it is edge space that defines the in-between).

Stay with me, as I share what I learned from dying.

Read the first four verses in the biblical book of Genesis. It talks about "In the beginning, God . . ." Nothing else existed then except what was called God. Earth was without form, void, and darkness was upon the face of the deep. Recognize this?

Dark space, dark energy, void = Creation's trio. So what jiggles all of this? God's movement in a desire for companionship.

What about the shimmer one finds in the void? This is the light that God called forth to partner with the darkness.

Noted physicist and mountain climber Heinz R. Pagels wrote: "I dreamed I was clutching for a shrub, but it pulled loose, and in cold terror I fell into the abyss." He went on: "What I embody, the principle of life, cannot be destroyed. It is written into the cosmic code, the order of the universe. As I continued to fall into the dark void, embraced by the vault of the heavens, I sang to the beauty of the stars and made my peace with the darkness." Six years later he died in the same way he'd dreamed and written about.

That man met truth—not as a prediction for his demise, but rather as an acknowledgement of the transcendent truth beyond truth. There is an edge space, a gap that exists that we can neither define nor describe. It's there. In the Book of Genesis, it's there. In every religion or holy ritual or spiritual revelation, it's there. In near-death experiences that transcend storylines, it's there. In my life—always—it's there.

Edges.

In-Betweens.

Fractals.

A little science here . . . fractals are emergent properties that are both unpredictable and deterministic *at the same time*. We recognize them as swirling, ever-changing, flowing, mesmerizing spirals. Think Mandelbrot, a peculiar geometric form shaped like a pear (actually more like a squatting Buddha). Benoit B. Mandelbrot (1924-2010) is the father of fractal geometry (those spirals that occur everywhere in nature—the same, yet different—movement moving).

Fractals are what's in the edge-space forming in-betweens.

You're going to love what comes next, so keep reading.

Now, think about inner world/outer world. Collapsing/expanding. Direct/indirect. Can't see/never discovered. The Mandelbrot fractal is a mathematical analogy of how things work. It shows us how all black holes in the universe are connected and how only fractal geometry can bend space without breaking it. Only about four percent of matter is actually visible, so the invisible (dark matter/dark energy) constitutes what can become the emergent world, revealed by the event horizon of the Void.

Far out?

Attention all near-deathers who experienced seeing, meeting, and feeling the Void: It's a harbinger of the consciousness within you that was freed once you experienced what you did. It is the silent non-existent "wayshower."

The Mandelbrot shape (like a squatting Buddha) is literally a picture of consciousness itself . . . because . . . consciousness is the unified field—the emergent property between mind and thought that enables things to come into existence.

The event horizon is the same thing as the emergent world.

I saw this, all of it, and it is true. And there's more.

The colloidal condition releases and unveils the power present in an awakened mind, a mind that is now capable of operating as if it were a fractal.

Has the universe evolved as science thinks it has? No. Besides fractals there are also muons . . . tiny particles that do not always obey the known laws of physics. The discovery of muons means that what we think we know isn't necessarily true. Don't you love it? Transformations of consciousness turn around, twist, or alter the worlds of every adult and child. That's because *consciousness itself constitutes the unified field*—the emergent reality between mind and thought.

What does all of this mean? Everyone of us, as a soul, brings eternity into the world of time. This is us. This is our job. It's what we do. How does this work? You cannot have light without darkness or darkness without light—for each defines the other. Without such contrast, life does not exist . . . nothing is learned.

What else? The left brain/right brain—the meandering intuitive and the logically precise—are necessary in order to produce businesses and societies and governments and households and medical advancements and art in a living breathing society capable of advancement.

Get that?

Characters like me who can sit on a stage tossing rune stones for the Professional Psychic Counselors hotline, yet faithfully do the kind of logical precise research I've done, are living examples of consciousness freed to be itself. Both vertical and horizontal realities are necessary for *any of us* to even begin to fathom the scope of who we are, where we came from, and the very meaning of life itself.

Here's the clincher to all I've just said: we live in a four-percent world. What we don't see—that 96%—is dark matter. We don't see it because we *can't* see it . . . unless we're born different or have gone through a colloidal condition that literally changed our brain—enabling and enlarging how we perceive the world inside and outside of us. Dark matter holds together what belongs together.

In that 96% is also dark energy, or life force—the creative shimmer of vitality that moves and holds and heals and helps. Auras offer us a glimpse of this vitality, this power. So does the vibratory component of what actually does the healing during the healing process.

Really real? Look at any aura again—person or object. What you are seeing, really, is a "signature" of whatever power is there.

Dark matter and dark energy are the enablers of creation's thought form. The interpreter that communicates betwixt and between is DNA.

The universe is organic, symphonic—existent in swirling orbs light-years away or a single flower blooming on my porch. And, as near as anyone can tell, there are five basic forces in our world:

electromagnetism, gravity, the strong nuclear force, weak nuclear force, and torsion waves.

Don't grimace. All of this is fun stuff. Truth always is. And that's what we're exploring here . . . how existence manages to exist. If you want to know more about the Void that so many near-death experiencers encounter when they die (me included), you need to tackle the reality of torsion waves. And we are going to do just that . . . right here, right now.

Torsion waves are the information carriers that ensure nothing is ever lost. They transmit order and preserve information to prevent the increase of entropy. They warp and modify space and time and are associated with "psychic" phenomena. Russian scientists call torsion waves "biogravity." They are also known as orgone, bioplasma, and bioenergy (associated with sacred sites and crop circles). Torsion waves are known to travel at tremendous speeds, far greater than the speed of light. They can propagate in the future and past, as well as the present. They can be influenced by consciousness, pass through all shielding, and are not weakened by distance. They have a role in the healing process. Torsion waves exist in two forms: one spins to the left, the other to the right; one slows time, the other speeds it up; one increases order in a system, the other decreases that order.

(It's fascinating to me that those about to die, whether in a hospital, at home, or somewhere else, almost always see spirits to the left. Sculptors, painters, and carvers also tend to report "visitations" from the left. "Doorways" such as these are torsion wave portals.)

As you have guessed by now, there is no such thing as junk DNA. DNA is both particle and process *at the same time*. It was never just coded proteins. Rather, DNA forms the patterning of how Creation functions, manifests, and moves. The number of strands doesn't matter as much as "the language" DNA speaks. For instance, *if you see auras, you're seeing DNA*. Remember that.

Einstein said that time, space, and light curve back on themselves—that everything moves in circles. Accordingly, mass and energy are equal. So does this mean the universe is conscious? Before we all scream "absolutely," let's reconsider the Void.

I encountered the Void during my second near-death experience. The Void: a place of darkness that is neither dark nor light, where nothing is, yet everything that could ever be or ever was . . . is. The Void: just entry alone can invoke madness or enlightenment. Those who are insane or lost in a nothingness that has no descriptive words and no helpful language may have accidently slipped into the Void. Experiencers of near-death and other transformative states who encounter this "non-place" struggle too. What can you do with a nothing that is a something?

Think of the good old days—about what shamans or psychics or healers or spiritual elders had to go through in their training in order to reach a point of no return where they either "flew" or "crashed." We have an edge place in our minds—not insanity, but expansive realities. It's that 4%. Just knowing about what it is invites all of us to rethink the reality we live and play and die in. But there's another way of looking at that 4%. It comes to us from the science of fluid dynamics, and it's easy to imagine. So join me.

Watch how birds flock, how they maintain an organized group. If one member swerves, neighboring birds will attempt to follow. That error spreads sideways across the formation until it diffuses among more and more birds, then vanishes, enabling the original formation to keep heading in the original direction. Adam Rogers, who wrote the *Newsweek* article "Going With The Flow," expands on this by pointing out a number of such examples—like watching how folks cram into subways at rush hour, or how crowded highways turn into parking lots, or how people muscle their way out of football games. These examples follow the same exact pattern as those birds do. Why? Fluid dynamics.

How groups move, how we behave in groups, hangs on that 4%. That's the magic number.

Allow me to explain. In the science of fluid dynamics, it only takes 4 to 5% of any group to change the whole group, condition, or situation. If you exceed that number, energy excites too much and can no longer be contained. The estimated number of near-death experiences in the general population worldwide is . . . 4 to 5%. Once that 4% is reached, the world as we know it begins to inch past that threshold. Energy excites. People begin to wake up, see more, and do more. Good or bad depends on us, the choices we make.

Threshold experiences (near-death and similar transformative states) comprise the vehicle that advances the human species. No other form of adaption or pressure can compare to the power unleashed by a consciousness freed to know itself.

Science has shown us that the entire universe is a fractal hologram. We can only see 4% of it. We move through the living of it in clusters of 4%. Look around where you live. Run out the door. See everything there: buildings, sidewalks, trees, ghettos, people, trash cans, dogs. You are only seeing four, maybe five percent of what is there. Can anything change or alter this? Threshold experiences. You see beyond 4% after such an experience. That's why so many people think they're going crazy. No, not crazy . . . waking up.

One of the Delphic maxims inscribed in the forecourt of the Temple of Apollo at Delphi in the 4th century B.C. is *Know Thyself.* Our elders knew this. Now it's our turn to wake up.

Tickle the Void and see what happens. It's the buffer shielding the dimensions of time.

Chapter 32

Edges

"Look well to the growing edge. All around us, worlds are dying and new worlds are being born."
—Howard Thurman

I have thrived on research since I was a small child. I still have a number of experiments ongoing, plus gadgets to clean the water and power coming into our home. Small pyramid grids extend the life of food left out, as well as any pills selected for the day. Gold spirals on the wall of my office uplift energy and enliven air. Plants just out the door from my computer desk grace a porch full of fascinating flowers and cacti. Shapes and spirals are everywhere, as well as crystals, paintings, Native American rugs, macrame (hanging from the yoke of a bull who once helped pull a load up White Bird Hill in central Idaho), and an orgone blanket (draped across my rocking chair). It was made to order via the research instructions of Wilhelm Reich, one of the greatest inventors of our time (who died in jail because the American Medical Association thought he was a phony and believed all the lies made up about him). Yup, I'm one of those—always experimenting, always finding out for myself what is true and what isn't.

A pride-place: our photographic bathroom. On all the walls (from ceiling to floor) I have photos of loved ones, special places visited, book covers, and a photo of dear Myriam. Why keep precious photos and mementos in a box or file when they can smile daily in a place often visited?

In our living room there is a huge framed photo of stars being born, plus an artist's rendition of the hour-glass-shaped-cyclones I saw in my third near-death experience. I was raised with guns—a cop's kid. Now I dwell in stars, watching those who go out (souls leaving their bodies) and those who suddenly blink in (souls entering babies-to-be). Every moment, every day, there are souls blinking on and off as they both accept and discard the gift of life provided on planet Earth. Since we need something to push against in order to grow, darkness is as valuable as light, and tragedy is as important as success.

Those who have gone through a colloidal shift of some type recognize that consciousness—intelligence—exists everywhere. Even in research on slime molds (pardon the comparison), scientists discovered and obtained positive proof that *intelligence does not need a brain in order to solve complex problems. Even slime mold can figure things out.* Intelligence, true intelligence, transcends thinking and feeling and seeing and touching. True intelligence knows itself and operates accordingly. And everything talks to everything else. Nature knows when earthquakes are about to start, when fire seeks to cleanse, when drought says "enough" because land is used/abused. Those who have gone through a colloidal state come to live more in line with natural rhythms. They become . . . edge walkers . . . like me.

Go back to the very first pages in this book—my walk along the edges of canyon walls—the crowd floating over Shoshone Falls made up of relatives, friends, people I had long since forgotten, those who were convinced I was a hopeless spoiled brat and those who knew I wasn't any such thing, people who loved me and people who hated me: everyone I ever met since birth. Whether part of my everyday experience or just brief interveners, a whole crowd of people filled my life. I love them all and I'm eternally grateful to each and every one of them—even those who only occupied a small snippet of time.

Always I have lived on the edge of things.

Recent photos of the war in Ukraine are similar to the newsreels I saw as a child . . . of Europe and the entire world caught up in the maniacal schemes of Hitler, Stalin, and Mussolini. Then Pearl Harbor happened. In the little town where I lived there were air-raid drills, rationing laws, victory gardens, and metal was taken to a special drop-off place for the war effort. In the world we now inhabit, Stalin is back. Ukraine is fighting a Russia supported by Iran and China, as China buys up all the farmland that it can in the United States. For years this has been happening with almost no one complaining, noticing, or asking why.

Yesterday I watched the PBS special, "The U.S. and the Holocaust," and learned the extent to which our country refused to take part in "Europe's War." We even openly traded with the Reich. Flying hero Charles Lindberg praised Hitler and denounced Jews. There were rumors at the time that President Roosevelt withheld information he'd received about Japan's plans to bomb Pearl Harbor. But when it happened, "the sleeping tiger awoke." Military signups in the U.S. went through the roof because so many volunteered. And I cried. All those gold stars. People dying everywhere. Symbols of death on my way to school and back home again. Air raid drills.

In tackling this book, Ken Ring kept telling me: "Write about your life. We want to know about the *real* you, not the research you!" I began doing that five years ago—at least I thought I had. His voice was right there from the start. I could hear him saying, "No, no, no. Not what you did . . . you." "Research *is* me," I'd reply. "It's who I am, who I've always been since I was no more than a toddler."

Ken just badgered more. Slowly I began to notice things I hadn't noticed before . . . how quickly experiencers flow in and through other worlds and discover healing abilities that are like miracles. How they come to speak "the language of spirit," and live in ways foreign to those who know them. How an experiencer's change is a remarkable; wondrous really. Many travel to other worlds, coming back with volumes of material they feel inspired to share about "the real truth behind what we think is true." Doing this enabled me to finally recognize that "unconditional love" is what undergirds even the ideas we have about reincarnation. Love or lack of it pushes the curiosity we have to explore varied themes and storylines in our living and dying.

The Voice Like None Other made it very clear to me in 1977 that I had a job to do, a specific one. Leave the miracles alone. Hunt instead for clues. What happens to people who die or nearly die and then return? My own stuff? Taken care of. And it was. For over forty-four years I wiped the slate clean, seeking patterns, aftereffects, and truths that so many others simply missed. I specialized in people, being with them, watching them, visiting in their homes whenever I could, listening, asking questions.

Ken kept saying over and over, "You. What about *you*?"

Well, in writing this book, I've discovered, in many ways, that I'm still that five-year-old wondering why mud pies can appear in different colors, depending on where they're located. I've realized how deeply I love and care, and how important it is that my mother never liked me, right from the start. I would never have learned what I did if I'd been a welcomed child.

Oscar Wilde, the famous Irish poet and playwright from the 1880's, once said: *"Without order, nothing can exist. Without chaos, nothing can evolve."*

How can we handle this truth? Through the Law of Reflection, which clearly reveals that order and chaos are *not* opposites, but instead reflections of what life is and what it needs in order to grow. You cannot have one without the other. All life begins in darkness. All of it. As we grow, we discover the power of order, how we can build our lives and our future, be who we can be through the light of discovery, consistency, application, sharing, and companionship. Question: if you hate the way your natural resources are being exploited and poisoned, ask yourself—are you willing to hang your clothes on an outside line to save energy? There are always alternatives. Like when I broke my left arm/wrist/hand. I healed. In a most incredible miracle I healed, because of my willingness *to step aside.*

What have I learned from the many lives and deaths I've had?

- *Facing my attackers and talking with them works wonders and solves most of the problems between us—plus it saves everyone a lot of money.*

- *My attackers actions were motivated by fear—fear that I would not credit their work and honor their sacrifices.*

- *Any new idea or unique method/finding is an automatic flag for attack. No one wants a newcomer messing up their theories.*

- *A long walk on "the dark side" is good for you. It keeps you humble and helps you find different ways to accomplish what you want to do.*

- *Your attackers are the best gift God could ever give you because they keep you honest and enable you to learn what you need to know . . . about yourself.*

- *Bless what hurts. That's just your soul trying to catch your attention.*

- *Bless the peace that follows listening to your soul.*

- *Love is the base of existence itself. Joy or lack of it, the driver. Everything results from this simple equation.*

I'll be almost eighty-six when this book is published. No regrets. I did the best I could each step of the way. My husband is my angel and my joy, God's gift to me. I leave you my work, what I discovered and proved. I leave you my laughter and my life and my books, and a host of questions still to be answered.

What we think is love, even unconditional love, isn't really what we think or feel. The bigness of this centers around breath. Everything breathes. The universe, every speck of all that is, breathes. Until we can flow into and through breath we have yet to discover the life and death of existence. Until we feel the breath a tree feels, the breath a rock feels, the breath that rolls throughout existence and non-existence, we have learned nothing. What we think life is alludes us, teases our sense of existence. We know nothing until we know the power and source of breath.

I discovered clear light several years ago. I got up from meditation and there it was: clear air, clear space . . . everything was clear. I knew, immediately knew, that when clear light appeared once more, I would walk into it and disappear. Forever gone.

Oh. The Voice Like None Other spoke to me again in August of 2022, outlining one more research project I'm supposed to do. Yes, I argued about it mightily. Didn't do a lick of good. I find it interesting that this new project will enable me to talk about what I've successfully avoided for four decades. A brief allusion to the subject is in my book, *Coming Back to Life* (Anomalies Chapter).

Thank you Ken, for refusing to give up on me.

Thank you dear Terry, for always being there.

Blessings to all,

PMH

Me, one-and-a-half years after my near-death experiences.

Me, thirty years later.

Terry

Terry and I today.

References

Elisabeth Kübler-Ross, *On Death & Dying: What the Dying Have To Teach Doctors, Nurses, Clergy & Their Own Families.* Simon & Schuster, New York, NY, 1969 (a bestseller still)

Art Yensen's book *I Saw Heaven*, was self-published and kept in print for many years after Art's passing by one of his sons. But it is no longer available.

P. M. H. Atwater, *Runes of the Goddess: A Joy-Filled Guide to Illuminating Your Inner Wisdom with One of the Oldest Known Rune Sets.* Galde Press, Lakeville, MN, 2011. This title has reverted back to me and I'm currently looking for another publisher. There are copies left, available at www.pmhatwater.com.

Spiritual Mind Treatments, a five-step process of affirmative prayer taught by Centers for Spiritual Living (formerly Religious Science/ Science of Mind), 573 Park Point Drive, Golden, CO 80401; (720) 496-1370; www.CSL.org.

Diane Pike & Arleen Lorrance, The Love Project teachings, through Teleos Institute, www.teleosinstitute.com, and www.consciousness-work.com. Teleos Institute, 12000 N 90th Street, #2025, Scottsdale, AZ 85260-8631.

Kenneth Ring, Ph.D., *Life at Death: A Scientific Investigation of the Near-Death Experience.* McCann & Geoghegan, New York, NY 1980. Also, *Heading Toward Omega: In Search of the Meaning of the Near-Death Experience.* William Morrow, New York, NY 1984.

Raymond A. Moody, Jr., M.D. *Life After Life.* Mockingbird Books, Covington, GA, 1975.

The International Association for Near-Death Studies, 2741 Campus Walk Avenue, Bldg. 500, Durham, NC 27705; (919) 383-7940; services@iands.org; www.iands.org. "The Book of Columns" (which contains a copy of each column I once wrote for their newsletter "Vital Signs") can still be obtained via their website.

Several more of the Rune Books I wrote—*The Magical Language of Runes.* Bear & Co., Santa Fe, NM, 1986/1990 *Goddess Runes: A Comprehensive Guide to Casting and Divination with One of the Oldest Known Rune Sets.* Avon Books, New York, NY, 1996. Currently, ownership has reverted back to me. Am currently looking for another publisher- contact me at www.pmhatwater.com.

Jeffrey Long, M.D., with Paul Perry. *Evidence of the Afterlife: The Science of Near-Death Experiences.* HarperOne, New York, NY, 2010. Dr. Jeffrey Long and his wife Jody have the largest computer collection of NDE accounts—4,000 in more than 23 languages: https://www.nderf.org.

Jane Roberts. *Seth Speaks: The Eternal Validity of the Soul.* New World Library, San Francisco, CA, 1972.

Machaelle Small Wright. *Behaving as if the God in All Life Mattered.* Perelandra Ltd., Jeffersonton, VA, 1997.

Perelandra Garden Workbook: A Complete Guide to Gardening with Nature Intelligences. Perelandra Ltd., Jeffersonton, VA, 1987.

The Findhorn Community. *The Findhorn Garden: Pioneering a New Vision of Man and Nature in Cooperation.* Harper-Collins, New York, NY 1976.

Edgar Cayce, considered the father of wholistic health, was a psychic of incredible gifts and unparalleled accuracy. The Association for Research and Enlightenment (A.R.E.) carries on his work through a myriad of activities and learning opportunities. Contact: Edgar Cayce's A.R.E., 215 67th Street, Virginia Beach, VA 23451-2061; 1-800-333-4499.

Ernest Holmes. *The Science of Mind.* Dodd, Mead and Company, NY, 1938. To contact Centers of Spiritual Living (formerly Science of Mind Centers and inquire about their classes), contact CSL.ORG, 573 Park Point Drive, Golden, CO 80401; (720) 496-1370. Their 5-step Affirmative Prayer classes are what enabled me to retrain my thinking process after I died.

The American Society of Dowsers has a training program for those interested, print a digest called The American Dowser, have chapters all over the U.S. Contact: ASD, P. O. Box 24 Danville, VT 05828-0024; (802) 684-3417; asd@dowsers.org.

The International Institute of Integral Human Sciences, P. O. Box 1387, Stn.H, Montreal,QC, Canada, H3G 2N3; www.iiihs.org; info@iiiha.org; (514) 937-8359. Inquire about their full list of opportunities, classes, workshops, conferences. My Honorary Ph.D. in Therapeutic Counseling was awarded by The Open International University for Complementary Medicines, Colombo, Sri Lanka.

Dr. James DeMeo continues the work of Wilhelm Reich. To reach him use demeo@mind.net. There is a video out now about Reich: The Scientific Discoveries of Wilhelm Reich and Their Repression; http://bolenreport.com/scientific-discoveries-Wilhelm-reich-repression/.

Brad Steiger delved into universal myths of a great flood and a race of gods in his book "Atlantis Rising." He wrote over a hundred books in his lifetime and became a dear friend.

Tape of "Coming Back to Life" has yet to be picked up by a sound library for distribution. "As You Die," however, is doing well. Can be purchased from me through www.pmhatwater.com, or from the distributor. There has recently been a buyout from the original group in Louisiana. It is now available through Focus On The Immaculate Heart, 909 S. IL, Route 83, Suite 201, Elmhurst, IL 60126; www.focustv.org; (630) 359-3277.

Robert O. Becker, M.D., and Gary Selden. *The Body Electric: Electromagnetism and the Foundation of Life.* William Morrow and Company, NY, 1985.

To sign up for my free monthly newsletter "For The Curious," simply get on my website www.pmhatwater.com, go over to Newsletter and sign up. There is an Archive for viewing past editions. I also produce a monthly blog. Read it at http://pmhatwater.blogspot.com.

Todd Burpo and Lynn Vincent. *Heaven is for Real.* Story of Colton Burpo's near-death experience when not quite four. Thomas Nelson Publishers, Nashville, TN, 2010.

Christy Wilson Beam. *Miracles from Heaven: A Little Girl, Her Journey to Heaven, and Her Amazing Story of Healing.* Hachette Books, New York, NY, 2015.

Alex Malarkey and Kevin Malarkey. *The Boy Who Came Back from Heaven.* Tyndal House, Carol Stream, IL, 2010.

"The Results System" developed by Margaret Fields Kean. Since her death, it was turned over to Rita Hartman, C.H.T., 1430 Williamette Street, PMB8, Eugene, OR, 97401-4049. You can also contact Leonard Kean, leonardkean@yahoo.com.

Todd Murphy's work, especially in Thailand with child NDErs, is in *Sacred Pathways: The Brain's Role in Religious and Mystic Experiences.* Create Space Edition, 2014 (self-published). Read Chapter 2, *Reincarnation in Human Evolution,* www.sacred-pathways.org.

Melvin Morse, M.D., with Paul Perry. *Closer to the Light: Learning from the Near-Death Experiences of Children.* Villard Books/Random House, Canada 1990

P. M. H. Atwater, L.H.D. *The Forever Angels: Near-Death Experiences in Childhood and Their Lifelong Impact.* Bear & Company, Rochester, VT 2019. Dr. Atwater created the *Animal Lights Series* (available only on Amazon), artwork by Eva M. Sakmar-Sullivan, to help parents discuss "what can you remember about birth and when you were a baby." The six animal stories (*horse, monkey, skunk, hedgehog, fawn, kitten)* cover conception through birth and afterward.

Also refer to *The New Children and Near-Death Experiences.* Bear & Company, Rochester, VT 1999-2003. And, *We Live Forever: The Real Truth About Death.* A.R.E. Press, Virginia Beach, VA 2004.

VOICES: Personal Stories From The Pages Of NIB: Healthcare After A Near-Death Experience, printed by John Hopkins University Press, and available free as a download: https://youtube/QQikr9-9Gz0.

Pim van Lommel, M.D. *Consciousness Beyond Life: The Science of the Near-Death Experience.* HarperCollins, New York, NY, 2010.

Rev. Karen E. Herrick, Ph.D. *Psychology of the Soul and The Paranormal.* Self-published: Herrick, 205 Broad Street, Red Bank, NJ 0771; (732) 530-8513. On pages 151-152 of this book is a description of the vagus nerve.

Rocco A. Errico, Th.D.,Ph.D. A student of George M. Lamsa and expert on Biblical translations, he is the founder and president of Noohra Foundation, Mableton, GA 30126; (678) 945-4001; www.noohra.com.

Freddy Silva. *The Lost Art of Resurrection: Initiation, Secret Chambers, and the Quest for the Otherworld.* Inner Traditions, Rochester, VT 2014

Bruce Greyson, M.D. *After: A Doctor Explores What Near-Death Experiences Reveal about Life and Beyond.* St. Martin's, New York, NY, 2021

Judith Pennington. *Mind Mirror*: Discovered and Developed by A.Maxwell Cade, Biophysicist and Psychobiologist, later teamed with Anna Wise, Humanistic Psychologist. Contact Pennington at judith@awakenedmind.org; (610) 570-1107. Atwater's results on her website at www.pmhatwater.com.

Claude Swanson, Ph.D. *Science of the Soul, The Afterlife, and The Shift.* Poseidia Press, 7320 North LaCholla, Suite #154-304, Tucson, AZ 85741. Published 2018. Very large, very thorough. Excellent research.

Newsweek Magazine article "Going With The Flow," by Adam Rogers, Issue 10-19-98, page 65.

J. R. R. Tolkien. *The Lord of the Rings (3 volumes).* Houghton Mifflin Company, Boston, MA 1965.

Ram Dass. *Be Here Now.* Harmony Books/Crown Publishers, New York, NY 1971.

John Lobell. *Between Silence and Light: Spirit in the Architecture of Louis I. Kahn.* Shambhala, Boston, 1979.

Cleve Backster spent 36 years researching biocommunication, the link between science and metaphysics. He wrote only one book: *Primary Perception: Biocommunication with Plants, Living Foods, and Human Cells*, published by White Rose Millennium Press, Agawam, MA 2003.

For a deep yet easily understandable interpretation of the Mandebrot and fractal geometry/chaos theory, get on the website of Lori-Anne Gardi: www.theOMparticle.com. She is a wonderful, clear, funny teacher. The class I took with her was in Canada through International Institute of Integral Human Sciences. This has been a study of mine for years.

U. S. Psychotronics Association, 525 Juanita Vista, Crystal Lake, IL 60014; www.psychotronics.org. Psychotronics is defined as the science of mind-body-environment relationships, an interdisciplinary science concerned with the interactions of matter, energy, and consciousness.

"The Secret of Slime Mold," and the extensive research done proving intelligence without a brain can be viewed at https://www.pbs.org/video/secret-mind-of-slime-oa3w89/.

Torus: for more information about the torus refer to the work of Robert Grant. His thought-provoking show on the torus can be viewed on https://www.gaia.com/series/sacred-geometry-spiritual-science.

Sancta Sophia Seminary, founded by Rev. Carol Parrish-Harra, Ph.D. She is the founder of Sancta Sophia Seminary, Sparrow

Hawk Village, 11 Summit Ridge Drive, Tahlequah, OK 74464-9215; www.sanctasophia.org. Her "The New Dictionary of Spiritual Thought" is outstanding.

The Challenge of September 11, A Memorial, is available at no cost from my website at www.pmhatwater.com.

As concerns 4G and 5G energy, read *The Invisible Rainbow: A History of Electricity and Life* by Arthur Fistenberg. Contact: Cellular Phone Task Force, P. O. Box 6216, Santa Fe, NM 87502 for more information.

About the Author

PMH Atwater, L.H.D., is an international authority on near-death states and the author of nineteen books. Her writings have appeared in numerous magazines and newsletters and some of her research has been validated in clinical settings. PMH has been mentioned in the *Lancet Medical Journal*, been given numerous citations, appeared on a variety of radio and television shows, and spoken at the United Nations. She donated the copyright of her book, *The Big Book of Near-Death Experiences,* to the International Association of Near-Death Studies so it could be used as an encyclopedia of the phenomena (with all monies going to IANDS for their work in the field). To date, her research covers nearly five thousand adult and child experiencers. Her latest book, *The Forever Angels: Near-Death Experiences in Childhood and their Lifelong Impact*, challenges the entire field of near-death studies and changes the conversation about death, reincarnation, and the life continuum. PMH publishes a free monthly newsletter—for the curious—and a blog for questions about near-death experiences and related matters.

Rainbow Ridge Books publishes a variety of spiritual, metaphysical, and self-help titles. To contact authors, peruse our titles, and see submission guidelines, please visit our website at www.rainbowridgebooks.com.

Made in the USA
Middletown, DE
07 October 2023